Melvin Tinker's collection of essays c
Evangelicals have finally realised tha
are divided and impotent in the counc
because they do not think their positions through. In this book
Evangelicals are given a clarion call to wake up and take concerted,
responsible action to proclaim the gospel to a new generation. There
is no time to lose, and Melvin Tinker's bold, prophetic witness comes
at what may turn out to be a key turning point for the future of the
church.

Gerald Bray
Anglican Professor of Divinity
Beeson Divinity School, Samford University
Birmingham, Alabama, USA

Christians need to think deeply, and biblically about the issues facing
society today. Melvin Tinker offers us a refreshing and insightful
way into many such issues. You may not agree with all he says, but
whoever reads the collection will be compelled to reflect more
carefully and thoughtfully on how Christians should respond.

Dr David Cook.
Fellow and Chaplain, Green College, Oxford
Director, Whitefield Institute, Oxford

These Essays show an acute perception of the way that
evangelicalism is going, and of the ways of returning it to the 'old
paths'. Although they are written in the first instance for Anglican
evangelicals, their intelligence, breadth of learning, and readability
offer important and timely lessons for evangelicals of all hues. The
essays show how it is possible to re-present the faith with freshness
and verve. They amount to a trenchent and courageous reaffirmation
of classic evangelicalism.

Paul Helm
Professor of the History and Philosophy
of Religion at King's College, London.

Evangelical Concerns

Melvin Tinker

Mentor

© Melvin Tinker
ISBN 1 85792 675 7
Published in 2001
by Christian Focus Publications,
Geanies House, Fearn, Ross-shire,
IV20 1TW, Great Britain

Cover design by Owen Daily

Printed by Bell and Bain Ltd, Glasgow

Contents

For Clive and Margaret West
who have modelled
what it means to be Gospel People

Preface

Back in 1963 Harry Blamires, the student and friend of C.S. Lewis, penned these words: 'There is no longer a Christian mind. The Christian mind has succumbed to the secular drift with a degree of weakness and nervelessness unmatched in Christian history. It is difficult to do justice in words to the complete loss of intellectual morale in the twentieth century Church' (*The Christian Mind*, p.3). Some would feel that Blamires overstates his case somewhat, but nearly forty years on it is difficult to say he has missed the mark entirely. Most serious commentators on the Western Church in general and evangelicalism in particular have noted an increasing tendency to flow with the 'secular drift' Blamires mentions. Just before he died, Francis Schaeffer lamented: 'We as Bible-believing Christians are locked in a battle. It is a conflict on the level of ideas between two opposed views of truth and reality. Sadly, we must say that very few in the evangelical world have acted as if these things are true. Rather than trumpet our accomplishments and revel in our growing numbers, it would be closer to the truth to admit that our response has been a disaster' (*The Great Evangelical Disaster*, p. 32). More recently David F. Wells has made similar observations in his two books, *No Place for Truth* and *God in the Wasteland*, charting the increasing 'worldliness' of the evangelical church, which he defines as 'that system of values and beliefs, behaviours and expectations, in any given culture that have at their centre the fallen human being and that relegate to the periphery any thought about God' (*God in the Wasteland*, p. 29). Wells, citing example after example, shows how such a process has occurred in the name of 'evangelicalism' until the heart has been taken out of what was once a dynamic and clearly theologically motivated movement. What has been transplanted may have a superficial similarity to its robust predecessor, but is far removed in terms of both message and method.

It would be wrongheaded and plain misleading to paint a picture

7

which is all 'doom and gloom'. There have been many notable signs of God's grace in reclaiming 'the Christian Mind'. There are many fine evangelical scholars coming through the sterling work of bodies like Tyndale House in Cambridge, the Whitefield Institute in Oxford and Trinity Evangelical Divinity School in Illinois, to name but a few such fruitful institutions. At the 'coal face' level the work of Proclamation Trust and the '9:38' web designed to encourage Word ministry have been particularly heartening developments. But still we are left with the eerie feeling that evangelicals stand in the shadows of a collapsing culture with nothing but two alternatives open to us: either to retreat into a ghetto and form a cosy club for the like-minded or sell the pass on fundamental issues of truth.

There is, however, a 'third way', which evangelicals have always advocated – to engage with the world while being firmly rooted in the Word. God has richly blessed us with many who have faithfully done that in the 20th century-Dr Martyn Lloyd-Jones, John Stott, Francis Schaeffer, Carl Henry and J.I. Packer to mention some of the more notable names. All of these men have influenced in varying degrees the present writer, who, writing primarily (though not exclusively) from within an Anglican context, wishes to raise 'Evangelical Concerns'. What is presented is a collection of essays written over a wide period which touch on fundamental issues seeking an evangelical perspective with which to resist the 'secular drift'. Many of these chapters originally appeared in the Anglican theological journal *Churchman*, and have been subject to editing to bring them up to date and to avoid overlap with other chapters. It is hoped that busy ministers and students of theology will find material here which will be of value in assisting the development of a fully orbed biblical approach to a whole range of issues from science and faith to socio-political involvement, no doubt taking what is found here and improving on it in the light of Scriptural reflection.

Schaeffer was surely right when he stressed we are locked in a battle, a battle of ideas, but at root a spiritual battle for the souls of men and women. May grace be increasingly given to us to follow the apostle Paul's example in this regard: 'For though we live in the world, we do not wage war as the world does. The weapons we fight with are not weapons of the world. On the contrary, they have divine power to demolish strongholds. We demolish arguments and every pretension that sets itself up against the knowledge of God, and we take captive every thought to make it obedient to Christ' (2 Cor. 10:3-5). This doesn't mean retreating into a defensive pietism; rather by standing firm upon God's self-revelation in Scripture, we humbly and prayerfully seek to 'contend for the faith once and for all entrusted to the saints' (Jude 3).

Soli Deo Gloria

Melvin Tinker
St John Newland
2001

1

Battle for the Mind

Introduction

Evangelicals have been far more influenced by non-Christian ideas than is realised, often in a subtle fashion. They have perhaps unconsciously adopted certain ways of thinking, values and attitudes which originate not so much from the Word of God but from the World which stands in opposition to God, although such ideas may be given a Christian guise.

Of course this is not anything new; in varying degrees it has always been so amongst God's people. Given this fact it is somewhat anomalous, therefore, that evangelicals should fail to be alert in order to detect and counter trends which are at variance with Scripture. The Apostle Paul's parting words to the elders of Ephesus in Acts 20:28-31 should be sufficient to cause us to take this responsibility more seriously than we do:

> Keep watch over yourselves and all the flock of which the Holy Spirit has made you overseers. Be shepherds of the church of God, which he bought with his own blood. I know that after I leave, savage wolves will come in among you and will not spare the flock. *Even from your own number* men will arise and distort the truth in order to draw away disciples after them. So be on your guard! Remember that for three years I never stopped warning each of you night and day with tears.

We must allow the full implications of this passage to come home to us with some force. From *within* these congregations, ones nurtured and taught by the apostle Paul himself, what we may, at the risk of being anachronistic, call 'evangelical' congregations, there will come men who will distort the truth. The question of sincerity or motivation is not an issue, it is the fact that such a thing can occur that is Paul's concern. How justified that concern was is born out by what we read in 1 and 2 Timothy, that within a generation this prophecy was sadly fulfilled.

In his first letter, the Apostle John pinpoints what the root of the problem is within his context:

> Dear children, this is the last hour; and as you have heard that the antichrist is coming, even now many antichrists have come. This is how we know it is the last hour. They went out from us, but they did not belong to us. For if they belonged to us, they would have remained with us (2:18-19).

Then in 4:1ff.

> Dear friends do not believe every spirit, but test the spirits to see whether they come from God, because many false prophets have gone out into the world. . . . They are from the world and therefore speak the viewpoint of the world and the world listens to them. We are from God, and whoever knows God listens to us; but whoever is not from God does not listen to us.

Here are teachers claiming new insights from God which are experientially based. The way John counters this is not by appealing to some other experience, one more authentic, but by appealing to the truth – the apostolic testimony which forms John's opening words in chapter 1: 'We proclaim to you what we have seen and heard so that you may have fellowship with us' (v.3). What is more, one cannot help but notice how strong and intemperate John's language is in referring to such persons and their teaching as 'anti-Christ'. Why does John use this sort of terminology? The prefix *anti* could mean that what is taught takes the place of Christ or that which stands in opposition to Christ, which amounts to much the same thing, and so constitutes an accurate description of what is occurring. But it is also an indication of the seriousness with which John views such developments, which he claims are in line with the 'world's view'. After all, nothing less than the integrity of the gospel is at stake and the eternal well-being of men and women which depends upon that gospel. The issue remains the same today – the health of the gospel and the health of the church. Evangelicals are not in the business of preserving a 'tradition' called evangelicalism; the real burden of concern is with that which evangelicalism claims to embody, viz., the integrity of the gospel understood in its richest and broadest sense; what Paul calls the 'whole counsel of God'. It is this which is in danger of being compromised and distorted in various ways from within evangelicalism itself, a situation which needs to be faced with humility and courage.

The locus of the battle

We are engaged in a spiritual battle which centres on the mind – a battle for presuppositions, beliefs and values which in turn determine our behaviour. The passage which focuses this truth for us most clearly is Romans 12:2:

> Do not conform any longer to the pattern of this world but be transformed by the renewing of your mind. Then you will be able to test and approve what God's will is – his good, pleasing and perfect will.

Cranfield draws out the implications of these verses in these terms:

> In the situation in which he is placed by the gospel, the Christian may and must, and – by the enabling of the Holy Spirit – can, resist the pressures to conformity with this age. And this command is something which he needs to hear again and again. It must ever be a great part of the content of Christian exhortation, so long as the church is 'militant here on earth'. For the pressures to conformity are always present, and always strong and insidious – so that the Christian often yields quite unconsciously. . . . However he is to allow himself to be transformed continually, remoulded and remade . . . and it is by the renewing of your mind that this transformation is effected.[1]

The overall context of Romans makes it plain that such a renewal occurs by attending to the Word of God applied by the Spirit of God in the church of God, which then issues in sacrificial service.

In his perceptive book *The Gravedigger File*, Os Guinness comments:

Christians are always more culturally short-sighted than they realise. They are often unable to tell, for instance, where their Christian principles leave off and their cultural perspectives begin. What many of them fail to ask is 'Where are we coming from and what is our own context?'[2]

That is the question this chapter seeks to consider. As evangelicals, where are we coming from? What are some of the major trends in thinking in our society which are manifesting themselves within Evangelicalism? It is self-evident that there is no simple cause-and-effect relationship here. The claim is not being made that patterns of thinking and certain beliefs are being adopted consciously, as if a deliberate decision is being made to put the Bible to one side or subsume the teaching of the Bible to current, popular thought. The process is often more subtle and gradual than that. The more modest suggestion proposed is that the prevailing intellectual climate – what is called 'modernity' – is more conducive to certain ways of thinking and behaving than others.

Discerning the trends

What follows is a sketch of the prevailing currents of thought which are present in our society and which appear to find expression within Evangelicalism.

First of all there is *secularism*, or 'trad is bad and the latest is the greatest'. This is characterised by a debunking of history and of what is not immediate. It is the process of secularization which gives rise to the predominating secular mentality. The process is the gradual freeing of sectors of society and culture from the decisive influence of religious ideas and institutions. The secular mentality is well described by Harvey Cox, viz., that 'Man turns his attention away from worlds beyond to this world and this time.'[3] In other words, this world – the world of sight, sound, taste and touch – is all that there is; or, in a diluted form, it is the most important aspect of reality. The net effect is that religious ideas and language become less meaningful and the church is marginalised, while concerns relating to 'this world' predominate and set the agenda for people's thinking and action.

There are two negative responses to secularism. First, there is the intended secularization of the gospel, which, while retaining traditional theological language, provides new content and emphases, usually of a political nature. The various liberation theologies of Guttierez and Cone are obvious examples of this. In a concern to make Christianity 'relevant' and 'meaningful' the net effect is to transmute it into something else.

But what of evangelicals? Are there signs of a drifting in this general direction? For an evangelical, one would perhaps expect the gospel to be defined in terms of Christ, the atonement, the regenerating work of the Holy Spirit and reconciliation with God. But according to one evangelical writer:

> The good news we love is defined in the Scripture as good news to the (physically and socially) poor; and that means that what the good news means to poor Christians (in scripture and today) should set the criteria for focusing what the good news means to others.[4]

The fact that it would be impossible to find such a definition or focusing of the gospel in such terms in either Acts or the epistles seems to have escaped the writer's notice. How can one explain such a development in thought which is linked to an inadequate view of the kingdom of God which, for this author is an 'old rule affirmed', viz., 'God rules'?[5] A clue as to what the answer might be is given in a statement made by the same writer in a subsequent article:

> There are two sources of theology. One is the Bible and the Christian tradition that has developed from it. The second is Christian experience.[6]

While one may go so far as to agree that 'Christian experience' in its widest sense may form the context in which theology is done and to some extent determine its shape and application, surely there is only one source which provides the material for theology, and that is Scripture. Even the tradition built upon it is itself the product of the theological enterprise the fount of which is the Bible, and it needs to be tested by the Bible.

The danger is to adopt what Francis Schaeffer in his book *The Great Evangelical Disaster* calls the 'blue-jeans mentality'. In expressing concern about the accommodation in which evangelicals are engaging, he likens it to some of the young people who used to arrive at L'Abri wearing 'blue jeans' as an expression of their rebellion but which in fact was a mark of their accommodation, because everyone was wearing blue jeans! Therefore he writes:

> What they [accommodating evangelicals] are saying is this: 'We are the "new evangelicals", the "open evangelicals"; we have thrown off our cultural isolation and the anti-intellectualism of the old fundamentalists.' But what they have not noticed is that they have nothing to say which stands in clear confrontation and antithesis to the surrounding culture. It is so easy to be a radical in the wearing of blue jeans when it fits in with the general climate of wearing blue jeans.[7]

However, if the first response to secularism is to accommodate the Scriptures to the prevailing trends of the day, the second is to withdraw, which leads to the next heading – *privatisation* or 'You in your small corner'. Here questions of belief and behaviour are withdrawn from the public sphere into the domain of 'private life'. Religion, therefore, is something 'very personal', which in practice means that it is not open to discussion and scrutiny. This is the end route of the worst excesses of pietism, which is still a great temptation for evangelicals. What is more, because belief is largely seen in our English culture as being restricted to the private world, Christianity is then viewed as being little more than an optional hobby with no universal truth claim.

The pressure is certainly on to quarantine religious belief and morality to the world of the individual and the world of 'values' in contrast to the world of 'facts'. This pressure is given added potency when linked to *pluralism* or 'Variety is the spice of life'. By pluralism one does not simply mean the sociological fact that we live in a society made up of a plurality of cultures and beliefs, but rather to the ideology of pluralism which states that such a variety of beliefs is good, reflecting a certain understanding of truth and reality. We now find ourselves in a situation in this country in which there is no one substantially shared world view; instead there is a whole host of what Peter Berger calls 'plausibility structures' – beliefs and practices which enable people to try and make sense of life. When one contemplates the tremendous variety of religions and philosophies now on offer today, many in popular form, the result can be quite bewildering, producing what can be called the 'fairground effect'; just as the old fairgrounds had a number of stalls each with a man clamouring for people's attention, so today there are promoters of different beliefs calling out from every quarter. Therefore the question arises: which do you choose? Which in turn begs the prior question: how do you choose? Some, of course, would ask whether such questions have any place. John Hick for example would have us see religions as being different but complementary, all forming part of the universe of faiths.

However, pluralism along the lines just described has its advocates within evangelicalism. Not in terms of Christianity and other religions, but in terms of evangelicalism and other traditions within the Church of England, what is sometimes referred to as 'internal ecumenism'.

In an article which appeared in *The Church of England Newspaper* a number of years ago, one Anglican evangelical urges a more positive approach by evangelicals to those of other traditions and writes:

> As evangelicals it is important for us to ask where we draw the line. At what point are we to see ourselves out of communion with those with whom we disagree? When Paul and Peter disagreed fundamentally over the issue of circumcision, the latter had a defective understanding of the gospel of salvation. What bound them together was not the fact that they agreed with each other. They clearly didn't. Presumably they were bound together because, as Paul urged the factious and disagreeable Corinthians, they were 'the body of Christ'. It was their common allegiance to Jesus as Lord that held them together. Instead of writing Peter off and refusing to have anything to do with him, Paul urgently engages in debate about salvation. St. Luke tells us that those who were insisting on circumcision were nevertheless 'believers' (Acts 15:1 and 5). Their understanding of the doctrine of salvation was wrong. Yet they were

still 'believers' – in our terms, Christians. Paul was able to persuade the errant Peter about the truth of the gospel as a fellow believer.... We should argue the truth of the gospel with a commitment to the unity of all believers in Jesus even when we question their understanding of something as fundamental as the nature of salvation. As an evangelical I am continually disappointed by the questioning of the bodily resurrection of Jesus. There are good reasons for believing the biblical account.... But when I meet Christians who question the Biblical account I engage them in debate not as enemies but as believers in Jesus, who like Peter, have failed to grasp sufficiently the doctrine of salvation.[8]

However one may sympathise with the intentions of the writer, one cannot but be concerned both by the confused thinking and careless exegesis exhibited as well as by the logical consequences of what is proposed.

In the first place, a number of categories of people are grouped together without making the much needed qualifying distinctions. The common factor linking them all is what can be called 'problems of belief', but the groupings must be teased out and distinguished to avoid theological confusion.

Firstly, there are those who are true believers but who may be suffering a spiritual lapse or failure of nerve. Peter at Antioch falls into this category. In Galatians 2, the issue is not that Peter and Paul were disagreeing over the question of circumcision, but over table fellowship with Gentiles (Gal. 2:12). It is clear from Acts 11 that by that time some agreement had been reached that Gentiles belonged to the church, and therefore what Paul is charging Peter with is inconsistency and not unbelief (Gal. 2:14). Peter, being true to character, seems to have weakened at this point and given way to what Paul calls 'false brothers'. Paul saw the serious consequences that this sort of behaviour would eventually have and was forced to have a public showdown over the issue. Therefore it was not that Peter and Paul were at odds about the nature of salvation, as suggested in the above article, but that Peter was failing to marry belief to behaviour.

Secondly, there are those who are spiritually immature, like the Corinthian Christians. Paul seeks to correct this and we too must help those struggling in this way.

But there is a third category which the writer seems to ignore, viz., those who out of conviction hold to non-apostolic beliefs and teach them. Acts 15 is mentioned in the article, but there is an error of fact, for verse 1 does not say that the folk who went to Antioch were 'believers'. Luke uses the term *tines* [some] as if to deliberately create a distance between those men and the church. Certainly in verse 5 we have former Pharisees who are called believers insisting on circumcision, but that is quite understandable: after all, former ingrained beliefs cannot be shaken off overnight. But once the decision is made that circumcision is not necessary for Gentiles, although for the sake of brotherly love certain concessions are made, where would such men have stood had they continued to insist on circumcision? Would they not have come under the anathema of Galatians 1:8? Paul's argument suggests that the answer would be in the affirmative.

The writer appears to be saying that it is possible to have a valid Christian unity apart from the gospel, especially when he writes that we 'should argue the truth of the gospel with a commitment to the unity of all believers in Jesus even when they question something as fundamental as salvation.' But surely the New Testament's requirement for being a believer, and therefore of being united in Christ, is an embracing of Christ by faith? Otherwise one is forced into the unbiblical position of believing that one can be a Christian without accepting Christ, or in some cases even repudiating the biblical view of acceptance with God.

It is quite irresponsible, both with regard to the truth of God and the eternal well-being of people, simply to assume that because, say, a fellow minister 'believes in Jesus' (although not necessarily as the redeeming Son of God) he is a Christian. In the context of the liberal–evangelical debate it is not a question of there being an entity called 'the gospel' with two different ways of viewing it. Rather there are different and rival concepts of what the gospel is – in Paul's language it is 'another gospel'. Greshem Machen's argument in his *Christianity and Liberalism*[9] has yet to be refuted. Full-blooded liberalism is not a version of Christianity: it is a different religion.

This pluralistic mind-set is, one would suspect, the dominant one in Anglican evangelicalism today and will eventually be its undoing, but it is an outlook which extends well beyond these denominational borders. It is now only a short step from pluralism to *relativism* or 'That's just your way of looking at it'. The issue of relativism is philosophically quite subtle and one would refer to Jeffrey Stout's helpful handling of this in his *Ethics After Babel*.[10] However, at the popular level it is characterised by the notion that objective truth is out. Nothing, especially in the areas of belief and morality, can be claimed with certainty and as being universally binding. What is true for one person is not necessarily true for someone else. Alan Garfinkel's response to the relativist is telling when he says: 'I know where you are coming from but, you know, Relativism isn't true-for-me.' What is 'true', therefore, is relative to one's culture, upbringing, gender and even churchmanship. How many an argument has been thought to have been settled by the retort: 'Well, you would say that, because you are an evangelical'? C.S. Lewis referred to this as 'Bulverism' and effectively made short work of it.

Are evangelicals in danger of opening the door to a relativism of this kind? In a paper entitled 'How can the Bible be Authoritative?'[11] one evangelical scholar certainly appears to be prising that door open. There are many things one could say about this paper, not least about the acerbic tone in which reference is made to 'evangelicals', presumably mainline evangelicals. However, it is the main proposal and its consequences which are our concern. It is argued that the primary category for our understanding of the Bible is 'story' or 'narrative' which has an authority of its own. To help us grasp how this idea may be worked out in the life of the church the following model is proposed:

> Suppose there exists a Shakespeare play whose fifth act has been lost. The first four acts provide, let us suppose, such a wealth of characterisation, such a crescendo of excitement within the plot, that it is generally agreed that the play ought to be staged. Nevertheless, it is felt inappropriate actually to write a fifth act once and for all: it would freeze the play into one form, and commit Shakespeare as it were to be prospectively responsible for work not in fact his own. Better, it is felt, to give the key parts to highly trained, sensitive

experienced actors, who would immerse themselves in the first four acts and in the language and culture of Shakespeare and his time, and *who would then be told to work out the fifth act for themselves.*[12]

This model is then applied to the Bible with Creation being Act 1, the Fall Act 2, Israel Act 3, Jesus Act 4, and the New Testament as the first scene in the fifth act. But, and this is the critical point, we are still living in the fifth act and the church is called to 'offer something between an improvisation and actual performance of the final act', under the guidance of the Holy Spirit of course. How, then, is the gospel to be communicated? Certainly not in terms of 'timeless truths', which the writer says is precisely what we should not translate the Bible into, but in terms of a 'story' which people are to be caught up in so that we 'make our unique, unscripted and yet obedient improvisation'.[13]

Apart from this thesis marking the end of the belief in the finality and sufficiency of Scripture as traditionally understood, there are no adequate checks that what someone would consider to be 'improvising' the Christian faith is in fact the Christian faith. There are two routes which this suggestion opens up. One is the route of Newman and some form of Catholicism. The other is relativism, so that David Jenkins can improvise in one way and John Stott in another and both could claim that what they are doing is broadly in line with God's story in the Bible. If it is objected that the way of checking whether such improvisation by the likes of Jenkins or Wiles is authentically Christian is by referring back to Scripture (so that while they claim Jesus is not God incarnate we may say Scripture indicates that he is), they can reply on the basis of this writer's own argument, that the Bible is not that kind of book, it is not a theological compendium, but a story which is incomplete, with one's beliefs fitting into it in a way that is no worse or better than anyone else's.

Pluralism flows into relativism and relativism easily spawns *subjectivism*: 'I rule, O.K.' Here one wonders whether recent interest by evangelicals in certain aspects of 'Catholic spirituality', and particularly mysticism, is an indication of this. The use of Scripture to encourage 'visualisation' is a disturbing trend which calls for a critical response.

We are acutely aware that our society is saturated with *hedonism*, or as Dr David Cook likes to put it, 'Eat, drink and be merry for tomorrow we diet.' The love of pleasure, good feelings – those are the things that are sought and offered. But we need to ask, To what extent is the church pandering to this? Not only in its evangelism ('Are you unhappy? Come to Jesus'), but in its worship has hedonism taken hold? One thinks of one evangelical church which alternates its midweek meeting between prayer and bible study and a praise and prayer. The former attracts twenty people, the latter sixty. What values and outlook does this reflect? The Puritan notion of Christians having their 'losses and crosses' is quite alien to many today.

Finally, there is *materialism*, or 'It's as real as I feel'. This can be understood in two ways. The first is philosophically, that only what is open to the senses and empirical investigation is 'real' – seeing is believing. The other is a more general intuition that significance and security are to be found in possessions – possessing a good home or healthy body. John Wimber in *Power Evangelism*[14] challenges Western Christians for adopting a post-modern world view and so being sceptical of the miraculous. But this argument can be turned around, for it could be asked whether a dominant concern for healing, health and material well-being, as well as the need to demonstrate the gospel's power in miraculous signs and wonders (seeing is believing), is itself reflecting a western materialistic mind-set rather than a biblical one. Even a cursory consideration of the place of signs and wonders in Jesus' ministry as presented in both Mark and John's Gospels would suggest that it is.

Such moulding forces have been extensively in operation throughout the worldwide Evangelical movement. In a paper entitled 'Mission in the Face of Modernity,'[15] Os Guinness contrasts Lausannes I and II:

> Under the influence of the 'terrible trio' (advertising, television and pop culture), modernisation has caused profound changes in public discourse: above all a shift from word to image, action to spectacle, exposition to entertainment, truth to feeling, conviction to sentiment and authoritative utterance to discussion and sharing. Most of these

wider cultural shifts have been well exemplified here (Lausanne II]
and the general diminishing of any sense of 'Thus saith the Lord'
has been marked.

If we are still left in any doubt about the moulding effect of such
forces upon Evangelicalism, such doubt may be dispelled by a
consideration of this short extract which described the now notorious 'Nine O'Clock Service' in Sheffield in its very early days:

> The Nine O'clock service has taken a conscious step of distancing
> itself from a narrow view of things charismatic, drawing its identity
> holistically rather than being identified with any one tradition. It
> identifies itself with the orthodox and catholic traditions. Moreover
> it has opened itself to the challenge of rational engagement with the
> world, and discourse with the liberal tradition. It is exposing its
> practices and theology to the rigours of critical scholarship. It has a
> catholic-orientated sacramental theology and has majored on the use
> of the symbolic in worship, yet it contains some of the most modern
> expressions of worship in the world. It has sought to establish a radical
> community life, and to align itself with the poor.[16]

Here all the different streams seem to flow into one pool. The
tragic and scandalous collapse of this enterprise and the shameful
exposure of its leader Chris Brain was a tragedy waiting to happen.
Sexual impropriety and psychological manipulation were just some
of the unsavoury goings on which eventually came to light. Some
would say it was an inevitable consequence of the syncretistic
beliefs and practices adopted with no scriptural checks in place.
When there is a conscious departure from biblical doctrine, it is
not long before there is a clear move away from biblical behaviour.

The way ahead
How can such ideas gain credence? Part of the answer is that there
is some measure of truth in all of them. There is a legitimate
pluralism among evangelicals; we acknowledge a measure of
relativism in our approach to Scripture and its application – the
question of feet washing for instance; even hedonism perversely
reflects the notion that God has created material things for us to

enjoy (1 Tim. 4:4). Where things go wrong and error evolves is when ideas which have a legitimacy in a certain context begin to occupy an improper place in our thinking, becoming exaggerated and disproportionate to the detriment of fundamental Christian truths. One definition of a weed is a troublesome plant which is a problem by virtue of its growing in an unwanted place and crowding out other more wholesome plants. That is a fair picture of what seems to be happening in the church today.

What should our response be? At least the following three things: own up, speak out and stand together.

We need to own up that things are not as they should be. We have to face, however painful it may be, that some have veered off course and that perhaps the alleged strength of evangelicalism in Britain is rather deceptive, being more apparent than real.

Secondly, we need to speak out. Not simply by reacting to events, but by creating opportunities to state positively and unashamedly where we stand, and by refusing to be manoeuvred into positions which compromise our evangelical beliefs. However, when we do speak we need to do so in love and out of concern for the glory of God and the well-being of our brothers and sisters in Christ.

Thirdly, mainline evangelicals need to stand together. Can we not think of ways whereby we can go beyond talking and complaining and move on to doing things to encourage and support one another? Is it time for 'new wineskins' for such evangelicals?

The days ahead are critical. May God give us the grace and wisdom to proceed cautiously but boldly.

NOTES

1. C.E.B. Cranfield, *Romans*, T. & T. Clark, 1985.

2. Os Guinness, *The Gravedigger File,* Hodder and Stoughton, 1983.

3. H. Cox, *The Secular City,* London, 1965.

4. Christopher Sugden, *Passage to India*, Evangelical Roots, 1988.

5. Christopher Sugden, *The Impact of Conversion-Entering the Kingdom*, MARC 1986.

6. Christopher Sugden, 'Conference *Theology'* in *Themelios,* Vol. 16, No.2, 1991.

7. Francis Schaeffer, *The Great Evangelical Disaster*, Kingsway, 1985.

8. James Jones, 'Drawing the Line', *The Church of England Newspaper*, June 16th 1989.

9. J. Greshem Machen, *Christianity and Liberalism*, Eerdmans, 1981.

10. J. Stout, *Ethics After Babel*, James Clarke, 1990, Chapter 4.

11. N.T. Wright, 'How Can the Bible Be Authoritative?', *Vox Evangelica*, XXI, 1991.

12. *Ibid.*, p.18 (italics mine).

13. *Ibid.,* p.25.

14. J. Wimber, *Power Evangelism*, Hodder and Stoughton, 1985, Chapter 5.

15. Os Guinness, 'Mission in the Face of Modernity' in *The Gospel in the Modern World*, Eds. Eden and Wells, Inter-Varsity Press, 1991.

16. Robert Warren and Chris Brain, 'Crisis Time for Revival' *Anglicans For Renewal*, Vol. 44, 1991.

2

Does The Christian View Of
Death Need Reviving?

Introduction

Although it may be something of an exaggeration to say that whereas for our Victorian forefathers sex was the taboo subject in polite company, today it is death, this is a saying which nonetheless contains more than a grain of truth. Twenty-first century Western man finds death a difficult subject to handle. Accordingly, there are three broad approaches commonly adopted in dealing with death.

First, death, is romanticised. One not only sees this with blockbuster films like 'Ghost', but with the increased popularisation of the belief in reincarnation.

Secondly, death is trivialised as being of no consequence: 'when you're dead, you're dead,' the saying goes, or as Bertrand Russell put it: 'When I die I rot.' If one can accept the philosophical conundrum posed, death is simply part of life.

Thirdly, death is dramatised. This is particularly seen in the works of the French existentialists like Camus and Sartre. Here, death is seen as the ultimate absurdity in a world of absurdities, and either one capitulates to a meaningless existence in the face of death or one creates some sort of significance for one's life in defiance of death.

For many people the prevalent attitude towards death is best expressed by that oft-quoted saying of Woody Allen: 'It's not that I am afraid of death, I just don't want to be there when it happens.' Christians of all people should not be surprised at this reaction, for it touches a very important part of the human *psyche* as God has made us – he has put 'eternity on our minds'.

What follows is a presentation of the key elements which

constitute a biblical view of death and the afterlife, elements which must be grasped if Christians are to be preserved from drifting along with the prevailing currents of thought on the subject and are to retain a cutting edge in evangelism. We shall take as our starting point the nature of man.

The Nature of Man

The psalmist in Psalm 8 ponders the question, 'What is man?' He feels towards an answer in terms of creation: God has made him 'a little lower than the angels'. The writer to the Hebrews also ponders this question in chapter 2 and refers to the same psalm, but he considers the question Christocentrically against the two further dimensions of the fall and redemption. Throughout the Bible those three interlocking themes of creation, fall and redemption, are crucial for understanding ourselves in relation to God and especially in obtaining a fully rounded picture of the Christian view of death.[1]

Man at creation

At creation man is presented as the image bearer of God: 'God created man in His own image, in the image of God He created him – male and female He created them'(Gen. 1:27). We are not given any precise explanation of what the term 'image' means, but as Christ is the fulfilment of this (Col. 1:15) we can work backwards from him and suggest that it at least embraces the ideas of ruling and caring for the world under God and relating to each other in a dynamic of love (cf. Heb. 2). Some commentators, notably Karl Barth, see in the male-female relationship a reflection of the trinitarian relationship and thus it is together as male-female that the image of God is expressed.

Man is more than a physical body. In that wonderful picture of intimacy and dependence in the second chapter of Genesis we see the life-giver God breathing into Adam so that he became a 'living being' – *nephesh* – a soul, or as moderns might say prosaically, a psychosomatic unity. The term *nephesh* throughout Scripture has more than one meaning, but whatever the varied nuances of terms like *nephesh-psuche* (soul) and *ruach-pneuma* (spirit) – the overall direction of biblical evidence (let alone experiential evidence) is as C.S. Lewis stated, that man cannot be reduced to being either wholly a material or an immaterial being; he is both.[2] Put simply and generally, the terms soul/spirit refer to man's immaterial aspect, describing the relationship of man's immaterial dimension to God and the world. (In some contexts the terms soul and spirit are interchangeable, cf. Isaiah 26:9; Luke 1:46,47.)

Man at the fall

However, it is the account of the fall, man's rebellion against God, which provides the most fundamental understanding of the origin and nature of death: Genesis 2:17: 'When you eat of the fruit you shall surely die.' Death is nothing other than God's judicial sentence. It is not an accident; it is God's doing, and so Moses boldly writes:

> *You* turn men back to dust saying: 'Return to dust O sons of men!' For a thousand years in your sight are like a day that has just gone by or like a watch in the night. You sweep men away in the sleep of death (Ps. 90:3-5).

Or as Paul puts it in Romans 6:23: 'The wages of sin is death.' In Scripture, the verdict of death embraces three dimensions. Firstly, spiritual death – alienation from God. This was immediately experienced by Adam and Eve (Gen. 3:10). Everyone born into this world is in this state (Eph. 2:1). Secondly, there is physical death – the lot of us all, a fact made plain by Psalm 90. It is upon physical death that the essential unity of man is torn apart, *cf* Ecclesiastes 12:7; James 2:26. Thirdly, there is the second or eternal death which occurs on the final day of judgement (Rev. 20:14).

The question arises: why did God choose death as the judicial punishment upon our rebellion? In a very helpful discussion on this point, Don Carson[3] draws attention to the fact that death is presented as God's limit on his creatures whose rebellion consisted in them wanting to become like gods (Gen. 3:5). God is such that he will not be relativised. We are human, and death destroys all our pretensions to the contrary. The outworking of this is that death is not something to which we relate passively. We die because we are sinners attracting God's judgement for our transgressions. Death is therefore God's personal response to my personal rebellion. This does not mean that we should not grieve or rage at death. The theological point is that our anger should not be directed against God, as if he were being unfair in pronouncing death; this would be as unreasonable as a thief shaking his fist at a judge for delivering his sentence against his crimes.

Thus, against the backdrop of God's original purpose for man and his judicial verdict upon our rebellion, death is an 'abnormal-normal'. It is linked to the moral and spiritual pollution of sin. Does this mean, therefore, that the Christian response is one of passive resignation? If this is God's decree, is it only right to acquiesce and not fight it? Surely the answer is no. For it is the biblical concept of redemption that provides the key to understanding how death is transformed by God and, in one sense, is opposed by him. Here we come to the heart of the paradox which runs throughout Scripture, viz., that the God who is against us because of our sin, is also the God who is for us because of his grace. It is only the one who is our judge who can be our Saviour. What is more, that which is man's undoing – death – becomes, through the death of another man – the God-man Jesus Christ – the means of eternal life.

Man at redemption
There are several biblical passages which focus this for us. We begin with Hebrews 2:9: '[Jesus] suffered death so that by the grace of God he might taste death for everyone'; and in verse 14: 'Since the children have flesh and blood, he [Jesus] too shared in their humanity so that by his death he might destroy him who holds the power of death – that is, the devil – and free those who all their lives were held in slavery by their fear of death.' Paul writes in 1 Corinthians 15:21: 'For since death came through a man, the resurrection of the dead comes also through a man. For as in Adam all die, so in Christ all will be made alive'; then in verse 54 Paul writes: 'When the perishable has been clothed with the imperishable, and the mortal with immortality, then the saying that is written will come true "Death has been swallowed up in

victory." ' Paul describes death as the last enemy, which in principle has been conquered by Christ's death and resurrection, and so Jesus is described as the first fruits of the harvest; but death will finally be abolished at the general resurrection of the dead when Christ returns and a new heaven and earth is established:

> Brothers, we do not want you to be ignorant about those who fall asleep [a metaphor for death], or to grieve like the rest of men who have no hope. We believe that Jesus died and rose again and so we believe that God will bring with Jesus those who have fallen asleep in him (1 Thess. 4:13-14).

It is because the Christian recognises that he is caught between the now and the not yet, between the first and second coming of Christ, that he has an ambivalent attitude towards death. On the one hand it is still an enemy, it retains a sting, it is an abnormal-normal. Christians, therefore, grieve and find death disgusting. There is no question of romanticism about death for the believer. But on the other hand, death, through the redeeming work of Christ, has been transformed into a doorway into heaven and there will come a time when the sting will be removed. Thus, while he will grieve, the Christian will not grieve as those who have no hope. Tears are still shed. Grief is no less profound, but there is no grim despair, instead there is that quiet reassurance that the best is yet to be. Carson states this well when he writes:

> Because death is fundamentally God's imposed limitation on human arrogance, his stern 'Thus far and no farther', the deepest terror of death is being cut off from him forever. But where there is reconciliation with God, where faith in the Son of God and his death on the cross has brought a man or a women into vital union with the living God himself, death no longer holds all its old threats. Death has not yet been abolished, but it has been stripped of its power (1 Cor. 15:57).[4]

It is at death that the authenticity of Christian belief is put to the test, a belief which admits no superficial triumphalism of the 'name it and claim it' variety, but a sure determination that God will keep his promise which is assured in Christ. One of the most moving and poignant expressions of such faith is found in the account of Martin Luther and his daughter Magdelene. In September 1542, as Magdelene lay dying, her father weeping by her side asked her, 'Magdelene, my dear little daughter, would you like to stay here with your father, or would you be willing to go to your Father yonder?' Magdelene answered, 'Darling father, as God wills.' Luther wept, holding his daughter in his arms, praying that God might free her; and she died. As she was laid in her coffin, Luther declared, 'Darling Lena, you will rise and shine like a star; yea like the sun. I am happy in spirit, but the flesh is sorrowful and will not be content, the parting grieves me beyond measure. I have sent a saint to heaven.'

Life after death

But what happens at death? While no precise details are given by Scripture, there are passages which indicate two important points. Firstly, that the one who dies *in* Christ goes to be *with* Christ. This is sometimes referred to as an 'intermediate state', a term which is a little misleading as we shall see. Secondly, when Christ returns and history is wound up, all believers will be given a resurrected body and then redemption will be complete.

When the phrase 'intermediate state' is used, it does not mean that the Christian who has died inhabits a place in between heaven and hell, a special intermediate resting place for the departed. Rather, it refers to the fact that although the believer is constituted as a centre of awareness (as a self), that centre of consciousness is not corporeal – that is, embodied. As the Westminster Confession puts it, believers at death, 'being then made perfect in holiness will be received into the highest heavens'. We refer to some New Testament passages which indicate this.

In Matthew 17:1-3, where we are told that Moses and Elijah met and conversed with Jesus who was transfigured before them. Whatever mysterious circumstances surrounded Elijah's departure from this world, the evidence is quite clear that Moses died (Deut. 34:5). Yet here is Moses in our space and time, conscious in the afterlife.

The passage in the New Testament which most clearly indicates that a believer goes to be with Christ in heaven after death is Philippians 1:21-32 (NEB): 'For to me life is Christ and death gain; but what if my living on in the body may serve some good purpose? Which then am I to choose? I cannot tell. I am torn two ways: what I should like is to depart and be with Christ; that is better by far.' Here Paul is wrestling with the inner conflict of desires: the desire to be with Christ and the desire to continue serving him on earth for the benefit of God's people. He makes it quite clear which he would prefer-to die and be with Christ. Since no allusion is made to the resurrection, *prima facie,* one must take this to mean that Paul considers that consequent upon his death he will be 'with Christ' in a heavenly state. Note too, that Paul uses the personal pronoun 'I' – the self, ego, or the soul – dwelling in his body which departs at death.

Hebrews 12:22-24 is also suggestive:

> But you have come to Mount Zion and to the city of the living God, the heavenly Jerusalem, and to myriads of angels, to the general assembly and church of the first born who are enrolled in heaven, and to God the Judge of all, and *to the spirits of righteous men made perfect,* and to Jesus...

When believers on earth congregate, they congregate before and with the heavenly church. F.F. Bruce thus writes:

> No distinction in meaning can be pressed between 'spirits' here and 'souls' there. It is plain that, for him, the souls of believers do not need to wait until the resurrection to be perfected. They are perfected already in the sense that they are with God in the heavenly Jerusalem.

However, there is a minority of evangelical scholars who are challenging this traditional understanding by propounding the idea of 'soul sleep'.[5] This is the way in which one writer describes it:

> Probably the best solution is the view that the moment of death for the believer is the last day for him or her because in death the Christian moves out of time, so that death is experienced as the moment when Christ returns.[6]

There are several problems associated with this view. The first is that it does not do justice to the texts just cited. Exegetically it is found wanting. Secondly, it assumes a certain relation between time and eternity which is difficult to square theologically with the Bible, for what happens is that for each believer who dies the 'second coming of Christ' – the Parousia – takes place, that is it occurs outside time, when the whole thrust of the Bible is that it takes place in time. But thirdly, this position largely rests on a forced interpretation of the term 'sleep' as it is used to describe those who have died 'in Christ', for example, in 1 Thessalonians 4:13-18. But why is the term used? Are there limits to its intended sense? Surely, it is a term which functions as a metaphor primarily to describe the posture of the deceased and possibly to indicate a lack of finality about their state. Greeks and Egyptians used the term to describe their dead, and they certainly believed in continued existence immediately after death. J. Jeremias summarises the evidence as follows: 'The notion of soul sleep is just as foreign to the New Testament as to Judaism; the image of sleep is introduced ... simply as an euphemistic description of death.'[7]

A bodily resurrection?

Nonetheless, for the Christian the story does not end there, for central to the biblical scheme of the flow of creation – fall – redemption is the belief that there will be a *bodily* resurrection. In one of the most extensive passages in the whole of the New Testament which deals with the question of the resurrection (1 Corinthians 15) the apostle Paul writes in verse 53: 'The perishable *must* clothe itself with the imperishable, and the mortal with immortality.' Why this emphatic emphasis on the *must?* It is tied to the certainty of God's promise and the nature of redemption achieved by Christ. Earlier in the chapter Christ is described as the 'first fruits'. His resurrection, which in 1 Corinthians 15 and the Gospels is conceived of as a bodily resurrection, is a pledge of what will follow for those who have died in him. How do we know that believers will rise again at the end of time? It is because Christ has been raised from the dead in time. What is more, if there is no bodily resurrection but only some disembodied spiritual existence, then redemption will not be complete, for death will have gained the victory in that it will still reign over our bodies. Death, as we have seen, occurs because of sin, and if death is not reversed in resurrection, then sin has triumphed. But Paul's argument is that Christ has conquered sin and the consequences of sin, including death.[8] As we have already established, God's judicial verdict on sin is death – spiritual, physical and eternal. Christ by his substitutionary death and resurrection reverses all of these and so reverses the effects of the fall. Therefore, when a person becomes a Christian, spiritually they are made alive and reconciled to God (Eph. 2:5), physically they are given a resurrected body at the Parousia (1 Cor. 15:52ff.) and they need not fear the second death on the Day of Judgement (Rev. 20:6).

It is helpful to follow the apostle Paul's line of argument in 1 Corinthians 15 as he tackles the question: 'How are the dead raised? With what *kind* of body do they come?' In essence Paul stresses both continuity and discontinuity between our present and future state. He uses three analogies to put over this point.[9]

Firstly, there is the analogy of the seed in verses 37 and 38. The point is that the resultant plant is markedly different from the seed from which it has sprung. Furthermore, the burial of a seed is reminiscent of the burial of a man in a tomb.

Secondly, attention is drawn to the different kinds of bodily forms in the world (v. 39). There are differences within the created order in terms of bodily composition ('flesh'), each suited to its own environment. Therefore, why should there not be a resurrected body composed in such a way that it is suited to its new environment? (Paul's target here is crass literalism).

Thirdly, a distinction is drawn between terrestrial and celestial bodies to make the same point (vv. 40~41), with the conclusion, 'so it will be with the resurrection of the dead.'

There then follows a series of contrasts between our present fallen bodily existence and our future resurrected existence. One is perishable, subject to decay, the other imperishable. Our fallen body dies in dishonour, but will be raised in glory. It is sown in weakness, but will be raised in power. However, the fourth and final set of contrasts has caused much perplexity as to whether

Paul is in fact talking about a 'spiritual' rather than a bodily existence at the Parousia, for he says that our body is sown a 'natural body but raised a spiritual body'. We must understand however that Paul is not setting a spiritual existence over and against a corporeal bodily one. The terms Paul uses are these – it is sown a soulish body (*soma pseuchikon*) and raised a spiritual body (*soma pneumatikon*). Here Paul is referring to orientation and not composition. By speaking of a soulish body, or a natural body, Paul is referring to the orientation of fallen man which is away from God, and towards self. This is the dominating principle by which we live our lives. However, at the resurrection, that orientation will change. Then it will be the Holy Spirit who will dominate as we are orientated towards God, as we were originally meant to be.

But what are we to make of verse 50 which says that 'flesh and blood cannot inherit the kingdom of God, nor does the perishable inherit the imperishable'? Here we have a Semitic idiom which simply means 'fallen human nature'. It is a summary of all that Paul has said so far, that this body, frail and weak, with selves warped in their basic scheme of priorities, cannot as presently constituted enter the world to come; it has to be transformed so that it becomes like the body of Jesus Christ himself. It will only be at that point that the fulness of redemption will be experienced:

> *Then* the saying that is written will come true: 'Death has been swallowed up in victory. Where O death is your victory? Where O death is your sting?' The sting of death is sin, and the power of sin is the law. But thanks be to God! He gives us the victory through our Lord Jesus Christ.

All that has been spoken of so far refers to the believer in Christ, but what of the unbeliever? Here we enter upon the awesome and delicate question of judgement and hell.

Eternal punishment or temporal?
The consistent testimony of the New Testament is that there is to be a future judgement and that God's judicial sentence upon the unpenitent is eternal punishment. Although such a teaching may

sound alien to our liberal western ears, it is woven into the fabric of the gospel itself and is an irreducible part of Jesus' message: Matthew 7:21ff.

> Not everyone who says to me, 'Lord, Lord,' will enter the Kingdom of heaven, but he who does the will of my Father who is in heaven. Many will say to me, 'Lord, Lord, did we not prophesy in your name, and in your name cast out demons and perform many miracles?' And then I will declare to them, 'I never knew you, depart from me, you who practise lawlessness.'

Matthew 10:28: 'And do not fear those who kill the body, but are unable to destroy both body and soul in hell...';

Mark 9:47: 'It is better for you to enter the kingdom of God with one eye than to have two eyes and be thrown into hell where "their worm does not die, and the fire is not quenched" ';

Matthew 25:31: 'Then he will say to those on his left, depart from me you who are cursed into the eternal fire prepared for the devil and his angels';

2 Thessalonians 1:8: 'He will punish those who do not know God and do not obey the gospel of our Lord Jesus. They will be punished with everlasting destruction and shut out from the presence of the Lord.'

These are just a few sample texts which are not simple 'proof texts' taken out of context. The plain meaning of Scripture is clear and sobering: 'man is destined to die once and then to face the judgement' (Heb. 9:27).

Lack of general acceptance is not to be mistaken for lack of truth. Belief in judgement and hell has been weakened. This is part of the general weakening of belief in the gospel. Also, it is difficult to grasp because we in the West tend to think of punishment as essentially being corrective and remedial rather than punitive and penal. With such a mind-set, the doctrine of hell seems to serve no purpose, except, according to the late John Robinson,[10] acting in Jesus' teaching as an existential thunderbolt designed to make people take his message seriously. (But obviously not that seriously, if there is no objective hell!) Another factor which has led to a weakening of belief in hell is the widespread diminution of *personal* responsibility in our society, for the whole basis of judgement proceeds from the premise that we are all personally accountable for our actions and will be judged accordingly (Rom. 2). However, for those who profess the Christian faith, it is the difficulty of squaring this doctrine with a certain view of the character of God that constitutes the major problem. The cry thus goes out: 'How can an all loving God ever consign people to eternal perdition?' If the character of God were to be reduced to pure benevolence, then one would be forced to agree with the sentiment contained in such a question; it does seem incongruous. But the Bible does not engage in such reductionism. God's love is a holy love, a righteous love. Love and justice are not two opposing traits in God, rather the justice of God expresses his loving desire that right be done and seen to be done. God's wrath is his measured response to our rebellion. Some of that wrath is being revealed now as God gives up rebellious human beings to the consequences of their godlessness (Rom. 1:18ff.). But the full extent of God's reaction is reserved for the end of time. It is in this sense that the doctrine of judgement and hell is integral to the Christian Good News, for it is precisely from this 'wrath to come' that we are saved (1 Thess. 1:10). What is more, without this doctrine the cross of Christ makes little sense and certainly does not accord with the Bible's own explanation of this event, *viz.* that Christ is offered as a 'propitiation for our sins' (1 John 2:2; Rom. 3:25).

Sin is to be punished. Either it is punished in Christ on our behalf or it is punished in ourselves, and that is hell. Hell is the place of absolute justice, which is dispensed impeccably by the one before whom everything is 'uncovered and laid bare' (Heb. 4:13). The arrangements will be just, because God is just and no one will have the least cause to complain.

Why should hell be without limit? The simple answer is that God has decreed it to be so. But, following the various biblical strands through, we might suggest that it is because the offence being punished is against one of immeasurable holiness. Does this mean that all will suffer equally? No. Not only is that alien to the idea of justice revealed in Scripture, but also to what is explicitly stated in Scripture – for example, in Luke 12:48 where we read that those who did not know the Lord's will are beaten with *few* stripes, that is, the punishment is commensurate. This may also be behind the discussion in Romans 2 that all those who have sinned outside the law – that is, in ignorance of the revealed law of Moses – will be judged outside the law, that is, they will be tested against their own standards of morality. This does not mean that they will escape punishment ('all who sin apart from the law shall perish apart from the law'), rather they will be rendered culpable for their sin and punishment will be meted out accordingly.

It is sometimes pointed out that the language which the Bible uses to describe hell is figurative, with the implication that somehow its force and meaning are weakened. While it is self-evident that the language is figurative, then so is the language used to describe heaven. However no-one would take this fact to mean that heaven does not exist or is less of a reality than the language used to describe it. To say that a statement is metaphorical or figurative only tells us something about the *nature* of the language used, not the ontological reality to which it refers. Indeed, the metaphorical nature of heaven and hell language only serves to highlight how much *more* awesome the reality will be; the imagery is but a feeble attempt to describe the indescribable.

Universalism and Annihilationism

Theologically, the traditional doctrine of hell has come under attack from two quarters. The first is universalism: that all will be saved in the end. This view takes a variety of forms.[11] But whatever the particular variety, universalism does not do justice to the Biblical revelation, let alone the theological framework founded upon that revelation. The universalist teaching acts like a Procrustean bed, upon which biblical texts which do not fit are lopped off or grossly distorted in their meaning. The second attack comes from those who argue that the unbeliever is annihilated after judgement, a position referred to as conditional immortality. This has some notable evangelical proponents, writers like John Stott,[12] P.E. Hughes,[13] John Wenham[14] and Michael Green.[15] Formidable names indeed! However, it must be said that the arguments adduced remain unconvincing, of which in the main there are two.

The first is that the idea of the 'immortality of the soul' is more platonic than biblical. Only God is described as having 'immortality' (1 Tim. 6:16). While it is true that immortality is intrinsic to God in a way that it is not intrinsic to men, it does not follow that it is not bestowed upon man and maintained by divine *fiat*. The reading of texts such as Matthew 10:28; Daniel 12:2; John 5:27 suggests that it is so. What is more, as Professor Donald Macleod has stated:

> We still have the huge improbability that the soul should be preserved alive through death, resurrection, judgement and the dissolution of the universe only to founder at some point not even mentioned in Scripture.[16]

The second major argument is that the terms the Bible uses suggest annihilation – fire, for example, destroys. Indeed the term destroy, *apollumi,* is the very term applied to the fate of the wicked in the texts already quoted. Thus John Stott writes: 'If to kill is to deprive the body of life, hell would seem to be deprivation of both physical and spiritual life, that is the extinction of being.'[17] The language of *Gehenna,* hell, argues Michael Green, is also suggestive of annihilation as this was the local rubbish dump

> where the maggots were always active and fire smouldering. It says nothing at all about constant unending torment; rubbish does not last long in a fire. The image indicates total ruin.[18]

Ruin yes, but annihilation no. This rabbinic metaphor taken up and used by Jesus has its origins in Isaiah 66:24. It did indeed mean torment, as is evidenced by the inter-testamental books Judith and Ecclesiasticus:

> Woe to the nations that rise up against my kindred. The Lord Almighty will take vengeance on them in the day of judgement in putting fire and worms in their flesh, they shall feel them and weep for ever (Judith 16).

'Humble thy soul greatly; for the vengeance of the ungodly is fire and worms' (Eccl. 7:16).

W.E. Vine's *Expository Dictionary of New Testament Words* states that the idea behind such words as *apollumi* 'does not mean extinction but ruin, loss, not of being but of well being. This is clear from its use'.

While both Stott and Green shun any literalistic interpretation of Hell passages, it is such literalism that drives them to the conclusion of annihilationism, so 'fire destroys totally'. Surely we must consider how the language functions in the light of other Scriptural statements regarding the nature of man, death and judgement. When this is done we see that such language points to ruination, which involves sorrow, pain and loss. It is an undue literalism which also renders some scholars incapable of holding together what are perceived to be two irreconcilable concepts - destruction and ruin; for if the former is taken as exhaustive, that is, absolute destruction, it leaves no room for the latter. But why cannot something be destroyed (even continually) leading to its perpetual ruination? For example, at the end of the Second World War Germany was 'destroyed', and so ruined at practically every level. The survivors were 'destroyed' and continued to suffer, but were not annihilated. No contradiction is involved.

This is not a subject on which one wishes to dwell. However, a fair amount of space has been devoted to it because it is a point of contention between evangelicals, and the Bible does speak clearly on the matter. We therefore should avoid two extremes. The first is going further than the Bible in describing this state. The second is falling short of what the Bible says, modifying and curtailing its teaching to make it say what we would prefer it to say.

Solid hope or shifting sand?

A month before his death, Jean Paul Satre wrote these words in his journal:

With this third world war which might break out one day, with this wretched gathering which our planet now is, despair returns to tempt me. The idea that there is no purpose, only petty personal ends for which we fight! We make little revolutions, but there is no goal for mankind. One cannot think of such things. They tempt you incessantly, especially if you are old... the world seems ugly, bad and without hope. There, that's the cry of despair of an old man who will die in despair. But that's exactly what I resist. I know I shall die in hope. But that hope needs a foundation.

How true! But what a contrast to the words of another 'old man' about to die:

For I am already being poured out like a drink offering, and the time has come for my departure. I have fought the good fight, I have finished the race. I have kept the faith. Now there is in store for me a crown of righteousness which the Lord, the righteous judge, will award me on that day – and not only to me but also to all who have longed for his appearing' (2 Tim. 4:6-8).

Here is hope based upon a solid foundation indeed.

NOTES

1. Cp. R.A. Morey, *Death and the Afterlife*, Bethany House (1984), for a thorough study of this subject.

2. C.S. Lewis, *Miracles*, Fount.

3. D.A. Carson, *How Long O Lord?* IVP (1990).

4. *Op. cit.*, p 129.

5. John Yates, ' "Immediate or Intermediate?" The State of the Believer upon Death', in *Churchman*, 1987 (Vol. 101:4).

6. K. Giles, quoted by John Yates, *supra.*

7. J. Jeremias, *Theological Dictionary of the New Testament* (ed. Kittel), Vol.1.

8. See Paul Helm, *The Last Things*, Banner of Truth (1989).

9. See W. Craig, 'The Empty Tomb of Jesus', in *Gospel Perspectives*, Vol II, ed. R.T. France and D. Wenham (J.S.O.T., 1981), for an elaboration of this text.

10. J.A.T. Robinson, *In the End God*, James Clarke (1950).

11. See Richard Bauckham, 'Universalism – a historical survey', *Themelios* (Vol. 4, No.2).

12. John Stott and David Edwards, *Essentials*, Hodder and Stoughton (1988).

13. P.E. Hughes, *The True Image*, IVP (1988).

14. John Wenham, *The Goodness of God*, IVP (1974).

15. Michael Green, *Evangelism through the Local Church*, Hodder and Stoughton (1990).

16. Donald Macleod, 'Must we all become annihilationists?' in *Evangelicals Now*, June 1991.

17. *Op. cit.*, p. 315.

18. *Op. cit.*, p.70.

3

Conflicts in Science and Faith: Ministers Beware

Introduction

The aim of this chapter[1] is a modest one, albeit in parts provocative. As the title suggests, it is an attempt to put in place a few 'Danger– Warning' signs in some areas where Christians, and in particular Christian ministers, need to tread a little warily in considering the relationship between the scientific enterprise and the Christian faith. I will be focusing on those issues which are seen to have some apologetic value – where perhaps something is advocated by the scientific community which is felt by some to be at odds with Christianity and therefore needs to be confronted as such; or where there are developments in science which appear to come to the aid of the Christian faith, maybe being perceived as providing corroborating evidence for some of its truth claims. But for the most part I will be discussing matters against a backcloth of what is still widely perceived – rightly or wrongly – as a basic conflict between science and religion.

Back to the Beginning

First of all it is necessary to go back a little and take a brief look at the contrast between pagan views of nature and the biblical view in order to see how it was this biblical outlook which not only provided the rational grounding upon which modern science could develop (as well as much of its motivation), but also positively laid upon man the obligation to engage in this enterprise, it being seen as part of the creation mandate to 'fill the earth and subdue it' (Gen. 1:28). Such a comparison and contrast between the two views will not only serve to show that at root there is no final conflict between science and the Christian faith, but should also sound a note of caution against running after pagan notions of nature which might be dressed in Christian guise.

The contrast between Greek views of nature and that of the Bible, together with the seminal influence of biblical Christianity on the development of modern science, has been well documented by Professor Hooykaas.[2] He summarises the Greek understanding of nature, going back through the Stoics, Aristotle, Plato and the Eleatic philosophers of the fifth century, under four points:

1. The Greeks did not admit creation; to them nature herself was eternal and uncreated. Nature worship was never totally removed from Greek thought, although it developed into a highly intellectualised form. Therefore it was simply 'not on' to pry too closely into her secrets – the legend of Prometheus captures the Greek understanding well. What is more, it was held that it was impossible to do anything against nature. Even for Plato in his *Timaios*, the demiurgos who shaped the world according to a definite plan had his hands tied in two important respects. Firstly, he had to follow the model of eternal ideas, and secondly he had to put the stamp upon recalcitrant matter which he had not created.

2. The Greek conception of nature was not only rational, it was rationalistic. To the Greeks, what was not rational was not real, and only what was real (that is, not subject to change) could be known. In nature logical necessity reigned. Therefore, mathematics with its ideal and unchangeable objects was the type of true knowledge. Astronomy was slightly inferior and the terrestrial sciences, where there is so much change, were hardly worth bothering with at all.

3. The disregard of matter led the Greek idealistic philosophers to undervalue observation and experiment. Plato, for example, mocked the Pythagoreans for their 'torturing instruments' in order to obtain knowledge.

4. The disregard of manual labour led not only to the undervaluing of experimentation but also to that of applied

science. Aristotle was of the opinion that all useful things had already been invented.

The contrast with the biblical view on the other hand could not have been greater. For one thing, the Bible spells freedom from any tyranny to 'nature', for even this is put under the dominion of man (cf. Psalm 8), so that in principle there is no aspect of creation which is a scientific 'no go' area. Experiment, technology and even art does not have to copy nature: they can actually go against it without any fear of reprisal. According to the biblical account, God created according to his own sovereign free will, so that one cannot say beforehand that certain things are impossible; he is not bound by what we would claim to be 'objective reason'. God has established rules in his creation, and it is by humble investigation that we are to discover the extent to which they are conformable to our reason. What God has created he pronounced good, so that the study of material nature is a religious duty; matter is not to be looked down upon. Furthermore, manual labour is not some inferior activity: God instituted it and he himself did not shrink from becoming a carpenter's son.

Hooykaas puts the contrast as follows:

> The Bible knows nothing of 'Nature' but only knows of 'creatures' who are absolutely dependent for their origin and existence upon the will of God. Consequently, the natural world is admired as God's work and as evidence of its Creator, but is never adored. Nature can arouse in man a feeling of awe but this is conquered by the knowledge that man is God's fellow worker who shares with Him the rule of the fellow creatures, the 'dominion over the fish of the sea and the fowl of the air. . . .' Thus, in total contrast to Pagan religion, nature is not a deity to be feared and worshipped, but a work of God to be admired, studied and managed. In the Bible, God and nature are no longer both opposed to man, but God and man together confront nature.[3]

One cannot over-emphasize the radical and liberating effect of this biblical outlook. Now, science becomes an activity which is actually pleasing to God. Obedience to the truth – what you find by observation and experiment – becomes central, so that one is no longer bound by preconceived ideas of what can or cannot be the case: to put it crudely, if you want to know what a thing is like – go and look. Science could be seen as part of Christian charity, a duty whereby the findings of science could be used to benefit one's fellow man. We see, for instance, in the works of Francis Bacon the ideal of science being used in man's service, and so he concludes his preface to his *Historia Naturalis* with the prayer:

> May God, the Founder, Preserver and Renewer of the Universe, in His love and compassion to men, protect the work both in its ascent to his glory and its descent to the good of Man, through His only Son, God-with-us.

Certainly, as Bacon himself stressed, such activity was to be done in a spirit of humility – humility before God and the creation as he has made it. Also, as we see in Newton, the founders of the Royal Society and the Puritans, men like John Wilkins (Cromwell's brother-in-law), whatever is done is to the 'glory of God'. Thus it was within the milieu of Protestant Christianity that modern science was launched.

Why the suspicion?

Given that the roots of modern science extend deep into the rich soil of biblical Christianity, why the suspicion – in the popular mind at least – that somehow science and Christianity, far from being the best of brothers, are the worst of enemies? Why do we still need apologetic talks such as 'Science versus Religion'? Why, in spite of the sterling work of bodies like Christians in Science and the Victoria Institute, does this perception of science being at odds with the Christian faith still persist? A number of reasons can be adduced, but let me mention just two:

First of all, there has been plain mischief-making by some notable scientists who make no pretence that they have a particular axe to grind, and usually a humanistic one at that; men like Sir Julian Huxley, G.G. Simpson, Jacques Monod, B.F. Skinner, Francis Crick, to name but a few. Some of these men, with access to the media, have propounded worldviews which are decidedly at odds with Christianity and have given the appearance that such philosophies are the product of science itself. And so one can forgive the unwary reader or viewer for thinking that it must be a case of either modern science or antiquated Christianity. Certainly, as we shall see, there is an either/or situation, but it is not in these terms.

Secondly, we must admit to the feebleness of some of our Christian apologetics in this area which have tended to foster the idea that whatever science is related to, it certainly is not the Christian faith. There have been those who, with good intentions, have employed bad arguments. The classical instance of this is the celebrated debate at the Oxford meeting of the British Association following the publication of Darwin's *Origin of Species*, between T.H. Huxley and Bishop 'Soapy' Sam Wilberforce. I think that Huxley's reply to the Bishop in which he demolished his argument as a piece of ignorant and 'aimless rhetoric' is certainly correct. Indeed, more or less from those days the picture of the churchman as the dogmatic, reactionary ignoramus, over and against the brave scientist who is open–minded, rational and willing to 'boldly go where no man has been before' (yes, even *Star Trek* has done its work in perpetuating this idea!), has persisted up to the present time. But in spite of the caricatures, we must admit that there is more than a grain of truth in this. Later I hope to give some more modern day examples where, from men whom I admire and to whom I owe much, there has come rhetoric and faulty thinking which has not really served the cause of Christ and truth – men like Francis Schaeffer, C.S. Lewis, and more recently Professor Oliver O'Donovan.

Putting the Cards on the Table

Let me make my theological position clear so that the reader might know from which direction I am coming. I stand within the tradition generally referred to as the Reformed or Calvinist tradition. I also acknowledge my immense debt to the work of the late Professor Donald MacKay whose thinking is referred to on a number of occasions throughout this paper. This is said so that when criticisms are made of other positions, they are made as it were from 'within the family'.

So, what are some of the areas of science and religion which need to be approached with some caution? Let me suggest five such areas:

1. Where there is less than a full–rounded appreciation of what science is and its limits

I suppose that the commonly held view of the way by which scientific investigation and acquisition of knowledge proceeds is along the lines proposed by Francis Bacon – generally referred to as the 'scientific method'. Ideally this can be set out in the form of six steps:[4]

1. Gather data.

2. Formulate a general rule (hypothesis) according to the data.

3. Derive predictions from the hypothesis.

4. Check the predictions by making experiments.

5. If the predictions are true, then give the hypothesis the provisional status of a law (theory).

6. If the predictions are false, return to step 1 and attempt to derive another hypothesis.

Underlying the scientific method are the following assumptions:

1. Data are hard facts and beyond dispute.

2. Hypotheses arise from seeing some sort of pattern in the data and making an inductive generalisation from them. This maintains that all cases fit the pattern.

3. Predictions from the hypothesis are derived by simple deduction from the hypothesis itself.

4. Discarding or retaining a hypothesis is a simple matter, depending upon whether additional experimental data support it.

5. Confirmed hypotheses are simply added to a long line of existing general laws. Progress in science is made by making such additions to the list. This is what Professor Hilary Putnam of Harvard calls the 'treasure store' approach to science.

This is the way many 'lay' people would conceive of science operating; and of course there is some truth and validity in this approach, although as pointed out earlier, the steps outlined are very much idealised.

In 1962, however, a book was published which was to cast considerable doubt upon this conception of scientific methodology, *The Structure of Scientific Revolutions* by Thomas Kuhn.[5] He argued that progress in science does not take place in this step-by-step approach. Research always takes place against the background of assumptions and convictions produced by previously existing science, so that to a certain extent, what actually count as data will be dependent upon the particular disciplinary matrix in which the investigative scientist operates. This disciplinary matrix (what Kuhn calls a 'paradigm') is made up of the scientific community to which one belongs. Without going into detail regarding Kuhn's work which has been adequately critiqued elsewhere[6], it might be helpful to outline the counter-presuppositions underlying his thesis in contrast to the Baconian method:

1. There are never hard data. All data are theory laden. It is presupposed that things are organised in a certain way which is compatible with the way science is organised at the time.

2. Hypotheses do not arise in a vacuum: they arise out of the combined influence of the paradigm as a whole.

3. It is not possible to deduce a prediction from an isolated hypothesis, it is also dependent upon an existing body of

theories which specify how it is to relate to any experimental set up.

4. Discarding an hypothesis is rarely an easy affair. Sifting an invalid hypothesis from a cluster of valid ones can be a subtle business.

5. Advance in science does not take place by piecemeal additions: sometimes 'revolutions' occur when a whole body of knowledge is recast.

Kuhn argues that there are, as it were, three stages of development in a particular scientific field:

1. Immature science, where the parameters are poorly defined and there is dispute between workers as to what are the relevant data.

2. Mature science, in which advances are made and a fundamental theory is proposed which becomes the 'exemplar' for others and acts as an organising principle. This is characterised as a period of problem solving.

3. Extraordinary science, which leads to scientific revolutions. Here particular anomalies cannot be ignored and indeed fall into a pattern of their own. Consequently more energy is devoted to working on these which leads to people producing alternatives to the established disciplinary matrix. Traditional ideas become increasingly challenged and a new paradigm more fruitful than the old is produced which accounts for the anomalies. The most well–known example of this is the 'revolution' from Newtonian physics to Einsteinian physics and now the 'new' physics. Working with these two understandings of science, where have Christians gone astray? Let us look at two examples where this has occurred.

First, by some creationists who, working with the first understanding of the scientific method, have claimed that evolutionary science is not 'true science'.[7] For example, one creationist writes:

> it is manifestly impossible to prove scientifically whether evolution took place or not . . . the events are non–reproducible and, therefore, not legitimately subject to analysis by means of the so–called 'scientific method'.[8]

Although repeatability is important in science it is by no means the sole or sufficient criterion by which it is distinguished from non-science. Here there is a failure being made to distinguish between nomothetic science – aiming to establish laws describing infinitely repeatable events, and ideographic science concerned with understanding and explaining unique events like the origin of species.

Some creationists have gone further by invoking Karl Popper's 'principle of falsification', which stresses that a theory must be testable in the sense that conditions must be specified under which it could be demonstrated as false. It is claimed by some creationists that according to this principle the theory of evolution is not open to falsification. However, there are two problems for the creationist at this point. The first is that it is inconsistent with what they are trying to do, namely, to demonstrate that the theory of evolution is false. Secondly, one must ask that if what is maintained about falsification holds, then where does this leave creation science, which, by its own admission, is non–falsifiable? Does this mean that it is a non–science or pseudo–science? It looks like the creationist is hoist with his own petard.

There are other Christians, who perhaps because of a misreading of Kuhn, have seized hold of the belief that objectivity in science is some sort of 'myth'. Thus one Christian writer can say: 'The social sciences . . . give lie to any simple model of value-free objectivity in science.'[9] It is then concluded that since value-free knowledge cannot be obtained in any pure form, then the whole concept of value-free knowledge is somehow meaningless – so it is one in the eye for the hard–nosed scientist! Nevertheless such reasoning is misplaced. Because we cannot obtain precise detailed knowledge, say, of a DNA molecule, this does not mean that the molecule is a 'myth'. Certainly the pursuit of knowledge, and how we use that knowledge, will to a lesser or greater extent be influenced by questions of value – what to do, how to do it and when. But it simply does not logically follow that the concept of value-free knowledge is a 'myth'. On a purely day-to-day basis there is a growing amount of evidence that in so many ways science has 'got it right' every time we get into a car or cross a bridge or switch on the television set. In other words what has been proposed as scientific knowledge actually accords with reality – there is something 'out there' with which we have to reckon whether we like it or not. Just as the terrain must be allowed to determine what a map-maker will show, so it is with the data that the scientist handles, he in his own way being a kind of map-maker. But to listen to some of the more extreme advocates of the 'myth of objectivity'[10] one would think that it was our ideas which shaped reality rather than the other way round.

It is not incidental either that those who dispute the ideal of objective knowledge mostly come from the social sciences and not the physical sciences, and one can see why. Here there is an inherent problem in gaining access to objective knowledge because in the main they are dealing with people. Thus, for example, the moment a survey is conducted in which a 'representative unreflective member of the public' is interviewed, the subject has so been 'shaped' by the questions that he ceases to be 'representative and unreflective' – he was until the interviewer stepped in! The vital point which must be maintained is that objectivity in science is commendable as an ideal: the scientist needs to check himself against bias and ensure that what is presented is open for others to check and double check. This, of course, is very much in line with biblical thinking about the nature of the world and of God who, after all, is the one who does know what is objectively true.

If some Christians attack science on the basis of a faulty conception of what science is and what it means to be objective, others do so by claiming that there are areas in which it is neither possible nor permissible for a scientist *qua* scientist to enter. Again we need to be clear about what is being claimed. To suggest that there is a territorial limitation, so that for instance 'religion' lies outside the proper study of science because it is a 'spiritual matter', is wide of the mark. The fact is that science can and does study 'religion', for example the psychology of conversion. Indeed, there is much that the Christian could learn from such findings, particularly concerning the dangers of psychological manipulation in preaching. Would it not be more appropriate to think in terms of methodological and conceptual limitations in science? Thus, the scientific method is fine if you want to obtain a certain type of knowledge. But it is next to useless if you want to obtain other types of knowledge such as personal knowledge (for example, the love of another). A failure to recognise this limitation was the gaping error of logical positivism. For the scientist, detachment is an ideal, but if that principle is carried over into some other areas of life it would not produce more knowledge but less.

What is more, there is a conceptual limitation to science in that while a description of a phenomenon may be given by a scientist which might be complete within its own terms of reference, this does not rule out other levels of description which are logically 'higher' and complementary. A chemist might give an exhaustive description of the contents of this page in terms of colour pigments and cellulose composition without mentioning what to me is the most important description of all – what the essay is all about! It might therefore be suggested that in principle there is no area in life which is *ipso facto* ruled out for scientific investigation, although there may be good practical and ethical reasons why such investigations should not be carried out. Sometimes the objection is framed in terms of the scientist wanting to 'play God'. But what does this mean? If it is a criticism of an attitude of arrogance and scant disregard of the consequences of research, motivated out of personal ambition, then the point can be taken; but if it is the suggestion that there are certain areas, say of human functioning at the genetic or brain level, into which in principle the scientist should not enter because it is 'interfering with nature', then it is misplaced. For if we are to take the Bible's teaching seriously concerning our responsible stewardship before God, then in some circumstances not to act would be morally reprehensible (Matt. 25:14–30, *passim*). Far from 'playing God', the scientist in his investigations may be doing no more than being an obedient steward before his Creator.

2. A failure to distinguish clearly between legitimate scientific methods and conclusions, and an illegitimate worldview which is parasitic upon science.

There is little doubt that some highly extravagant claims have been made in the name of 'science' with an anti-Christian slant, which, upon closer inspection, have more to do with a worldview which by sleight of hand has been linked to science and all the prestige it carries in the minds of some. The most obvious example is that of evolutionism, which some Christians think is indistinguishable from the theory of evolution itself. Consequently, some adopt the tactic of trying to show that the scientific theory is false in the hope that any atheistic philosophy built upon it will come tumbling down. But this is to concede too much too soon. It is far from certain (given that one cannot derive an 'ought' from what 'is') that evolutionism as a worldview follows from the theory of evolution. As a philosophy, evolutionism leaves much to be desired. Indeed, as some Christians have argued, the theory of evolution is just as congruous with a biblical perspective, perhaps even more so than with an atheistic one. This failure to tease out sufficiently scientific investigation and any accompanying philosophical views shows itself in other ways too. In his booklet *Back to Freedom and Dignity*,[11] Francis Schaeffer engages in a wide-ranging attack upon the teachings of Jacques Monod, B.F. Skinner and Francis Crick, as well as expressing concern about research on the human brain. He admits that much of what these men teach arises not so much out of their scientific research but their philosophies, which in most cases are reductionist – that is, man is understood solely in terms of his constituent parts and nothing more. Unfortunately, instead of Schaeffer attacking the reductionist philosophy and demonstrating that it is philosophically bankrupt, he uses rhetoric to attack scientific practices which, while needing the correct ethical safeguards, may in principle be regarded as legitimate methods of enquiry. He writes:

> While we would add that man is more than a brain, our brain is a good brain. God made the human brain. But the fact is that man is fooling with it. Electrical stimulation of the brain, genetic engineering, chemicals in the drinking water – the human brain will be drastically changed.[12]

Certainly to 'fool' with anything as delicate as the brain is reprehensible, but who is talking about 'fooling'? To speak of our brain being 'good' because God 'made it' needs some qualification in the light of Christian belief in the fallen human condition. Surely there are instances when the brain is evidently far from 'good' (schizophrenia, for example). If the brain in such circumstances could be improved (again with the appropriate safeguards), then it would be incumbent upon us to do so. Also Schaeffer fails to make the important distinction between physical determinism and metaphysical determinism: 'When one accepts the presuppositions of determinism, whether chemical or psychological, moral values disappear.'[13] But as Donald MacKay has shown[14] even if one were to grant physical determinism, metaphysical determinism (the denial of the reality of human freedom and responsibility) does not logically follow from it. We need to make sure that our criticisms are aimed at the right targets.

3. A failure to appreciate the relationship between science and hermeneutics

How are we to understand the relationship between the findings of science and biblical interpretation? Is it a matter of science (and for the moment, we include archaeology) augmenting or verifying the biblical revelation? Certainly archaeology provides helpful background material, enabling us to tackle some of the historical and cultural questions with which the Bible presents us. But given the sufficiency of Scripture for the purpose for which it was divinely inspired, namely, to teach, rebuke, correct and train in righteousness so that we might become wise with regards to salvation (2 Tim. 3:16), are these the two primary alternatives set before us? Could it not be that when one wants to ask more sophisticated questions beyond, as it were, the 'spiritual' meaning of the passage (making us wise unto salvation etc.), what the facts of science, as distinct from speculation, provide us with is a check or corrective to ensure that we are looking at the passage from the right angle. In other words, science might perform a negative function in eliminating faulty interpretations of the Bible. For example, Psalm 93 was taken by some teachers in the church as evidence against the Copernican claim that the earth revolved around the sun. It is not sufficient simply to retort that such teachers were more influenced by Aristotle than the Bible and this accounted for their error; the fact remains that divinely inspired Scripture was adduced in supporting their case. We now know that they were wrong. Does this cast doubt upon the divine authority or trustworthiness of Scripture? Not at all. But it does mean that the way such teachers interpreted Scripture was awry. In this case science provided a corrective as well as an incentive to go back and put right the hermeneutics. The God–given meaning of Psalm 93 had not been altered at all; indeed, in some ways it was perhaps highlighted and brought into sharper focus by this scientific discovery. Just in case there are those who think that this approach is a novel one, it is worth reminding ourselves that this was the hermeneutic of John Calvin. He held that the religious (what I called 'spiritual') message of the Bible is accessible to everyone and that God accommodated himself to our infirmities in the writing of Scripture, so that Moses 'adapted his writing to common usage'. Thus Hooykaas comments:

> It is to Calvin's credit that, though recognising the discrepancy between the scientific world system of his day and the biblical text, he does not repudiate the results of scientific research on that account.[15]

The Puritan John Wilkins, while making much of Calvin's commentaries on the Psalms and Genesis, stressed a non-literalist interpretation of Scripture when touching on scientific matters. One may therefore want to raise the question: Who is standing much closer to the hermeneutical tradition of the Reformers on the matter of the interpretation of Genesis 1–3: the creationists or the theistic evolutionists?

4. The problem of romance, nature and paganism

We live in an age in which 'science bashing' is the rage. One reaction to what has been perceived as the abuses of technology is to romanticise nature, so that if only we could go back to nature and conform to her designs, then many of our present problems would be alleviated. But far from this being a biblical idea, as we have seen, it is a strongly Greek and pagan one reminiscent of the Greek belief in a 'Golden Age'. One no less than C.S. Lewis fell into this trap in his book *The Abolition of Man*[16] in which he protested against Baconian technology, claiming that both magic and applied science share a common ground in that they both try to subdue reality to the wishes of man. He condemned human dominion over nature as being hubris and praised the ancient wisdom of conforming to nature.[17] But this is a Stoic conception and not a biblical one. Interestingly enough, Lewis did not adduce Scriptural support for his position! Hooykaas helpfully comments:

> It is true that the results of our dominion over nature have been unhealthy in many cases; the powerful river of modern science and technology has often caused disastrous inundations. But by comparison the contemplative, almost mediaeval vision that is offered as an alternative would be a stagnant pool.[18]

More recently this same 'back to nature', semi–Stoical view has surfaced in the writings of Oliver O'Donovan in his book *Begotten or Made?*[19] which explores developments in reproductive technology such as in vitro fertilisation. O'Donovan argues that technological interference with the 'natural' course of events in procreation (begetting) is expressive of western man's determination to 'free himself from the necessities imposed upon him by religion, society and nature'.[20] This 'project of human self–mastery' is identified with attempts to 'fashion the future' in contrast to simply 'acting together', an action being defined as 'an event which has a beginning and an end'; and 'when one completes what one is doing, one launches it, as it were, upon the stream of history. What happens to it then is out of one's control.'[21]

to act well, then requires faith in divine providence . . . but to 'fashion the future' is to refuse to let one's act go. It is to strive to extend one's control even to directing the stream of history . . . to assume a totalistic responsibility for what will happen.[22]

The language is impressive, but the reasoning is flawed. Would it be at all responsible or a denial of belief in 'divine providence' if a Christian helicopter pilot entered his aircraft (a product of technology), started the engine, and when in flight decided to 'act well' by 'letting go'? Of course not. O'Donovan appears to be focusing upon one type of action at the expense of another, viz. man acting in open defiance of God (which is reprehensible) and man acting as a responsible steward before God (which is commendable). The latter type of action, far from requiring a 'letting go', demands that all the resources and gifts which God has given (through divine providence) be used in a responsible manner. It is ludicrously wide of the mark broadly to claim that all such attempts to 'fashion the future' arise out of man's rebellion. What about controlling disease, averting floods, and saving the ozone layer?

O'Donovan does say that 'Christians should. . . confess their faith in the natural order as the good creation of God. To do this is to acknowledge that there are limits to the employment of technique', and that these limits are taught to us by 'the understanding of what God has made, and by a discovery that it is complete, whole and satisfying'.[23] But what sort of limits are envisaged: ethical or territorial? Again one must ask, 'What of the fall?' The world has disorder too and is in so many ways far from 'satisfying'. It is a world which requires control and subduing as our Lord by his example showed us. With more concern rightly being shown over 'green issues' and with the rise of new cults like the 'New Age' movement, Christians of all people need to resist any enticement back to paganism, even if it is wrapped up in Christian terminology. We need to set our feet squarely upon the rock of Scripture and the worldview that it promotes – a view which sees the world as God's creation and man as a responsible steward and not a passive participant.

5. The need to guard against an unhealthy fusion of science and theology

The most obvious example of an unhealthy fusion of science and religion is that of Teilhard de Chardin's work, an amalgam of evolutionary science, Thomism and pantheism. But more recently, with some remarkable developments in physics, there are those who are attempting to bring science and the Christian faith together in such a way that it is hoped science will provide insight into our understanding of theology. The most notable proponent of such an approach is Professor John Polkinghorne. In his *Science and Creation*,[24] Polkinghorne is concerned with exploring a revised natural theology. He fails, however, to make the important distinction between natural theology and natural revelation. He cites Scriptural passages like Romans 1:20 as encouraging an attempt at natural theology, but at most such passages legitimise belief in natural revelation, which is a far cry from the natural theologies of Aquinas or Swinburne, the difference lying in their epistemologies.

In *Science and Providence*[25] Polkinghorne states that 'The modern understanding of the physical process is indeed helpful in the consideration of God's possible action in the world' and that 'recent advances in science point to an openness and flexibility within the physical process'. He claims that 'the causal joint of divine action is located in those regimes where what we call chance has a role to play' (chance being understood in its technical and not popular sense). But not only is this a too restrictive notion of God's interaction with the world understood in terms of providence or miracles (he suggests the model of 'watchmaker' be replaced by that of 'divine juggler'), the theological price paid is too high, namely, a dilution of the biblical revelation of the sovereignty of God. At one point[26] Polkinghorne mistakenly analogises the omnipotence of God with his omniscience, so, it is argued, that just as God cannot change the past he cannot know the future, except by making highly informed conjectures. While the 'Book of nature' and the 'Book of scripture' need to be related, they should not be conflated. Still by far the best course to follow is the Reformed principle of the Bible providing the rationale, motivation and epistemological basis for science, but with theology and science being kept conceptually distinct – the former providing the higher category of meaning for the latter.

Conclusion

In his book *The Turn of the Tide*,[27] Professor Keith Ward devotes a chapter to science and religion under the title, 'The Phantom Battle', which admirably sums up the contention of this paper, that in so many ways the alleged 'conflict' between science and Christianity is more apparent than real. Questions of application still remain; ethical considerations which are inextricably bound up with religious convictions need constant review. Christians should have their critical guard raised in distinguishing good arguments from bad, and extravagant claims (in the name of 'science' or 'Christianity') from more realistic and modest ones which accord with Scripture.

We conclude with one more insightful remark by Hooykaas:

> We have to steer a middle course between an archaistic reactionary defence of pagan–nature worship in Christian disguise, and the progressive hubris of modern scientism: between a feeble submission to nature, and a belief in infinite progress achievable through pulling ourselves up by our bootlaces....[28]

Such a 'middle course' can only be charted if an attitude of humility is cultivated between the scientific investigator and him who said 'without me you can do nothing'.

NOTES

1. A paper originally given to ministers and students at Elim Bible College, Nantwich, December 1989.

2. R. Hooykaas, *Religion and The Rise of Modern Science*, Eerdmans (1974). Also, Hooykaas, *The Christian Approach in Teaching Science*, Tyndale Press (1966).

3. Hooykaas, *Religion and the Rise of Modern Science*, p.8.

4. This summary is helpfully expounded by Vern Poythress in his

excellent book, *Science and Hermeneutics*, Apollos (1988).

5. T. Kuhn, *The Structure of Scientific Revolutions*, Chicago Press (1962).

6. See Del Ratzsch, *Philosophy of Science*, IVP, Chapter 3 (1986).

7. For an excellent review of the creationists' claims see Poole and Wenham, *Creation or Evolution – False Antithesis?* (Latimer Studies 23/24, 1987).

8. H.M. Morris, *The Twilight of Evolution*, Baker Book House (1963), p.29.

9. Cited by D.M. MacKay in his essay 'Objectivity as a Christian Value', in P. Helm (Ed.), *Objective Knowledge*, IVP (1987), p. 26.

10. For example David Bloor, who is not a Christian, and one of the leading advocates of what has become known as 'The Edinburgh Strong Programme'.

11. F. Schaeffer, *Back to Freedom and Dignity*, Hodder & Stoughton (1973).

12. Ibid., p. 29.

13. Ibid., p. 27.

14. See D.M. MacKay 'Man as a Mechanism', in *The Open Mind*, M. Tinker (Ed.), IVP (1988), p.49.

15. Hooykaas, Ibid., p.120.

16. C.S. Lewis, *The Abolition of Man*, Fount (1978).

17. Ibid., Chapter 3.

18. Loc. cit. p.74.

19. Oliver O'Donovan, *Begotten or Made?*, Oxford (1984).

20. Ibid., p.6.

21. Ibid., p.7.

22. Ibid., p.8.

23. Ibid., p.12.

24. J. Polkinghorne, *Science and Creation*, SPCK (1988).

25. J. Polkinghorne, *Science and Providence*, SPCK (1989).

26. Ibid., p.79.

27. Keith Ward, *The Turn of the Tide*, BBC (1986).

28. Hooykaas, *The Christian Approach in Teaching Science*, p.19.

4

Content, Context and Culture:
Proclaiming the Gospel Today

'We evangelicals,' writes John Stott, 'are gospel people. The word *evangelical* contains within itself the word *evangel*. And if the first hallmark of the evangelical is biblical supremacy, the second is the centrality of the gospel.'[1] It is this passionate concern to define the good news of Jesus Christ clearly and to communicate it effectively that has not only helped set the criteria by which an evangelical is defined, but has also set the priorities by which an evangelical is to serve. Therefore, it is not merely a similarity of words which accounts for the confusion in many people's minds between being an 'evangelical' and being an 'evangelist', for one of the basic identifying features of evangelicalism is the activity of evangelism.

It is precisely because evangelicals are 'gospel people' that three questions are presently being discussed by evangelicals both within and outside the Church of England.

The first is the question of gospel content. Just what is to be included in the presentation of the gospel message? In short, what are the 'givens' of the gospel, the fundamental gospel truths revealed by God?

The second question revolves around the extent to which the cultural context in which the gospel is to be proclaimed leads to a reshaping of the gospel message. In other words, how flexible can we be in presenting the gospel without compromising it to such a degree that it becomes another gospel?

The third area of discussion concerns the nature of the relationship between gospel and culture. The main question here is, 'How does the gospel affect culture?, or at least shape the Christian's attitude towards culture?'

The three areas of concern – gospel content, gospel context, gospel and culture – are not simply matters of academic interest to those involved in teaching about 'mission'; they are of immense *practical* importance to us all. For whatever answers we give to these questions will determine both the nature of the church's message and the nature of the church's task in the world. Therefore, as we consider these subjects from the standpoint of evangelicals, it is vital that we are uncompromisingly biblical in our thinking and radical in our application.

The beginnings of the gospel

When we go back to the accounts of Jesus' ministry as recorded in Matthew, Mark and Luke, we discover that there is both a unity and a diversity in the way the term 'gospel' (good news) is used.[2] But whatever differences there are in detail between the synoptic writers, there is little doubt that the good news they have in mind centres upon the person and work of Jesus of Nazareth through whom the kingdom of God is made known.

A brief look at the first few verses of Mark's Gospel will serve to illustrate this: we read, 'The beginning of the gospel of Jesus Christ, the Son of God' (Mark 1:1) – words which not only form an introduction to the events which immediately follow (the ministry of John the Baptist) but to Mark's work as a whole.[3] What is more, it is the good news of 'Jesus Christ', both in the sense that it originates from him – he being the herald of the good news – and that he is its subject matter: it is about him. A little later, in verse 15, we are given a summary of what it was Jesus proclaimed, namely, 'The kingdom of God is near. Repent and believe the good news.' And so it is not incidental that this startling announcement is immediately followed by the call of Simon and Andrew to leave everything and follow Jesus, for this, in a nutshell, is what responding to the gospel entails.

The gospel and the kingdom

At this point we need to clear away some of the fog which has tended to surround the phrase 'kingdom of God', especially given the way this term has become something of a 'hooray word' among some evangelicals in recent years, almost to the extent that it is now in danger of becoming the mark of a new evangelical orthodoxy.[4]

Primarily, the term 'kingdom of God' refers to the dynamic rule or reign of God in which he reveals his *saving* and *judging* activity in *Jesus Christ*. This is something which should not be confused with God's universal sovereign rule. Yet this is an important distinction which is sometimes overlooked by some in their concern to provide a basis for social involvement grounded in what is called 'kingdom theology'.[5] However, as we shall see in a moment, the kingdom of God in the New Testament is thoroughly Christological in nature – centred upon Christ – and is not to be generalised simply to mean 'wherever God's will is done'. A warning against making such a generalisation was given by Sir Norman Anderson back in 1967 at the first National Evangelical Anglican Congress (NEAC) at Keele, a warning which sadly has largely gone unheeded. This is what he said:

> But is there a wider sense in which one can think of the Kingdom as advanced wherever the will of the King is done, even by those who do not give him personal allegiance? This, it seems to me, is dangerous ground, for we cannot regard the Kingdom of God as having materialised in a factory, for example, merely because social justice and harmony reign therein. Still, we should not deny for a moment that such is the will of God.[6]

The main thrust of the New Testament is that the kingdom of God has to be received or entered into, and it is only those who are 'poor in spirit' (Matt. 5:3), and obedient to Christ (Matt. 7:21), who can become members of the kingdom. Indeed, according to John's Gospel, one has to be 'born from above' even to *see* the kingdom of God, let alone enter it (John 3:5). It would seem that the popular expectation at the time was that God would decisively establish his kingdom in a manner which would be public and open for all to see, bringing immediate benefits to his people. But what we find in the Gospels is something radically different. In the ministry of Jesus, God is *already* acting, dynamically with saving effect, but also *secretly*. We have the 'veiled' mystery of the kingdom which proceeds like a tiny grain of mustard seed or a small lump of yeast. In the person and work of Jesus, God's kingly rule has already broken into history so that all that was promised in the Old Testament is being fulfilled in him and will be consummated at some point in the future when he returns.

How, then, does the kingdom of God find expression in Jesus Christ? In at least three ways.

The kingdom of God and the works of Jesus
First of all, the kingdom of God is revealed in the *works* of Jesus. In reply to John the Baptist's question from prison concerning the real identity of the Messiah, Jesus points to the signs of restoration taking place within his own ministry in which the effects of sin and the devil were being undone (Matt. 11:4). In Matthew 12 it is interesting to note that it is within the context of an exorcism – a direct encounter with dark spiritual forces – that the statement is made: 'The Kingdom of God has come upon you' (v. 28). What is more, it is the religious and social outcasts – the lepers, tax collectors and prostitutes – who are received into the kingdom, as indicated by the fellowship meals they had with Jesus. This was not only a sign of acceptance within the setting of Jesus' own ministry, but was also a deeper sign pointing to the messianic banquet to be enjoyed when the kingdom is brought to completion at the end of time (cf Luke 14:14; Matt. 8:5ff). Little wonder, therefore, that Jesus received that marvellous backhanded compliment of being 'the friend of tax collectors and sinners'. He was!

It is impossible not to notice that all those who were drawn to Jesus like moths around a flame were characterised by the same inner disposition in that they were all 'poor in spirit'. Although it is swimming against the popular Christian tide (but then popularity should not be confused with truth), it is being maintained here that when the term 'poor' is used in relation to the kingdom of God, for the most part the main sense in which it is to be understood is metaphorical and not literal.[7] The striking exception is Luke 6:20, but even here we do not have a universal commendation of the poor. Jesus actually says, 'Blessed are *you* poor,' meaning the disciples who had become materially poor in following Christ as members of the kingdom. Otherwise, as in Jesus' comment on Isaiah 61 in the synagogue in Nazareth (Luke 4:16-19), the term is used in a secondary transferred sense to speak of the spiritual demeanour required by all, whatever their material or social standing. The point of comparison between the materially poor and the spiritually poor is that of helplessness – they are those who are unable to pay back – and this is the condition of everyone before God and needs to be recognised as such.

The kingdom and the words of Jesus

As well as in the works of Jesus, the kingdom of God finds expression through the *words* of Jesus. Unlike the teachers of the Law, Jesus authoritatively declares the word of God firsthand, taking the unprecedented step of prefixing his statements with 'Amen' – 'truly I say to you' (Matt. 10:42; 18:3). It is Christ alone who unfolds the secrets of the kingdom to his followers (Mark 4:10), and is described as 'rabbi' – 'teacher'. From the lips of Jesus we hear the values of the kingdom, supremely encapsulated in the Sermon on the Mount. As the judge of the kingdom he declares the forgiveness of sins (Mark 2:5), corrects distortions about the Sabbath (Mark 2:33ff) and makes it clear in no uncertain terms that a person's response to him will determine their ultimate destiny (Matt. 10:32).

The kingdom and the person of Jesus

Third, in a deep and profound way, the kingdom of God is manifest in the *person* of Jesus. As we have already seen, as the Son of God – the King 'veiled' – Jesus brings about the Father's rule and will in saving and judging. But as the Son of Man – representative Man – he is obedient to the will of the Father on our behalf, therefore fulfilling God's original intention that man should be God's covenant partner. As Karl Barth put it, 'Jesus does what we refuse to do' in that he was obedient to the Father at every point, even to the point of death on a cross in satisfying God's holy love. In similar vein, P.T. Forsyth claims that it is in the obedience of Christ, and especially at Calvary, that the heart of the Lord's Prayer in one sense is already fulfilled. At the cross God's kingdom had come and his will was done on earth as in heaven.

The Christ-centred kingdom

We are now in a position to see why, for instance, Mark presents the *whole* of his account as 'The beginning of the gospel of Jesus Christ, the Son of God', with the theological emphasis falling quite clearly upon the cross. It is illuminating to turn to a story such as the rich young ruler in Mark 10 to see how all of the themes mentioned above are brought together: inheriting eternal life (v. 17) is linked to receiving the kingdom (v. 23), following Jesus (v. 28) and the gospel (v. 29). This is immediately followed in verses 32ff by Jesus teaching about his death and resurrection – they are all of a piece.

It is therefore not so strange a shift that the one who proclaimed the good news becomes, in the early church, the one who is proclaimed as the good news. What was pointed to and substantially realised in the earthly ministry of Jesus – the restoring of relationships between God and man and the bringing together of a formerly estranged people into a new community – is eternally established through the empty cross of Christ and brought home to people's lives by preaching the gospel in the power of the Holy Spirit. So let us briefly look at the gospel truths proclaimed by the apostles: the 'givens' of the gospel.

The given of the gospel

For the apostle Paul, like Mark, there is never *a* gospel, but only *the* gospel, a message with a definite recognisable shape and content. And just what that apostolic core content is, we have set before us in 1 Corinthians 15:1-5:

> Now brothers, I want to remind you of the gospel I preached to you, which you received and on which you have taken your stand. By this gospel you are saved, if you hold firmly to the word I preached to you. Otherwise, you have believed in vain. For what I received I passed on to you as of first importance: that Christ died for our sins according to the Scriptures, that he was buried, that he was raised on the third day according to the Scriptures, and that he appeared to Peter, and then to the Twelve.

As John Stott so rightly remarks:

> There is only one gospel, the apostolic faith, a recognisable body of
> doctrine taught by the apostles of Jesus Christ and preserved for us
> in the NT... it is still so today. If there is only one gospel in the NT,
> there is only one gospel for the church. The gospel has not changed
> with the centuries ... although its presentation may vary, its substance
> is the same.[8]

The substance of the gospel

That substance is focused on by verse 3 of 1 Corinthians 15. The
good news is first and foremost *Christ-centred: 'Christ* died for
our sins.' The primary focus of the gospel is God, highlighting his
nature and movement in love towards us, with the secondary focus
being upon men and women as the recipients of that gospel.
Second, the gospel is *cross-centred:* 'Christ *died* for our sins.' It
centres upon a work, not our work, but his work on Calvary, and
any so-called 'gospel' which does not have the cross at its centre
as an act of substitutionary atonement is simply not the gospel, no
matter how attractive and appealing it might be. But third, the
gospel is *grace-centred:* 'Christ died for our *sins.'* Here alone is
the basis for our acceptance before God whereby we are declared
to be in a right relationship with him, having been saved from the
future judgement (justified); made more and more like Christ
(sanctified); only eventually to be with him for evermore in the
life to come (glorified). Furthermore, this grace so wonderfully
free, is received solely by the empty hand of faith: 'For by grace
you are saved *through* faith' (Eph. 2:8). Bishop Stephen Neill
states the Christian position well when he writes, 'Christians are
bound to affirm that all men need the gospel. For the human
sickness there is only one specific remedy, and this is it. There is
no other.'[9] How, then, is this remedy to be communicated? To
help answer this question we need to consider the relation between
the gospel and cultural context.

Gospel and context

Both logically and theologically, the identification of the gospel's
content must precede the question of how we are to go about

communicating that message in any given social context. However, the process of gospel communication will inevitably call for a variety in gospel expression. In fact, it was the early church's versatility in doing just that which formed part of the key to its own success in evangelism.[10] Nevertheless, while it is true that we must creatively and sensitively establish points of contact between the gospel and those whom we are trying to reach with that gospel, we must ensure that the gospel's integrity is fully preserved. It is the gospel which addresses people in their situation, not the situation which determines what the gospel is. Or to put it another way, although the gospel will address a whole range of felt human needs, such as loneliness, guilt, meaninglessness, and so on, it is not the case that those needs define the content of the gospel, so that, for example, the gospel comes to *mean* 'Jesus frees you from loneliness' or 'Jesus heals your diseases.' Although these things may form a point of contact for the gospel – a starting-point – they are not identical with that gospel.

It is important that we stress this because there is always a temptation to think of what people need and then to tailor a 'gospel' to fit accordingly. To go down that road is to end up with some sort of situation theology similar to the situation ethics which caused so much damage in the 1960s. In so doing we will be prone to respond evangelistically, like the psychiatrist to his neurotic patient. The patient, realising that he had another appointment asked the psychiatrist, 'What time is it?'. To which the psychiatrist replied, 'Well, what time would you like it to be?'

Contextualisation

This balance between ensuring that the gospel is communicated and yet not compromised is a delicate one, and the word used to describe the means whereby it is achieved is *contextualisation*. This term was brought to the fore back in 1972 by the Theological Education Fund,[11] and essentially means the reformulation of the Christian message within the language and culture of its hearers in such a way that the original meaning is properly conveyed. The advantage of the term contextualisation, as the director of the TEF, Shoki Coe, points out, is that it is a dynamic concept, for cultures themselves are never static but are constantly in a state of change. We have seen in our own culture how much things have changed in the last thirty to forty years, and so it is vital that we are constantly open and creative in our evangelism (using satellites and all!).

Therefore, if we are to be faithful to the Great Commission to 'make disciples of all nations', then we have to be sensitive to the context in which the recipients of the gospel are to be found. To use the rather well-worn phrase, we have to start where people are, and this applies as much to the housing estate in Bolton as to the marketplace in Bangkok.[12]

The example of Paul

Just what is involved in communicating the gospel contextually is helpfully illustrated for us both by the principles the apostle Paul himself adopted, and also by what happened to him on the road to Damascus.[13] Let us start with that revolutionary experience first.

In his own account, given to Agrippa in Acts 26, Paul makes three points which are highly relevant. The first is that Paul was addressed by the risen Christ in his own native Hebrew tongue, not Aramaic or Greek, although Paul could understand both. Second, the Word that addressed him did not so much affirm his way of life as call it into question: 'Saul, Saul, why do you persecute me?' Up to that point he had thought that he had been doing God a favour! Third, the voice which can make such a demand can only be the voice of the sovereign Lord himself, there is to be no question of speaking on our own authority, based upon experience, or the church's authority, but only *his* authority which is the authority of Scripture.

Here we have a marvellous model of what it means to engage in cross-cultural communication, with the objective trans-cultural gospel being communicated in thought-forms and language appropriate to the hearer. However, if the gospel is properly being conveyed, then this will inevitably involve calling into question certain ways of understanding and behaving, calling for a U-turn of mind – a new way of looking at things and a new direction for living, which means following Christ.

This is precisely what we see being worked out in the apostle's own ministry as he outlines his principles of what we could call 'dogmatic contextualisation' in I Corinthians 9:19ff:

> Though I am free and belong to no man, I make myself a slave to everyone.... To the Jews I became like a Jew, to win the Jews. To those under the law I became like one under the law... so as to win those under the law.... To the weak I became weak.... I have become all things to all men so that by all possible means I might save some. I do all this for the sake of the gospel, that I may share in its blessings.

Here Paul avoids two polar extremes. One extreme is so to stress faithfulness to *the way* we have received the gospel that the result is a stifling of the gospel – in a particular form, to the point of fossilising it. The other extreme is to be so concerned with flexibility, being 'all things to all men', that this amounts to an unconditional surrender to the prevailing spirit of the age (the error of theological liberalism).

For anyone concerned with spreading the gospel it is obvious that both faithfulness and flexibility are required: faithfulness to the revelation received (after all, Paul made it his aim to preach the 'word of the cross', a revelation which he tells us in Galatians 1:1 came not from man but from Jesus Christ), and flexibility in our approach so that we might save some. Furthermore, it was because Paul occupied a 'third position', as one 'under a law to Christ', that he was able to combine both of these so confidently and effectively.[14]

Dangers to be avoided
The biblical balance between faithfulness and flexibility is not always so easy to maintain in practice, and there is a tendency in some quarters to allow the social context to determine too much the *content* of the gospel message and not simply the way it is presented. So, although it is true to say that every theology will to some extent be shaped and coloured by the particular culture in which it is planted, it does not follow that the resulting contextualised theology will be true to Scripture. Again, we must

stress the priority of the Bible as being supremely definitive for belief and practice.

This is far from being a matter of mere academic interest, for 'existential contextualisation' (when what is considered to be 'the gospel' will vary from situation to situation) is in danger of being adopted by some evangelicals to the detriment of true evangelism. For example, in an article in *Evangelical Roots,* the preliminary magazine to NEAC 3, we find the following statement:

> The good news we love is defined in the Scripture as good news to the (physically and socially) poor; and that means that what the good news means to poor Christians (in Scripture and today) should set the criteria for focusing what the good news means to others.[15]

Apart from it being highly questionable whether Scripture does define the gospel in the way here suggested, the move to place Scripture and present-day context ('today') on a par with each other is a very dangerous one, since the tendency is for the latter to gain the controlling upper hand. What is more, this is often accompanied by a drift into some form of cultural relativism, as the rest of the article shows signs of doing.

The *Manila Manifesto,* produced by the 'Lausanne' International Congress on World Evangelization, states the evangelical position clearly when it says, 'Evangelism takes place in a context and not in a vacuum. The balance between gospel and context must be carefully maintained. We must understand the context in order to address it, but the context must not be allowed to distort the gospel' (p 9).

God the evangelist

Even when we have been as faithful and as flexible as possible in presenting the gospel, there still remains a stumbling block, namely, the cross of Christ. In the light of an active ministry among Muslims, Basam Madany writes:

> No matter how much we might contextualize the gospel message, the stumbling block remains... we cannot avoid the offence of the word of the cross. The contextualization which the Muslims require

of us to make the message really acceptable to them is nothing less than unconditional surrender.[16]

Considering this, together with the predicament being heightened by the biblical teaching on humankind's natural hostility towards God (Rom. 8:7) and the blinding effect of Satan upon the mind of the unbeliever (2 Cor. 4:4), how can we have any confidence that the gospel will be heard, understood and accepted? The answer lies in the regenerating work of the Holy Spirit. After all, it is the Spirit of God who is the great cross-cultural missionary – something stressed by Paul in his 'missionary manifesto' in 1 Corinthians 2:1-5:

> For I resolved to know nothing amongst you except Jesus Christ and him crucified.... My message and my preaching were not with wise and persuasive words, but with a demonstration of the Spirit's power.

Professor David Wells is therefore not exaggerating when he writes, 'Outside the supernatural workings of God's Spirit, unbelief is invincible, cultures are impenetrable and doors are closed.'[17]

All that has been said so far in terms of the gospel's content and the need for it to be contextualised has implied a certain understanding of the way the gospel is related to culture. It is now time for that understanding to be made more explicit and to draw from it some of the practical implications it has for evangelicals committed to mission in our land.

Gospel and culture

In asking the question, 'What is culture?', a number of definitions are readily at hand: Louis Luzbetak describes it as 'A design for living';[18] Peter Cotterell as 'The totality of an individual's normal behaviour in his own society';[19] Charles Kraft as 'That set of guidelines, followed largely unconsciously and habitually in the living of life, which structure and pattern all that we speak, think and do'.[20] It is obvious from these all embracing definitions of culture that religion, too, is an important element which makes up a particular culture. But the gospel, given by God, although needing to be expressed in forms appropriate to culture, is not bound by culture. In this sense we can speak of the gospel as being 'trans-cultural' or 'supra-cultural'.

Getting the relationship right

But how might the two – gospel and culture – be related? In a highly influential book entitled *Christ and Culture,* H. Richard Niebuhr proposes that at varying points the relationship might be one of *antithesis,* where something is so wrong that it has to be opposed; *reformation,* the elimination of something wrong so that something better will result; *identification,* where elements which are good in themselves need confirming and defending; and finally, *transformation,* in which the mediocre and ineffective is changed into something beneficial.

This fourfold dynamic understanding of the relation between gospel and culture accords well with the major biblical themes of creation, the Fall and redemption. In the light of the Bible's teaching on creation, we are not to dismiss everything in a culture as 'evil' simply because it appears strange to us. But neither, in view of the biblical doctrine of the Fall, do we accept uncritically everything as good and God-given. What is more, against the backcloth of the Scripture's teaching on redemption, we should eagerly be at work for change in accordance with God's revealed purposes for his world.

At the 1988 Lambeth Conference, Bishop David Gitari showed how this process of evaluating culture by the truth of the gospel works itself out in an African context.[21] Dr Gitari perceptively supplies examples of where the gospel challenges culture (e.g. the Massai's belief that all the cattle in the world belongs to them); *tolerates culture* (at least *provisionally,* as in the case of polygamy among those who have just become Christians); *endorses and transforms culture* (e.g. the African corporate understanding of humanity and the need to win whole communities for Christ). Bishop Gitari concludes his address by saying:

> The Incarnational model invites us to proclaim the gospel not from a distance but rather by penetrating into communities and cultures whose customs are endorsed, challenged or transformed by the gospel. In this way we believe that we are obeying the Great

Commission and as a result 'The Lord is adding to our numbers those who are being saved' and the Church of Christ is growing.[22]

By drawing together the two approaches of Neibuhr and Gitari, what might we suggest are some of the implications of the relationship between gospel and culture for the British scene?

Antithesis and challenge
The writer Os Guinness has pointedly remarked that:

> Christians are always more culturally short-sighted than they realise. They are often unable to tell, for instance, where their Christian principles leave off and their cultural perspectives begin. What many of them fail to ask themselves is 'where are we coming from and what is our own context.' [23]

In terms of the general trends in thinking and practice in our own society, there are several which deserve special mention in that the gospel stands in opposition to them.

In the first place there is *secularisation,* and one of its effects, *privatisation.* Secularisation is the process whereby various sectors of society are gradually freed from the decisive influence of religious ideas and institutions. The net effect is that religious ideas, and more to the point Christian ideas, become less meaningful and the church is marginalised. In its turn, privatisation makes a sharp distinction between those beliefs and practices which relate to the public sphere of life and those which are seen as purely private. How many times have we heard it said that 'Religion to me is a very personal thing', meaning that it is private and not open for discussion and scrutiny? Morality, too, is largely seen in private terms, so that we set great store by 'personal morality', which need bear no relation to the morality of the office or parliament. The gospel, however, challenges both of these trends on the basis of the lordship of Christ as the Creator-Redeemer to whom all things are subject in heaven, on earth and under the earth. A rigid compartmentalisation between 'sacred' and 'secular' is not a Christian option.

Second, there are the trends of *pluralism* and *relativism:*

pluralism, in that there is no commonly shared 'worldview' or system of values, but rather a variety of what the sociologist Peter Berger calls 'plausibility structures' – ideas and practices which enable people to make some sort of sense out of life. The pressure is then on to adopt a relativistic stance with there being no absolute truth; everything, it is claimed, is relatively true to something else. This in turn means that the focus of our attention is upon the *act* of choosing. What then matters is *that* you choose, with *what* you choose being a secondary consideration (hence the prevailing fixation on 'freedom of choice'). Questions of right and wrong then turn upon either personal preference ('whatever turns you on') or consequences ('the maximisation of happiness'). As a result a consumer approach to belief and values reigns.

However, it is the objectivity of the gospel, the truth given by the God of truth, which in transcending all cultures in its judgement upon them stands in opposition to such trends and so 'relativises the relativisers'. Christianity is not just one option among many in the religious supermarket; it is *the* truth, with Christ being the way, the truth and the life, and no one coming to the Father except by him (John 14:6).

The predominance of pluralism and relativism within our culture has also to be challenged within the church, and not simply outside it. We might well ask to what extent are Anglican evangelicals especially guilty of capitulating to a view of 'comprehensiveness' in the Church of England which smacks more of the relativism just mentioned than the principled comprehensiveness that Scripture would urge upon us? Are Anglican evangelicals to see themselves simply as one group among many in the church, alongside liberals and catholics, sharing their distinctive 'insights'; or is it the case that in the words of Dr Packer, 'by historical and theological right Anglicanism is evangelicalism in pure form.'[24] Our commitment to the gospel would suggest that it is the latter.

But if the gospel challenges both pluralism and relativism, beginning with the 'household of God', it also counters *hedonism* and *materialism*. Hedonism is the consuming love of pleasure, with its corollary that pain is to be avoided almost at any cost.

Materialism, on the other hand, can be understood either philosophically, so that only that which is open to the senses is 'real' ('seeing is believing'), or more practically as the desire for possessions. But here, too, we need to ask whether we as a church have been infected by such forces more than we realise. Do such present emphases on 'health and wealth', 'praise and worship', 'healing and wholeness', truly arise out of 'the whole counsel of God', or are they the Christianised offspring of hedonism and materialism? Surely it is the eschatological perspective, which the gospel alone provides, which sounds a distinct note of caution to such movements. So, with Paul, we would affirm that 'this slight momentary affliction is preparing for us an eternal weight of glory' (2 Cor. 4:17), no matter what the 'wholeness' teaching might say. We are not to view all meaning and value in terms of the 'now', measured solely in material terms, whether brought about 'miraculously' or by social involvement, but we are to hold on to the 'not yet' which is to be revealed.

Identification and toleration

Variety in culture does provide us with a rich variety in life as part of God's gracious provision – variety in music, dress, language and communal living. And it is here that the church needs to learn and apply the principle of flexibility. Let us take just one example – the question of liturgical worship.

For those coming to an Anglican church from a non-book culture, for instance , is it necessary to immediately confront such folk with a Book of Common Worship which has a reading age of twenty (the *Sun* is thirteen), which by all accounts makes it difficult to read? Why not allow and encourage liturgical and non-liturgical expressions of worship to develop within the local community which are appropriate to that community? David Bronnet's comment at NEAC 2 still needs to be heard:

> If the church is middle class and intellectual in the language of the services, in the music employed, in the lifestyle expected of Christians, in its leadership, and in the methods of presenting the gospel, then the whole atmosphere is such as to repel those who are not middle class and intellectual.[25]

Transformation and reformation

The primary task of the church and the primary means of transforming culture is evangelism. This is our 'priestly duty' (Rom. 15:16). It is in making disciples and the working out of that discipleship in society that cultures are transformed and God is glorified. As C. S. Lewis so characteristically remarked: 'He who converts his neighbour has performed the most practical Christian-political act of all.'

Nevertheless, if Christians are to penetrate as 'salt and light', and work and pray for the changes required by Christ, then the church must have before it, as one of its main duties, to free and equip them for this task. In practice, this will mean that what is presently regarded as 'lay ministry' – the performing of liturgical functions – is replaced by true lay ministry whereby busy people are spiritually fed in the local church and so built up and encouraged to go into the world for Christ.[26] For all the tremendous steps that have been made in recent years regarding the role of 'laity', there is still a tendency to see 'Christian presence' in clerical terms when, in fact, *all* Christians are truly God's ministers in their respective situations.

It is by the faithful preaching of God's word in the power of God's Spirit that the Christian mind is informed, transformed and so equipped to deal with a whole range of situations at every level of society. After all, men like Wilberforce and Shaftesbury had no sophisticated 'kingdom theology' to act on, yet they, upon the basis of Christian love and obedience, achieved far more than many of us can claim.

Finally, when all has been done to remove archaic expressions, finding culturally equivalent terms, and so on, it remains vital that we help people to think themselves into the Christian account of things. The concepts and terms rooted in Scripture are fundamentally necessary for true *Christian* experience. All experience is interpreted experience, and so it is important that we interpret our experiences biblically and help others to do so. In an excellent treatment on this subject, Paul Helm writes:

Because there is a strong connection between the Word of God and
the Spirit of God and the vital place human understanding plays in
coming to Christ, a distorted presentation of the gospel will, in all
likelihood, produce distorted Christian experience. An evangelistic
proclamation which dispenses with the element of conviction of sin
and penitence, whose essential message is 'Jesus loves you come to
Jesus', will produce converts whose experience of sin and penitence
is either smothered or explained away.[27]

In other words, in sharing the gospel, whether to the most
down-to-earth docker or the most sophisticated scientist, scriptural
concepts such as 'sin', 'repentance' and 'faith' are not disposable
cultural commodities; they are non negotiables which are integral
to what being a Christian is; they cannot be bypassed; they have
to be explained.

Conclusion

As 'gospel people', evangelicals would want to contend humbly,
yet robustly, that there is only one gospel entrusted to the church,
the gospel revealed by God in the Scriptures concerning the unique
and final reconciling work of the Son of God upon the cross for a
rebellious and sinful world. It is the gospel which proclaims him
risen bodily from the dead, ascended, and Lord and Saviour of all
who put their trust in him. It is this gospel which the church is to
faithfully, sensitively and imaginatively proclaim to the ends of
the earth. In so doing, by God's grace, cultures will be transformed
as people are transformed by the Holy Spirit to the glory of God
the Father.

NOTES

1. J.R. W. Stott, *What is an Evangelical?*, Falcon (1977), p 10.

2. Mark prefers the unqualified use of the noun *euangelion* (good
news); Luke the verb *euangelizesthai* (to herald the good news);
and Matthew the qualified 'the gospel of the kingdom'.

3. See R. P. Martin, *Mark: Evangelist and Theologian*, Paternoster:
Exeter (1979) for a scholarly presentation of this idea.

4. As John Stott points out in his reply to Sider's *Evangelism, Salvation and Social Justice* (Grove Ethics, No 4).

5. As, for instance, Graham Cray's Sir Norman Anderson Lecture: 'The Kingdom of God and the Mission of the Church' (unpublished lecture delivered at the Salt and Light Conference, Swanwick, November 1988), in which he quotes with approval Lesslie Newbigin's statement that 'Jesus' proclamation concerned the "reign of God" – God who is creator, upholder and consummator of all that is. We are not talking about one sector of human affairs, one aspect of human life, one strand out of the whole fabric of world history; we are talking about the reign and sovereignty of God over all that is ....' Later, in an attempt to substantiate the belief that the kingdom of God is extended by the Spirit via non Christians, Cray says, 'Since Pentecost the Spirit has been poured out on all flesh, not just all Christians' (italics mine), a statement which has no scriptural support at all.

6. In J. I. Packer (Ed), *Guidelines*, Falcon (1967), p 231. More recently, Dr R. T. France has put the matter even more strongly when he writes, 'It is as wrong to identify the Kingdom of God with social reform as it is with the church or with heaven, and for the same reason: it is a category mistake'.... 'To talk of men, even Christian men, bringing about God's Kingdom is to usurp God's sovereignty. Yet this sort of language is increasingly being heard in evangelical circles. It is strangely reminiscent of the language of 10th century liberalism, which called upon men to create a just and caring society which was called "the kingdom of God", ' In D. A. Carson (ed), *Biblical Interpretation and the Church – Text and Context*, Paternoster, Exeter (1984), p. 41.

7. For a detailed defence of this position, see Hans Kvalbein, 'Jesus and the Poor: two texts and a tentative conclusion', *Themelios*, vol 12, no 3 (1987). Similarly, David Seccombe has argued that the Isaianic background to Luke 4 must be taken seriously as applying to Israel as a whole, but now (Luke 6:20) the inheritance belongs to the 'poor', i.e. the disciples. See 'Possessions and the Poor in Luke-Acts', *SNTU* Series B, (Linz: 1983), p 137.

8. J. R. W. Stott, *Only one Way – The Message of Galatians*, IVP, (1968), p. 7

9. Stephen Neill, *Crisis of Faith*, Hodder & Stoughton (1984), p.31.

10. For an excellent treatment of this subject see Michael Green, *Evangelism in the Early Church*, Hodder & Stoughton (1970).

11. *Ministry in Context*, Theological Education Fund (1972).

12. For a first-rate example of how to contextualise the gospel for today see Alister McGrath's *Justification by Faith – An Introduction*, Marshall and Pickering (1989), pp. 77ff.

13. Lesslie Newbigin develops this theme with considerable skill in his book, *Foolishness to the Greeks*, SPCK (1986), pp. 5-20.

14. The fact that Paul's principle of 'accommodation' was not without limits is argued in detail by D. A. Carson in his article, 'Pauline Inconsistency: Reflections on 1 Corinthians 9:1-23 and Galatians 2:11-14', *Churchman*, vol 1 (1986).

15. Christopher Sugden, 'Passage to India', in *Evangelical Roots*, Church of England Evangelical Council (1988), p. 27.

16. Quoted in *Outlook* (February 1986).

17. David F. Wells, *God the Evangelist*, Paternoster (1987), p.28.

18. Louis Luzbetak, *The Church and Cultures* (William Carey library: 1970), p. 61.

19. Peter Cotterell, 'What is Culture?', *Christian Arena* (December 1986), p. 2.

20. Charles Kraft, 'Gospel and Culture', *Christianity: A World Faith* (Lion: Tring, 1985), p 274.

21. David Gitari, 'Evangelization and Culture: Primary Evangelism in Northern Kenya' (unpublished paper of the 1988 Lambeth Conference of Bishops).

22. *op cit*, p 16. Similar proposals are made by the 'Willowbank Report', Occ Papers Lausanne no 2 (1978).

23. Os Guinness, *The Gravedigger File,* Hodder & Stoughton (1983), pp. 42, 45.

24. J. I. Packer, introduction to W. H. Griffith Thomas, *The Principles of Theology*, Vine (1978).

25. D. Bronnet, 'The Gospel and Culture' in J. R. W. Stott (ed), *Obeying Christ in a Changing World*, vol 3, Collins (1977), p. 126.

26. See Tony Walter, 'Against participation, for the Kingdom', *Churchman*, vol 2, (1988), pp. 14-150.

27. Paul Helm, *The Beginnings: Word and Spirit in Conversion*, Banner of Truth (1986), pp. 12-126.

5

Doctrine Matters:
Anglican Evangelical Theology Today

Introduction

There is a story of a group of British soldiers who became lost in the desert during the Gulf War. They eventually stumbled across an American General who was surveying the scene. 'Do you know where we are?' the men blurted out. The General, very annoyed that they were improperly dressed and hadn't bothered to salute or address him as 'Sir', indignantly replied: 'Don't you know who I am?' 'Now we are in real trouble,' said one of the soldiers, 'We don't know where we are and he doesn't know who he is!'

This is an attempt to ascertain where Anglican evangelicals are in terms of their theology, for it is our contention that certain cracks are appearing which indicate several weaknesses at the level of foundations. What is more, what can be said of Anglican theology in particular can be extended to much of Western evangelical theology in general. There is widespread uncertainty about 'who we are' as evangelicals.

Our purpose is to offer a critique of some present trends in Anglican evangelical theology, together with some constructive correctives. The hope is that this will stimulate a more consistent evangelical approach to matters of doctrine. What is offered are some select examples which illustrate such trends, with accompanying comments rather than in-depth analysis. There are two basic reasons for selecting the following examples for our study: first, they touch upon issues of fundamental importance for evangelical belief and practice, and second, the writers involved are quite influential amongst Anglican evangelicals and therefore their views require serious consideration.

The misuse of the biblical concept of the Kingdom of God
Certain biblical concepts are presently in danger of having their biblical sense obscured and other meanings gradually attached to them; concepts such as 'Kingdom' and 'Justice'. Some of these terms function as 'buzz words', creating an approving resonance in the minds of the hearers and so act as means in forwarding certain theological agendas. If the words are used often enough in this way, then it is only a matter of time before the new meaning takes over from the Scripturally intended meaning.

One example of this is the way the term 'The Kingdom of God' is being employed by some evangelicals.

Think of the way the term 'Kingdom' is now frequently used as an adjective. Books are appearing thick and fast with titles such as 'Kingdom Living', 'Kingdom Ministry', 'Kingdom Praying'. Indeed, it appears that one sure way of gaining a ready market for a book is to have the term 'Kingdom' appearing somewhere in the title. This, however, is not the way the New Testament uses the term. It is the Kingdom of *God (he basileia tou Theou),* the focus being God who exercises his kingship. But even this has to be qualified given the New Testament's emphasis upon God's saving kingly rule exercised through Jesus Christ. Hence, George Beasley-Murray's helpful rendering 'the *saving* sovereignty of God'.[1] In other words, a conceptual distinction has to be made between the 'universal reign of God' which carries the sense that God is sovereign ruler over all (Psalm 145:13, and God now ruling through Christ, Ephesians 1:20-23), and the 'kingdom of God' understood with specific reference to Jesus Christ and salvation. The latter is a kingdom which must be sought and entered into. It requires poverty of spirit, submission to the will of God and an entering through the 'narrow gate' (Matt. 5:3; 7:21; 7:13). Indeed, one has to be born from above even to see this kingdom (John 3:3). This is a spiritual kingdom, one which is 'not of this world', and therefore it is not appropriate to use worldly means to achieve its ends (John 18:36). To come into this aspect of the reign of God is to enter into eternal life – the sphere of salvation. As Don Carson rightly argues, the Kingdom of God understood in terms of salvation is a subset of the universal reign of God which is now mediated through the risen and ascended Christ.[2]

Why is it important that attention be drawn to this? For the simple reason that such a distinction is being overlooked by some evangelicals, with far-reaching implications for the way we understand both the nature of the gospel and the way in which God extends his saving rule in the world.

Amongst those who would wish to own the term 'radical evangelical', the New Testament sense of the term 'Kingdom of God' is seriously being misused and reduced to the idea that 'God rules'. Those who adopt this position maintain that wherever social justice and peace are promoted, there we are to see the Kingdom of God, even if Christ is not acknowledged or salvation experienced.[3] One leading advocate of the 'Kingdom' approach to social ethics writes: 'Jesus' rule and action are cosmic. He has disarmed the principalities which create division in society. Where we see barriers broken down, can we divorce this from God's will seen in Christ's victory over the powers on the cross? (e.g. between Jew and Gentile, slave and free in Galatians 3:28)' and 'this understanding gives us a basis for seeing God at work in society beyond the church applying the effects of Christ's victory on the cross through social change'.[4] Another leading exponent of this position states: 'The Kingdom comes wherever Jesus overcomes the power of evil... Jesus' death was also a decisive victory over the disordered, rebellious structures of our socio-historical existence.'[5]

Such statements are very reminiscent of the 'Social Gospel' movement which developed in the USA at the beginning of this century under the theologian Walter Rauschenbusch. Rauschenbusch was a thoroughgoing theological liberal, adopting a theology of the Kingdom of God espoused by Albrecht Ritschl. However, as White and Hopkins insist, 'The theology of Walter Rauschenbusch was rooted in evangelical piety.'[6] He condemned the toleration of sin in society and sought through social change to assist in the practical realisation of the kingdom of God in the world. He also saw the 'unChristianized' nature of American capitalism as being a stumbling block preventing non-Christian nations responding to missionary work. The cross, however, did not largely figure in his theological framework, whereas it is central to the understanding of the new radicals (e.g. 'Wherever evil is overcome in society it is due to the work of the cross'[7]).

Nonetheless, there are similarities between the old social gospellers and the new radical evangelicals. Both have the Kingdom of God as their theological centrepiece for mission. Both see social action as being integral to mission and forwarding the Kingdom in the world. Both see non-Christians as in some way experiencing the redemptive scope of the kingdom.[8] As Brian Stanley observes: 'This is extremely difficult to distinguish from the claim of Rauschenbusch that wherever corporations abandon monopoly capitalism for the "law of service" or undemocratic nations submit to real democracy "therewith they step out of the Kingdom of Evil into the Kingdom of God".'[9]

But in extending the term 'the Kingdom of God' to embrace people and actions which are not Christian, a most serious misuse of a fundamental biblical concept is taking place. What Scriptural warrant is there for claiming that 'Where evil is overcome in society this is due to Christ's work on the cross'? Much is made of reference in Colossians and Galatians to the defeat of the 'elements of the universe' (*stoicheia tou kosmou*), as if it is crystal clear both what these 'powers' are and that whatever influence they have in the socio-political sphere can be altered by political change which can be traced back to the cross.[10] However, it is highly questionable that this is a correct reading of the term as employed by Paul.[11] Certainly in Colossians it would seem that the main thrust of Paul's argument is that it is as people become *Christians,* now living under the Lordship of Christ, that such spiritual powers are denuded of their influences over them. Similarly it is questionable whether the 'principalities and powers' of Ephesians 6 can be identified with political structures as some like Ron Sider and John Howard Yoder have proposed.[12]

It is also implied that the miracles and healing ministry of Jesus can be understood not simply as signs of the inbreaking of the Kingdom into the present age, but as equivalent to present day efforts to bring about justice in society. Indeed, some go further and claim that *any movement,* Christian or not, which takes place to establish social justice and righteousness are to be interpreted as having the same character as Jesus' Kingdom acts of power and healing.[13] But one must ask whether the Bible is being handled properly to justify such thinking.

The great commission, the example of the early church in Acts and Paul's teachings to Christians, all show that the way the saving Kingdom of God relates now to God's wider rule is through people being converted, then adopting new priorities and values. Such people will seek to improve the lot of their fellow men out of obedience to Christ and his call to fulfil the law of love.[14] It is *in making disciples* and the working out of that discipleship in society that cultures are transformed.[15] The church itself, which although not to be identified with the Kingdom of God, is the locus in which Christ's rule should be most visibly and clearly expressed.[16] As such, Christians individually and collectively should both put society to shame and indicate the way forward to more wholesome God-approved patterns for living.

If the New Testament understanding of the Kingdom of God is not adhered to, what will result will be 'another Gospel', one in which redemption from sin is absorbed in policies for socio-political change. Salvation is then conceived as rescue from structural sin rather than from the wrath to come.

False relation between doctrine and experience
The relationship between Christian doctrine and Christian experience is much more intertwined than we often suppose. There is a sense in which doctrine enables us to interpret experience. For example, in talking with a non-Christian who may be experiencing some sense of meaninglessness, the doctrines of creation, the nature of man and the consequences of the Fall could be brought to bear so that the experience may be properly understood as a prelude to presenting the gospel. However, it is vital to stress that it is in and through Christian truth that one comes to experience God. Doctrine 'informs' experience; it structures and interprets it.

But not all view doctrine and experience in this way. One writer describes the relationship between doctrine and experience as follows:

Underlying the Christian faith is first and foremost an experience, rather than the acceptance of a set of doctrines. The New Testament bears powerful witness to the experiences of the first Christians – an experience of the presence and power of the risen Christ in their lives, charging them with meaning and dignity.... The essential purpose of Christian doctrine is to provide a framework within which the experience of the first Christians may become ours.[17]

Elsewhere he writes:

Experience of God provides the stimulus to develop doctrines about God. Thus the Christian belief in the divinity of Christ did not arise as an intellectual theory, but through the impact of experiencing Jesus Christ as God.[18]

But is this actually the case?

In countering what can be called incipient gnosticism, John in his first letter writes: 'That which was from the beginning, which we have heard, which we have seen with our eyes, which we have looked at and touched with our hands – this we proclaim to you concerning the Word of life.' Howard Marshall in commenting on these verses writes: 'Our writer here wants to emphasise that the Christian message is identical with Jesus; it took personal form in a person who could be heard, seen and touched.' In other words, the apostles' experience of Jesus was not simply some existential 'I-Thou' encounter which led them to search around for appropriate concepts to express that experience. Rather, the experience itself involved hearing propositional truths – teachings – received from Jesus about his person and work, explained within the framework of the Old Testament Scriptures.

What is more, the apostles' Spirit-enabled task was to 'witness' to Jesus, bringing other people to faith through their message (John 16:13; 17:20). It is by embracing this message (with definite doctrinal content) that fellowship is had with God and other believers (1 John 1:5). Certainly this is more than intellectual assent *(assensus),* it is wholehearted trust *(fiducia).* But doctrine does not follow some experience of God, it is the means by which we come to recognise him and so experience him. Furthermore, it is as revealed truth is embraced, animated by the Holy Spirit, that a whole host of other Christian experiences are to be had such as conviction of sin, repentance, forgiveness, joy unspeakable (1 Peter 1:3-12 is most instructive here). It is not the case that 'Experience and meaning are two sides of the same coin,'[20] but rather that in order to experience the gospel one must respond to its meaning.

The relationship between doctrine and experience is such that belief in erroneous doctrine can generate erroneous experiences, which if not anti-Christian may well be sub-Christian. To help us understand how this is so, let us think of the way language in general functions. Language is used to talk about things (informative) and to think about things (cognitive). It is also used to get things done and bring about a change of affairs; promises and commands do this (performative). Language is also used to express and elicit feelings (expressive and evocative) as well as bind people together in a common solidarity (cohesive). Doctrines function in much the same way. They relate truths about who God is and what he has done (informative). They provide categories by which we might think about God and ourselves aright (cognitive). They can bring about a state of affairs, so for example, in hearing and responding to the doctrine of justification we are declared to be in a right relation to God (performative). Through doctrines about the holiness of God, his saving righteousness and so on, our feelings may be stirred to adoration (evocative) and by using the appropriate language of praise and penitence we may express such feelings (expressive). Furthermore, through adherence to common biblical doctrines, we enjoy a common evangelical solidarity (cohesive).

Now we can see that far from Christian doctrine merely being some sort of mould by which formless experience is given shape, it actually gives Christian experience its character. Thus to change doctrines which function in the ways just outlined is very serious indeed, for if such changes are substantial what results is something *other* than *Christian* experience. What *counts* as Christian experience will, in part, be determined by the doctrinal grid through which it comes. If that grid is not biblical, the experience won't be Christian.

Let me give a personal example of what I mean. When I was a student we had a speaker at the Christian Union who, with impressive rhetoric, told us that he had received a 'word from the Lord' loosely based on John 15 that there were two types of Christian; those who were servants of God and those who were friends of God. The servants of God had a dutiful service, but the friends of God were those who having being baptised in the Spirit knew a joy and intimacy which the others could only envy. 'Which are you?' he challenged. 'Which do you want to be?' he enquired. The answer, of course, was a foregone conclusion. Practically everyone in the meeting, including myself, felt impressed, convicted, and cast down. But was such an experience 'Christian'? The answer must be 'no', for no such division of Christians is to be found in Scripture and no alleged 'filling' of the Spirit is proffered as a solution. The truly Christian experience came for me when, in reflecting upon what was said in the light of Scripture, I saw the teaching to be bogus and realised afresh the wonderful liberty of being a child of God.

Now we can see why a Bible-centred ministry is so vital to the spiritual well-being of the church and why evangelicals of all people should not give way to other things which would displace it. It is through such ministry, by the agency of the Holy Spirit, that people's minds are shaped and hearts are moved to know, obey and so experience God as he has revealed himself through his Word.

Subversive Hermeneutics

In an article entitled 'It seemed good to the Holy Spirit and to Us?',[21] one Anglican scholar has argued that those who have changed their mind on the issue of ordaining women to the presbyterate have done so in the light of certain recent changes. It is acknowledged that society has changed and is 'impatient' with the few remaining bastions of male privilege. The church, and therefore the gospel, is 'for many tarred with the brush of chauvinism and of injustice'. The church too has changed, 'moving away from the one man band form of ministry causing many to appreciate the ministry of women.' But thirdly, and perhaps most significantly, hermeneutics has changed, that is, the principles and methods applied in biblical interpretation and application, particularly, under the influence of what is sometimes called the 'new hermeneutic'. So now, says the writer 'we have come to realise that it is possible on some issues to argue in quite opposite directions from Scripture depending on what texts you take as your starting point, and what relative weight you give to different aspects of the whole scriptural revelation'.

Having acknowledged the traditional approach to this matter, namely considering those texts which seem to apply specifically to the issue –1 Corinthians 11, 1 Corinthians 14, 1 Timothy 2 and so on – he suggests a different approach. This is to look at the broader sweep of Scripture, one which sees women in the Old Testament from time to time taking a leading role, the way Jesus related to women and challenged conservative Jewish attitudes, and the alleged 'impressive way' Paul viewed women, as we glean from the way he greets and speaks of certain leading women in Romans 16. So he writes:

> The effect of this chapter is so striking that one wonders how it could derive from the same Paul who is responsible for 1 Timothy 2:12. If it does, as I believe, then the question must surely be raised whether Paul meant in that passage quite what he is generally understood to have meant, or whether there was something specific to the situation in Ephesus at the time which caused him to make a more restrictive ruling apply.

So we have a choice: 'Whether we take our stand on 1 Timothy 2 and related passages, and somehow make the prominent role of women in first century Christianity fit in with them or we start with the more general picture as it is summed up in Galatians 3:28 and ask how the more restrictive passages can be explained in that context.' In addition, he says, we have to face the more demanding hermeneutical question that even if we follow the traditional reading of Paul, how do we apply that teaching to the very different circumstances in which we find ourselves today?

There are several issues here

First, should we not detect signals when it is admitted that one of the main stimuli for a re-examination (and re-interpretation) of biblical texts is changing attitudes in society? Thus, Paul accommodated his teaching to the culture of his time (and from one point of view was inconsistent, going against the principle of Galatians 3:28) and we are to do the same. Does this mean that if our society developed in a more male dominant direction then we had better re-read Paul again and go back to a more traditional interpretation?

Secondly, the writer inverts a very important principle of Biblical interpretation. Instead of reading passages which clearly and specifically deal with an issue – e.g. eldership/teaching ministry within the church – and reading the less clear passages in their light, it is suggested that the more obscure passages, such as the listing of women in Romans 16, be taken as key and the more specific passages such as 1 Timothy 2 be viewed against this backdrop, thus not only explaining them but explaining them away as culturally specific.

The fact is, Paul, in the one passage dealing with the issue, refers back to the creation order for his ruling and not to the specific context of the church situation. Therefore, we need a hermeneutic which will enable us transpose this principle of headship, that is Christlike male leadership and teaching, to the situation in the church today, and not a hermeneutic which violates it.

The main concern with a hermeneutic which emphasises the difference between our world and the world of the New Testament over and against the sameness, is that too much weight and influence is given to the prevailing beliefs of the present day. One cannot help but see a parallel between the arguments used for the ordination of women – relativising those texts which address the issue – and the arguments for legitimising practising homosexual relationships. Supposing the prevailing attitudes in society were to change to such an extent that, to modify the words of our writer, 'it became impatient with the few remaining bastions of heterosexual privilege and began tarring the church, and therefore the gospel, with the brush of homophobia and injustice', does this mean that we should go back to the Scriptures and reinterpret those texts which appear to rule out such practice? If we are to be consistent, then the answer must be 'yes', and conveniently a hermeneutic is ready at hand to enable us to do so.

In fact this has already started to happen. Here is part of an article which appeared in a recent Anglican evangelical journal.[22] Notice the formal similarity in the argument used to legitimise homosexual relationships and the arguments we commonly hear to justify the ordination of women to the presbyterate. Referring to Romans 1:26-27 this writer states:

> Paul's argument is Greek in form. He draws on the notion of the natural (*phusis*) which was very important in a wide range of Greek philosophies (but relatively unusual in the biblical tradition). It is a word which means more than 'normal' or 'conventional', but it does not mean natural in the sense of a fixed law in physical nature of a purely factual kind. The natural is not that which is simply observed in nature, but rather it is a human moral reflection on the natural world. It includes a sense of human judgement which can be enshrined in cultures and laws. Thus, when Paul speaks of it being natural for women to wear their hair long (1 Corinthians 11:14), he is using the word in a typically Greek sense .... I suggest that Paul's argument in verses 26f is similar to that in I Corinthians 11:14, based on his own moral reflection of the natural order he comes to the conclusion that male/male and female/female sexual relationships are idolatrous ... my argument is that based on the openness to reflection of the concept *phusis*, we need not necessarily share his conclusion today. It is significant that Paul and his world had no word for homosexuality, they did not know that some human beings have sexual orientation that seems deeply fixed in a homosexual mode. As a consequence they lumped together pederasty, homosexual prostitution and sexual debauchery. It seems to me that we could claim today that living and committed homosexual relations are natural within the Greek sense of the word *phusis*...

He then goes on to say:

> Because it uses a moral argument based on the Greek *phusis*, Paul's reasoning in verses 26f means that in our different empirical and moral setting we can come to a different conclusion in the specific

case of committed homosexual relationships. We can thus remain faithful to the deep argument of Paul's text...

And the conclusion?

We ought to accept homosexual relationships that are not idolatrous as being part of the variety of creation. Those who are convinced under God that this is the form of life that they are called to ought to be respected whether they are lay or ordained.

Is there not something perverse in a hermeneutic which can lead us to say the exact opposite of what Paul is saying and at the same time claim that we are being faithful to him?

The development of a hermeneutic which has the effect of imprisoning Paul's teaching within the confines of his own culture and ideological preunderstanding, so relativising and silencing him, reached a new stage in a subsequent article dealing with the same issue.[23] Here it is argued that Paul's worldview need not be ours, indeed, the recent insights of psychology and sociology make it almost impossible for us to adopt Paul's 'weltenschaung' with integrity:

Current thinking generally considers homosexual orientation to be 'natural', physiologically present in a person. Sexual relations should be between equals and with consent of both persons.... Our world view is very different from Paul's. Paul condemned same-sex acts in the light of his differentiated and structured view of creation, in which the male and female roles should be distinct and hierachical. Is such a worldview normative for Christians today? There are many aspects of Paul's thinking that we no longer accept uncritically; we condemn slavery more forthrightly than he did; we do allow women to teach, and in few churches are women silent and hatted, and in those churches seldom do men lift up holy hands as part of their praying.

The writer concludes by presenting us with a stark choice of alternatives, either to use the Bible 'pre-critically', in which case, he argues, we have to go the whole way to be consistent, strict adherence to the Torah, speaking to one another in psalms, etc., or we adopt a 'post-critical' position, allowing our interpretation of Scripture to be the result of a 'dialogue' with 'the best of psychological and sociological insights'.

But surely this is a false antitheses. In the first place it is quite evident that this proposed 'dialogue' is a very unequal one, effectively rendering the authority of Scripture in any meaningful sense void. The presentation of the 'traditional' evangelical approach is a gross caricature which is most reprehensible. It has been demonstrated by eminently able evangelical scholars that it is possible to adopt an approach to interpreting Scripture, based upon the grammatico-historical-theological method, which enables us to make some distinction between those elements of Scripture which are solely or largely the cultural expressions of theological principles (wearing veils, lifting holy hands, etc.) and those which have absolute, universal application (e.g. the prohibition of same-sex genital relations).[24] To place Paul's treatment of homosexuality in the same category as wearing veils is naive and mischievous. In a variety of places and in a variety of ways, Paul propounds a theology of male-female relations, grounded in the doctrine of creation-fall-and redemption. It is this framework which makes same-sex genital relations 'unnatural'. To jettison such an understanding, as this professing 'evangelical' writer does, is to engage in a serious departure from a view of biblical inspiration and authority which has been one of the defining elements of evangelicalism. While one is wary of the 'slippery slope' argument, one wonders what, if anything, will be left of Paul's teaching which we can consider as having any validity today.

Several years ago Carl Henry commented:

> In recent years a type of theft has emerged as some fellow evangelicals wrest from the Bible segments that they derogate as no longer the Word of God, some now even introduce authorial intention or cultural context of language as specious rationalisations for their crime against the Bible, much as some rapist might assure me that he is assaulting my wife for my or her own good ... they misuse Scripture in order to champion as biblically true what in fact does violence to Scripture.[25]

This is a most pertinent comment on some trends presently taking place in Anglican evangelicalism.

A new commitment

Of all the weaknesses reviewed, the last is perhaps the most worrying. It has been a hallmark of evangelicalism that Scripture is supremely authoritative and sufficient for matters of faith and conduct. While the question of the authority of Scripture is the subject of another chapter in this book, it might be helpful to raise one or two points in conclusion.

What does it mean to hold to the authority of Scripture? One helpful way of considering this question might be to think of the way any form of communication functions. In this regard valuable assistance can be afforded by the insights provided by brain science at the level of communication engineering, as propounded, for example, by the late Professor Donald MacKay.[26/27] Put simply, any form of communication (whether true or false) is designed to shape the way we relate to things, what is called our 'conditional states of readiness'. How this works can be illustrated by way of analogy: In a railway shunting-yard there will be a signal box of levers. When the levers are set up in a certain pattern the yard is 'conditionally ready' to deal with traffic in a corresponding way. Change the pattern of the switches and you change the conditional readiness to cope with the traffic. Words can be thought of as specially designed tools for adjusting the switch settings of our brains – having a shaping function, so that we can become ready to act. So it is with God's communication with us in the Bible. It is designed to shape the way we relate to reality – the reality of God, the world, each other and so on. Hence, Jesus' often misquoted statement in John 8:31: 'If you *hold* to my teaching, you are really my disciples. *Then* you shall know the truth and the truth will set you free.' Understanding and obeying the truth of God co-inhere. It is impossible to have obedience without understanding.

The implications of this are quite far-reaching.

Firstly, it is an incentive to put teaching where it ought to be, namely, at the centre of Christian ministry. For it is through proclamation, teaching and admonishing (Col. 1:28), that people's states of readiness are shaped so that they will think and behave in God-approved ways. We must not underestimate what happens Sunday by Sunday or on any other occasion when God's Word is opened.

Secondly, it means that in addition to attempting to be as accurate as possible in conveying Christian doctrine, we must pay close attention to the non-verbal aspects of our communication which can be just as effective in their shaping effect on people's minds as the actual words used. By this one does not simply mean the manner, intonation and demeanour adopted in preaching (although these things are included), but, for instance, the 'style of worship', the form as well as the content of the services. Are these subject to God's authority? Are they designed to have the shaping effect in people's lives that God intends? Or is something else being conveyed such as: 'This is being done because it is sixteenth-century language' or 'Worship is having a happy self-indulgent time with good vibes all around'? To acknowledge the authority of Scripture in *practice* means acknowledging and submitting to God's right to shape our conditional states of readiness.

This brings us to our third point, namely, the extent to which we are submitting to that authority can in part be gauged by our responses to situations as they arise. In other words, our behaviour often serves as a fair indicator of what our true beliefs are and what is *really* exercising its authority over us. For example, in spite of what Article Six of the Thirty Nine Articles says about the authority of Scripture, in practice many Anglican evangelicals are more or less being required to adopt as an article of faith that only 'priests' can officiate at Holy Communion. This is not required by Scripture and one may argue that a good Scriptural case can be made that it should not be so. (A similar position has now arisen with the measure permitting the ordination of women to the presbyterate.) What are Anglican evangelicals' conditional states of readiness with regards to such matters? Are we being ruled by God's Word or by denominational regulations? What are we willing to do about it?

There must be a new and deliberate undertaking by Anglican evangelicals to promote the belief and practice of the authority and sufficiency of Scripture. This will involve exposing and resisting some of the trends that have already been noted. It will involve encouraging ministers in particular to develop and maintain the priority of the teaching ministry and to call for those who are so gifted to engage in doing the necessary theological graft to promote a coherent and contemporary evangelical theology for our generation. This will not be a matter of doing the theological equivalent of re-inventing the wheel, but it will be part of contending afresh for the faith delivered once for all to the saints. And it is to this task that all evangelicals must commit themselves with renewed vigour.

NOTES

1. G.R. Beasley-Murray, *Jesus and the Kingdom of God*, Paternoster Press (1986).

2. D.A. Carson, *The Sermon on the Mount:* An Evangelical Exposition of Matthew 5–7, Baker Book House (1982), pp.11-15.

3. So George Carey writes: 'The Kingdom comes when lives begin to open to the claims of Christ and surrender to him; it comes also when God's peace, love, joy and righteousness are reflected in human society; it comes as the bonds of alienation are cut from the lives of men.' *I Believe in Man*, Hodder (1977) p.125.

4. Sugden in *Kingdom and Creation in Social Ethics* (Grove Ethical Studies, No 79, Sugden and Barclay, 1990).

5. R. Sider, *Evangelism, Salvation and Social Justice*, Grove Books (1977).

6. R.C. White Jr and C.H. Hopkins, *The Social Gospel; Religion and Reform in Changing America* (Philadelphia, 1976) p.17; also p.249.

7. C. Sugden, *op cit*, p.13.

8. C. Sugden, *'The Kingdom of God in Social Ethics'*, unpublished paper 1984, p.10.

9. B. Stanley, *'Evangelical Social and Political Ethics: An Historical Perspective'*, unpublished paper 1986, p.11.

10. So R. Sider writes: 'Colossians teaches that Jesus' death did more than accomplish atonement for believers. Jesus death was also

a decisive victory over the disordered rebellious structures of our socio-historical existence.' *Salvation and Social Justice,* p.9.

11. For a thorough discussion of the meaning of the 'Elements of the Universe', see Peter O'Brien in his *Colossians, Philemon,* commentary, Word (1987), pp. 129-132.

12. See J.R.W Stott, *Ephesians,* The Bible Speaks Today Series IVP (1979), pp. 267-275.

13. See Vinay Samuel and Chris Sugden, 'God's Intention for the World; Tensions Between Eschatology and History,' in Tom Sine (ed), *The Church in Response to Human Need* (Montrovia 1983), pp.225-6.

14. For a discussion on how Christian ethics be commended to society at large see, M. Tinker, 'The Priority of Jesus: a look at the place of Jesus' teaching and example in Christian Ethics' in *Themelios,* Vol 13, No 1 1987.

15. Russell Shedd's comment is worthy of consideration within this context when he writes: 'Replacing unjust structures with more equitable ones will finally be crowned with failure unless a far more profound transformation is wrought in the men who establish them and wield their power. For this reason evangelicals must ever contend that the first responsibility of the church is the proclamation of the gospel and depend upon the consequential spiritual change wrought by the Holy Spirit to create a community in which the unconverted may see a model of the Kingdom of God.' 'Social Justice, Underlying Hermeneutical Issues', D.A. Carson, *Biblical Interpretation and the Church – Text and Context,* Paternoster (1984), p. 201.

16. See I.H. Marshall, 'The Hope of the New Age, the Kingdom of God in the New Testament', *Themelios* (Vol 11, No. 1, 1985).

17. A.E. McGrath, *Justification by Faith,* Marshall Pickering (1988), p.129.

18. A.E. McGrath, *Understanding Doctrine,* Hodder and Stoughton (1990), p.40.

19. I.H. Marshall, *The Epistles of John,* in New International Commentary on the New Testament, Eerdmans (1978), p.102. See footnote for discussion on the interpretation of verse 1.

20. A.E. McGrath, *The Genesis of Doctrine,* Blackwell (1990) p.70.

21. R.T. France, 'It seemed good to the Holy Spirit and to Us?' *Churchman,* 1994, Vol.3. Also see Melvin Tinker, 'It seemed good

to the Holy Spirit and us'? A reply to Dick France, *Churchman* (1994), Vol. 3.

22. M. Williams, 'Romans 1: Entropy, Sexuality and Politics', *Anvil* Vol 10/No 2/1993, pp. 105-6.

23. P. Reiss, 'Sexuality, Symbol, Theology and Culture: A reply to Francis Bridger', *Anvil,* Vol II, No. 1,1994.

24. *Hermeneutics, Authority and Canon.* ed. D.A. Carson and J.D. Woodbridge, IVP (1986).

25. C.F. Henry, 'The Bible and the Conscience of Our Age' in *Hermeneutics, Inerrancy and the Bible'* ed. Radmacher and Preus.

26. D.M. MacKay, *Human Science and Human Dignity*, Hodder and Stoughton (1979), pp. 80-102.

27. D.M. MacKay, *Behind the Eye*, Blackwell (1991), pp. 112-116.

6

Euthanasia – A Severe Mercy?

In 1992, Dr Nigel Cox was prosecuted for the attempted murder of Lilian Boyes, a longstanding patient of his who was suffering from rheumatoid arthritis. Her life expectancy was short and she asked Dr Cox to end it for her. At first he refused. But then he gave her a lethal injection of potassium chloride and she died within minutes. He was found guilty and received a twelve-month suspended sentence. He was reprimanded by the General Medical Council but continues in practice today. Here is an example of 'voluntary euthanasia'.

A few years earlier, a Down's syndrome baby, John Pearson, was given a deliberate overdose of dihydrocodeine by his doctor, Leonard Arthur. The doctor was acquitted and treated leniently by the medical authorities. This is an example of 'non-voluntary euthanasia'.

We now have well known figures like Ludovic Kennedy urging a change in the law to allow what is sometimes referred to as 'death with dignity' to take place under certain conditions. Over the years there have been several attempts to legalize euthanasia, and presently there is an all party euthanasia group which claims the support of 100 or more MPs. However, in 1936, 1969 and 1976 when bills were brought before Parliament seeking to allow voluntary euthanasia, they were all defeated, not primarily for moral reasons but for practical ones, which maintained that any such law would be unworkable and open to abuse.

What is Euthanasia?
'Euthanasia' literally means 'dying well', and as such is a fairly neutral term. However, in recent years, largely through the work of the Voluntary Euthanasia Society (formerly EXIT), it has taken on a more specialised meaning. Put simply, euthanasia refers to

'medically assisted suicide'. A more precise definition is: 'The deliberate bringing about of the death of a human being as part of the medical care being given him or her.' Immediately this might strike many people as odd, for it may well be argued that there is an internal contradiction involved: how can bringing about someone's death be conceived as being part of the medical care offered? Surely to terminate life is to terminate medical care also; it cannot therefore be part of it.

Clearing the Ground

Advocates of euthanasia often muddy the ethical waters by raising the question 'Should life be preserved at all costs?' and assume that if the answer is 'no', then euthanasia is legitimized.

Two things need to be said in response to this. Firstly, even Christians who would place a high value on the sanctity of human life would not advocate preserving life at all costs! One only has to think of the extraordinary lengths taken (which were politically motivated), to preserve the 'lives' of Tito and Franco in their last moments. This would not be considered justifiable, medically or ethically.

Secondly, there is a world of difference in terms of intention between deliberately shortening a life (euthanasia) and choosing not to prolong the dying process unnecessarily. The former involves the intention of killing, the latter the intention of not prolonging the dying. The difference between them is morally important and the two should not be confused.

There are basically three options available in the treatment of those who, as shown by medical criteria, are dying with no hope of recovery. One is euthanasia which, as we shall see, is immoral. The second is to prolong the dying artificially in a way that is disproportionate to any advantage that may be gained for the patient. This, although not immoral, may well be deemed to be unwise. The third option is to let die, but provide the best possible care and relief – an option well exemplified by the hospice movement.

It is important, however, that if the decision is made to 'let die', this is made using medical criteria and not more ill-defined or subjective notions such as 'quality of life'.

Let it also be said that the administration of drugs in order to alleviate pain (such as morphine), which at the same time may shorten the life expectancy of the patient, is not euthanasia. The distinction again turns on the question of intention, which is focused for us by the ethical principle known as 'double effect'. Thus the intention in such cases is to reduce the pain (the primary and wanted effect), the foreseen but undesirable secondary effect is a shortening of life. This is different from euthanasia, which has the primary effect in view of taking life away.

Sometimes reference is made to the difference between active euthanasia and passive euthanasia. The former involves taking positive steps to terminate a life (e.g. the injection of poison), the latter withholds treatment, which results in the loss of life. In some circumstances this is a distinction with no difference, when both the intention and the result are the same – death. Let it also be made clear that 'passive euthanasia' is to be distinguished from 'allowing to die' when it has been established that there is no reasonable hope of recovery, the distinction again turning on the matter of intention. In the case of passive euthanasia the intention is to bring about death by withholding treatment (on the general assumption that the sooner the better). In the case of allowing to die the intention is not to prolong the dying process unduly.

Perhaps a comment is in order concerning what is known as a 'persistent vegetative state' (PVS), a condition which received much attention by the High Court ruling, upheld by the Court of Appeal and the House of Lords, that the family and doctors for Mr Tony Bland, who was severely injured at the Hillsborough football disaster, were permitted to remove tubes which eventually led to his starvation. It needs to be said that some PVS victims have been known to recover substantially. While it is doubtful that this was the position of Mr Bland, nonetheless what was proposed was euthanasia. This is not a matter of prolonging the dying process artificially, but deliberately bringing about death by removing fundamental and basic care from a patient. While heartfelt sympathy and hopefully practical support should be given to any family in these very sad circumstances, ethically to take such action is wrong and the wider implications for our society are very far reaching indeed.

Biblical principles

There are at least three principles in the Bible which rule out euthanasia as an option and render it morally repugnant.

1. Life is a gift. God himself breathes into man the breath of life (Gen. 2:7). It is a gift which is precious because man and woman are made in God's image (Gen. 1:27; 9:6). To take away this life deliberately, as Genesis 9 and the sixth commandment make plain, is murder. This value people have, like life itself, is God-given and not man-determined; hence the Christian will be very wary of such dubious value-criteria such as 'biological quality' or 'usefulness'. As such, within the grand sweep of Scripture, life is seen as a good to be received gratefully, in contrast to death, which stands as an 'abnormal normal' in a fallen world.

2. Life is on loan. The gracious nature of life is focused for us in that well known response of Job: 'Naked I came from my mother's womb and naked I shall depart. The LORD gave and the LORD has taken away; may the LORD's name be praised' (Job 1:21). The life giver is also the life taker. Since life is on loan, it is not ours to do with as we please, but belongs to God, and therefore is to be handled with the care expected of good stewards. To choose death, our own or that of another, as an end in itself, without divine sanction is to take the place of God. To the question so often raised in this debate 'Whose life is it anyway?', the Bible gives the answer, 'It is God's.' It is perhaps this principle more than any other which runs counter to one of the most deeply entrenched assumptions of our age. One student, upon reading Karl Barth (the originator of the phrase 'life on loan'), remarked: 'What I don't like about him is that he seems to think that our lives are not really our own.' Autonomy is the order of the day. It is reasoned that if our lives solely belong to us, we then have the right to decide what should be done with those lives. It is the age-old question first raised in the Garden of Eden, 'Who is to be God?'

3. Life is to be redeemed. Christ came to redeem us from the

curse of the law (Gal. 3:13), to destroy the one who holds the power over death and to release those whose lives are held in fear of death (Heb. 2:14-15). Death is the final enemy which one day will be destroyed (1 Cor. 15:26), and what will be the case at the end of time, is tasted in time, in Jesus' own ministry (e.g. John 11) and supremely in his resurrection (1 Cor. 15:20). Here is the model and basis for medical care – the person and work of Jesus Christ, who sought to bring healing, relief and life. It is true that the Christian has an ambivalent attitude towards death – seeing it both as an enemy and as a release and therefore a gateway into glory (1 Cor. 15:56; 2 Cor. 5:1ff; Phil. 1:21f). Nonetheless, the overall direction of Scripture is to view death in negative terms, with a positive emphasis on caring for the sick and needy, no matter what the cost, and not deliberately hastening their demise, no matter who requests it.

Issues raised

It is the fear of prolonged and uncontrollable pain which in the minds of many seems to offer the most compelling *prima facie* argument for euthanasia – a situation which appears to have been focused by the Cox case. While one may wish to distinguish pain from suffering (the latter including mental, social and spiritual anguish), the situation regarding the alleviation of pain by palliative care is rapidly changing, largely as a result of the development of new drugs and methods pioneered by the hospice movement. Thus, in a report 'Cancer relief and palliative care' published by a World Health Organisation committee in 1990, we read, 'With the development of modern methods of palliative care, legalization of voluntary euthanasia is unnecessary. Now that a practicable alternative to death in pain exists, there should be concentrated efforts to implement programmes of palliative care, rather than yielding to pressure for legal euthanasia.'

But we must also consider the wider implications of legalized euthanasia.

How would voluntary euthanasia affect the medical profession and the doctor-patient relationship? In Holland, where voluntary euthanasia is part of accepted medical practice, there were 3,700 euthanasia deaths recorded in 1990, of which 1,030 were non-voluntary. This has had the most devastating effect amongst many of the old people in that country, who fear that they may be put to death against their wishes. The doctor-patient relationship is based upon trust. To legalize euthanasia would seriously weaken that relationship by replacing trust with suspicion.

Should doctors and nurses, whose training and action is based upon the fundamental drive to save life, be put in a position where by law they are required to take life away? This is a classic clash of 'rights', where the 'right' of one (an euthanasia patient) is an infringement on the 'right' of another – the doctor or nurse. While no doubt some 'conscience clause' would be involved in any legislation (which, if the effect of the 'conscience clause' in the 1967 Abortion Act is anything to go by, provides little cause for comfort), this does not deal with the basic issue of whether anyone in a caring profession should be put in a position where they actively assist in someone else's death. The psychological strain would be appalling (witness the strain upon those performing abortions), and the gradual erosion in motivation towards care would be inevitable. With increasing pressure upon our health service in terms of demand and expectations, and the concomitant need of increased funding and resources, coupled with an increasing elderly population, the temptation to take the easy option of euthanasia would be both understandable and great.

Perhaps a more insidious effect of legalizing euthanasia would be the further erosion of respect for human life in a society which already exhibits an unnerving valuing of property over and against persons. Increase in physical violence towards the elderly is one of the most appalling scandals of our day. What message would be received if euthanasia became widespread, of which the elderly would be the main recipients? It has long been suggested that there is a link between abortion on demand and child abuse (the one being an extension of the other). How long would it take for a similar link to be engendered between euthanasia and geriatric abuse? One suspects, not long at all.

7

Justifying Justification

In 1538 Luther expounded Psalm 130:4 and, referring to justification, claimed that 'if this article stands, the church stands; if it falls, the church falls.'[1]

From that time, through the teaching of men like John Owen in the seventeenth century, George Whitefield in the eighteenth, C.H. Spurgeon in the nineteenth and Martyn Lloyd-Jones in the twentieth, the doctrine of justification by faith alone has been the great hallmark of evangelical Christianity, the jewel in the crown of Protestant thought, bringing peace to many a troubled conscience and a deep assurance in the face of certain death.

It therefore strikes one as odd, if not perverse, that such a doctrine is having a hard time today within evangelicalism. When was the last time you heard an evangelistic address which spelt out this truth clearly? Certainly it is a doctrine which is an embarrassment ecumenically, as it still divides the Roman Catholic Church from all mainline Protestant churches. It may also jar in an age which tries to explain away sin and conceive of our estrangement from God in terms of 'existential alienation', rather than actual guilt which incurs God's anger. Were the Reformers so wrong in seeing this as central to our understanding of the gospel? Or are some modern commentators, like James Dunn, right in viewing this as one metaphor among many and not a central one at that?

Not ashamed
In order to clarify the meaning and significance of this doctrine, we shall focus on one passage which provides the springboard for Paul's programmatic unfolding of the gospel – Romans 1:16-17: 'For I am not ashamed of the gospel, because it is the power of

God for the salvation of everyone who believes; first for the Jew, then for the Gentile. For in the gospel a righteousness from God is revealed, a righteousness that is by faith from first to last, just as it is written: "The righteous shall live by faith." '[2]

Notice the logical link between verses 16 and 17. Paul is not ashamed of the gospel *because* it is the power of God for salvation ... *because* in the gospel a righteousness from God is being revealed. In Paul's mind, the gospel and the question of 'righteousness' are inseparable (both the noun 'righteousness' (*dikaiosune*) and verb 'to justify' (*dikaioun*) have the same root: the *dik*- group.

The key term is 'righteousness of God' (*dikaiosune theou*). What does this mean?

The righteousness of God
Three basic views have been put forward.[3]

First, righteousness is seen as a moral quality of God (possessive genitive), such that all his actions are just and in keeping with his character, so 'the Judge of the earth will do what is right' (Gen. 18:25). In Romans 3:25-26, we are told that God demonstrates his righteous character, his justice (*dikaiosune*), by presenting Jesus as a sacrifice of atonement. He does not ignore sin (v. 25b), but deals with it and at the same time shows himself to be the 'one who justifies those who have faith in Jesus'.

Second, the 'righteousness of God' is construed as a divine activity (subjective genitive) whereby God intervenes to save his people and so is acting in accord with his covenant promises. The most obvious background for this is the Book of Isaiah, especially chapters 40–66, where God's righteousness and action in saving belong to the same world of thought; e.g. 'I am bringing my righteousness near ... and my salvation will not be delayed' (Isa. 46:13).

Third, the term can be taken not as subjectively referring to God, but objectively, stating what God achieves *for* us, whereby we are declared to be acquitted by God (which we can call the negative aspect of justification – he 'justifies the wicked', Rom. 4:5) and then *positively* as now standing in a right relationship with the judge credited as righteous (as was Abraham: Gen. 15:6; Rom. 4, especially vv. 23ff). This is sometimes referred to as 'imputed righteousness'.

To understand this more fully it is helpful to have some knowledge of workings of the Hebrew law court which, it is generally agreed, stands behind much of Paul's use of the term 'to justify' in Romans and Galatians.

Jewish court
In the Jewish court, three people were involved: the judge, plaintiff and defendant. The judge is 'righteous' if he tries the case according to law, is impartial, punishes as sin deserves and supports those who cannot uphold their own cause (the widow and fatherless).

As there was no counsel for the prosecution or defence, both the accuser and defendant would argue their own case until one conceded defeat. The sign that such defeat had been admitted was the placing of one's hand over the mouth (which may be the background to Paul's statement in Romans 3:19: '... so that every mouth may be silenced'). The verdict would then be pronounced on which of the two was 'in the right'. In other words, the term 'justified' denoted a person's status, from the judge's ruling; it had nothing to do with their moral character, only that they were vindicated against their accuser.

Imputed righteousness
Some, like Dr N.T. Wright, take the term 'to justify' solely in this sense, denying that God 'imputes' righteousness as a category mistake, while at the same time taking the term 'righteousness of God' to refer solely to the saving activity of God in accord with his covenant promises fulfilled in Jesus the Messiah, the embodiment of all that Israel was meant to be.[4] But this fails to do justice to the plain meaning of texts such as 2 Corinthians 5:21 where Paul describes believers as having 'become the right-eousness of God', as well as the whole series of texts in Romans 4 which speaks of righteousness being accredited to those who have faith (a commercial term taken from the world of accountancy

– Paul was not averse to mixing his metaphors).

Which of the above interpretations is correct? Is 'the righteousness of God' a moral attribute, a divine activity, or a gift freely bestowed? Could it not be that the term is what philosophers call a 'polymorphous concept'? That is, while there is a common core of meaning, the term functions differently according to context. Thus arising out of the righteous character of God, he acts on behalf of the needy (those who cannot save themselves) in accord with his covenant promises, in such a way that he punishes sin while acquitting the sinner, conferring upon him the status of Christ's righteousness.[5]

Helpfully Philip Eveson defines 'justification' as 'a legal pronouncement made by God in the present, prior to the day of judgement, declaring sinners to be not guilty and therefore acquitted, by pardoning all their sins and reckoning them to be righteous in his sight, on the basis of Christ, their representative and substitute, whose righteousness in life and death is put to their account, when in self-despairing trust they look to him alone for their salvation'.[6]

Central message
Is this important? Our forefathers certainly thought it was (as did Paul, Gal. 1:6ff). Nothing less than our salvation is at stake. Luther's point that it is the article by which the church stands or falls still remains. Eveson puts the matter boldly, yet accurately, when he writes:

> If a body calling itself 'the church' loses this central message of justification, it will soon have no good news to present. It will become another superstitious religious institution, falsely bearing the name Christian. What is more, the people will continue to be in the dark, heading for hell, while at the same time trusting in a Jesus of faulty human thought and heretical church tradition.[7]

To neglect this teaching is to court disaster, to recapture it is the road to renewal.

NOTES

1. *Luther's Works*, *XL3, 352*, Weimar edition.

2. For a readable survey and critique of the present debate, read Philip Eveson's *The Great Exchange*, Day One Publications (1996). For a more technical discussion, D.A. Carson (ed.) *Right with God*, Paternoster (1992).

3. These are reviewed in John Stott's *The Message of Romans* IVP (1996), pp. 61-65, and N.T. Wright, *What Paul Really Said*, SPCK (1997), pp. 100-11.

4. NT Wright, ibid. p. 98.

5. John Stott in his commentary on Romans writes: 'For myself, I have never been able to see why we have to choose, and why all three should not be combined' (p. 63).

6. Eveson, *The Great Exchange*, p. 193.

7. Ibid. p. 175.

8

Language, Symbols and Sacraments:
Was Calvin's View of the Lord's Supper Right?

Introduction

In his insightful work on the eucharistic theology contained in the reformed confessions,[1] B. A. Gerrish postulates that amongst the reformed theologians there was a spectrum of belief about the significance of symbol in the sacraments, which can be reduced to three main varieties of outlook: symbolic memorialism, symbolic parallelism and symbolic instrumentalism. What is held in common between all three positions is the notion that the symbol 'points to something else'. What distinguishes them is the actual reference of the sign, and how the referent relates to the sign. In symbolic memorialism, the heart of Zwingli's sacramental theology, the referent is 'a happening in the past'. In the case of symbolic parallelism emphasised by Bullinger (Zwingli's successor in Zurich), it is to 'a happening that occurs simultaneously in the present' through the work of God *alongside* the sign itself. The third approach, symbolic instrumentalism, represented by John Calvin, stresses 'a present happening that is actually brought about *through* the signs'. This latter position may come as a surprise to many, given Calvin's outright rejection of the Roman Catholic belief in *ex opere operato*. But there is little doubt that he saw his own position as a *via media* between the Roman view on the one hand and mere memorialism on the other. One can take Calvin's comments on 1 Corinthians 10:3 as evidence of this:

> When Paul says that the *fathers ate the same spiritual meat,* he first of all gives a hint of what the power and efficacy of the sacrament is; and secondly he shows that the old sacraments of the law had the same power as ours have today. For if manna was spiritual food, it

follows that bare forms (*figuras nudas*) are not exhibited to us in the sacraments, but the reality is truly figured at the same time (*rem figuratam simul vere dari*). For God is not so deceitful as to nourish us in empty appearances (*figmentis*). A sign (*signum*) is indeed a sign, and retains its own substance (*substantiam*). But just as the Papists, on the one hand, are ridiculously dreaming of some sort of transformation, so, on the other hand, we have no right to separate the reality and the figure (*veritatem et figuram*) which God has joined together. The Papists confound the reality and the sign (*rem et signum*); unbelievers such as Schwekfeld and men like him separate the signs from the realities (*signa a rebus*). Let us preserve a middle position, that is, let us keep the union made by the Lord, but at the same time distinguish between them, so that we do not, in error, transfer what belongs to one to the other.[2]

The same 'symbolic instrumentalism' is evident in the *Institutes*:

I admit, indeed, that the breaking of bread is a symbol, not the reality. But this being admitted, we duly infer from the exhibition of the symbol that the thing itself is exhibited. For unless we would charge God with deceit, we will never presume to say that he holds forth an empty symbol.... The rule which the pious ought always to observe is, whenever they see the symbols instituted by the Lord, to think and feel surely persuaded that the truth of the thing signified is also present. For why does the Lord put the symbol of his body into your hands, but just to assure you that you truly partake of him? If this is true let us feel as much assured that the visible sign is given us in seal of an invisible gift that his body has been given to us.[3]

As Gerrish observes about Calvin's view of the Lord's Supper as sacrament, it is 'not that it brings about a communion with Christ, or a reception of his body that is not available anywhere else, but rather that it graphically represents and presents to believers a communion they enjoy, or can enjoy, all the time'.[4] It is little wonder that Calvin found himself not only meeting resistance from Lutherans, who thought that he did not go far enough in affirming the real presence of Christ under the signs, but also from Bullinger, who thought his position too close to that of the papists!

Bullinger and Calvin were able in some measure to come

together through the Zurich Agreement (Consensus Tigurinus) of 1549 in a statement which respected both their common concerns and fears. By the time Bullinger composed the Second Helvetic Confession in 1562 he understood the sign and thing signified in the Lord's Supper to be simultaneous occurrences – nonetheless he could not accept Calvin's belief that God performs the inward through the outward.

For Calvin, the sacrament consisted of both word and external sign and had to be received by faith to be effective,[5] but what is effected is the receiving not simply of the benefits of Christ, but Christ himself: 'That sacred communion of flesh and blood by which Christ transfuses his life into us, just as if it penetrated our bones and marrow, he testifies and seals in the Supper, and that not by presenting in a vain or empty sign, but by there exerting an efficacy of the Spirit by which he fulfils what he promises.'[6]

Was Calvin wrong to conceive of the relationship between sign and signification in this way?

What is presented in this article is an approach to the nature of the Lord's Supper, drawing upon four areas of study, which, it will be argued, throw light on the nature of the sacramental in such a way that Calvin's theological instincts regarding the sacraments are upheld as being fundamentally correct. While eschewing the Romanist error of transubstantiation on the one hand, he was also right to resist mere memorialism on the other. The four areas we shall be investigating are: the functional approach to language, the nature of symbolism, the doctrine of the Incarnation and the dynamic nature of the sacramental.

The Function of Language in the Lord's Supper

A useful classification of language according to function has been provided by G. B. Caird[7] who groups them under five headings. Words are used (a) to talk about people, things and ideas (informative); (b) to think (cognitive); (c) to do things and get things done (performative and causative); (d) to display or elicit attitudes and feelings (expressive and evocative); (e) to provide a means of communal solidarity (cohesive).

Of prime importance to our study is the idea of performatives as fathered by J. L. Austin[8] and brought to maturity by John Searle.[9] Performatives, as the term implies, perform rather than inform. Many statements set out in the indicative mood are not strictly true or false, but are designed to bring about a state of affairs. For example, in the wedding service the officiating minister asks: 'Will you take x to be your lawful wedded wife?' and the response is made: 'I will.' This is not a description of marriage, but part of the action of *getting* married. This type of speech act is distinguished from others which are mainly referential and called 'constatives'.

Later Austin considered *all* utterances as speech acts to be performatives.[10] Within his general theory there are two other specifications relevant to our study.

First, let us consider the distinction between speech acts in the narrow sense – making referential statements, proclaiming forgiveness, making promises, i.e. what we *do* with statements - and the *effect* of such utterances on people, in persuading, amusing or annoying them. The former is termed the illocutionary act and the latter the perlocutionary act. Secondly, within the illocutionary act a distinction is made between propositional content (the locutionary act, equivalent to 'meaning' in the traditional sense) and the *type* of act, the illocutionary force. One therefore could have several illocutionary acts, all having the same propositional content, but differing in force – e.g. 'Do you believe in God?' (question); 'Believe in God' (plea); 'You will believe in God' (prediction). Thus in relation to an illocutionary act, when one asks, 'What is meant by it?' one may mean (a) What type of speech act is it? or (b) What is its propositional content?

It is important, in relation to the Lord's Supper, to stress the functional view of language in order to guard against the common tendency to conceive of it as being solely referential, which could lead in two equal and opposite directions. The first would be to think of the elements as 'the body and blood of Christ' in terms of identity, the other would be to see the elements as simply referring to Christ's death on the Cross as a memorial. Words (and, as we shall argue below, symbols) can have a function which is more varied than referential; they can be vehicles whereby something is imparted to the hearer and certain states of affairs are established.

At this juncture it is necessary to draw attention to two other points made by Austin in connection with performatives. First, this type of language only functions if certain conventions hold; the shaking of hands by two businessmen to conclude a financial deal is only meaningful in a culture where this functions as a sign of agreement and trust. This point is akin to Wittgenstein's 'language games'[11] where he states that language functions within particular life settings. The meanings of concepts are in part derived from within the game itself. Thus the function and sense (cf referent) of the speech acts performed within the context of the Lord's Supper are determined by their place within the life setting of the Christian community. Secondly, Austin claims 'for a certain performative utterance to be happy, certain statements must be true'.[12] In other words, performatives in the narrow sense can only function within the wider context of a referential understanding of reality.

This second point is also relevant to our discussion of the nature of Holy Communion, for it underscores the fact that the celebration does not operate *in vacuo* but is grounded in a referential view of the reality of God's action in history in his Son, Jesus Christ. The claim that the body of Christ was 'given for you' makes no sense unless related to the one in history who actually gave his body. This will also set the limits to eucharistic interpretation, so that a New Age 'planetary mass' becomes something else with only a passing similarity to the Holy Communion of the Church.

Symbols and Sacraments

Sometimes the term 'sign' is used interchangeably with 'symbol', but a distinction between the two may be attained by pondering the nature of analogical discourse. Here it is suggested that whereas analogy is dependent upon some intrinsic likeness between itself and that which it illustrates, and is thus to some degree self-interpreting because of the shared core of meaning which acts as the point of correspondence, a symbol requires a greater degree of interpretation for its significance to be appreciated. J. Macquarrie states: 'The difference is that the best analogues are almost self-interpreting, whereas symbols frequently require much explanation of background before we begin to see where they are pointing.'[13] Thus, one may speak of the Cross as a 'symbol' of God's love, but this can only be perceived within the Christian tradition against the background knowledge of the nature of Christ's atoning sacrifice – that he is the Passover Lamb.[14] Those unfamiliar with such a background would be hard pressed to see any such connection between the claim of divine love and the normal method of Roman execution reserved for the worst possible criminal offenders.

A similar process is required when one comes to the symbolism of the Lord's Supper. The points of contact between the elements themselves and that which they signify require some teasing out. Calvin writes: 'By the corporeal things which are produced in the sacrament, we are by a kind of analogy conducted to spiritual things. Thus when bread is given as a symbol of the body of Christ, we must think of this similitude. As bread nourishes, sustains and protects our bodily life, so the body of Christ is the only food to invigorate and keep alive the soul.'[15]

How, therefore, might the 'symbolic' function in the Lord's Supper? While it might be argued that symbols are primarily evocative, there is no reason to suppose that they cannot operate at more than one level.

The symbolic gesture of the breaking of bread and subsequent distribution with the accompanying words are informative – conveying the truth of Christ's sacrificial death; evocative – drawing believers to praise and gratitude; cohesive – promoting unity and communal solidarity as 'one body', as well as being performative – constituting the illocutionary act of conveying the divine love with the consequent perlocutionary acts of thankfulness, including obedient Christian service.

Similarly, D. M. Baillie draws attention to the 'mediatorial' quality of a sacrament.[16] As sensible signs, the material elements and accompanying actions become channels whereby the personal can be conveyed. This happens, he argues, in everyday life by the use of gestures – smiles, handshakes, embraces etc. At one level they are symbolic, and yet they are capable of performing that which they represent, giving approval, creating agreement, conveying affection.

Revelation and Sacrament

Clues as to how we might understand the relation between the symbolic and sacramental may be gained by a consideration of how John handles his material in his Gospel.

The Fourth Gospel is full of symbols as John moves on two levels at once – the material and the spiritual. This is particularly to be seen in the 'I am' sayings.

S. S. Smalley argues that the 'sacramental' pervades the whole of the Fourth Gospel.[17] He argues that within a Christian context a symbol evokes and represents that which is spiritual and divine, whereas a sacrament conveys through the material elements themselves that which is spiritual and divine. He cites as an example the saying of Jesus: 'Whoever drinks of the water I shall give will never thirst' (John 4:14). This, according to Smalley, is a symbol of the life-giving power available to the believer through the living Christ.[18] But when Jesus says 'I am the resurrection and the life' (John 11:25) and demonstrates this truth by raising Lazarus from the dead (as well as embodying the truth and universalising it for all believers in his own resurrection), it is maintained that this is part of the sacramental dimension of John's Gospel.

Smalley contends that the principle underlying all the signs and which provides the theological basis for John's view of the 'sacramental' is the seminal statement 'The Word became flesh' (John 1:14). From this point on, history is to be seen in a new light as the potential carrier of the spiritual, and the temporal as the potential mediator of the eternal. Thus John takes a number of ordinary things such as bread, wine, water and light, and 'thinks them through with a truly biblical realism',[19] until they become what they represent. Jesus not only changes water into wine at Cana, but he himself is the source of the Kingdom to which the signs point. Smalley writes: 'whereas the sacramental in John is always symbolic, not every symbol is sacramental.' [20]

Karl Barth also takes the divine revelation in the Incarnation as foundational to what constitutes the sacramental: 'Revelation occurs in the form of this sacramental reality, i.e., in such a way that God elevates and selects a definite creaturely subject-object relationship to be the instrument of the covenant between himself the Creator and man as His creature.'[21] Earlier he writes: 'The humanity of Jesus as such is the first sacrament, the foundation of everything that God instituted and used in His revelation as a secondary objectivity both before and after the epiphany of Jesus Christ.'[22] Referring to John 1:14, Barth suggests that the sacraments underline the words *sarx* and *egenetō,* but always have their objective basis in the Incarnation.[23]

If Barth is correct that the incarnate Jesus is 'the first sacrament', then a link is immediately forged between revelation and sacrament. 'Revelation means the giving of signs. We can say quite clearly that revelation means sacrament, i.e., the self-witness of God, the representation of His truth, and therefore of the truth in which He knows Himself, in the form of creaturely objectivity and therefore in a form which is adapted to our creaturely knowledge.'[24]

None of this is far removed from the thoughts of Calvin:

We are taught by the Scriptures that Christ was from the beginning the living Word of the Father, the fountain and origin of life... hence John at one time calls him the Word of life ... but ever since that fountain of life began to dwell in our nature, he no longer lies hid at a distance from us, but exhibits himself openly for our participation. Nay, the very flesh in which he resides he makes vivifying to us, that by partaking of it we may feed for immortality. 'I', says he 'am that bread of life'.... 'And the bread that I will give is my flesh, which I give for the life of the world'. By these words he declares, not only that he is life, inasmuch as he is the eternal Word of God who came down to us from heaven, but, by coming down gave vigour to the flesh which he assumed, that a communication of life to us might thence emanate.[25]

He then goes on to draw a direct line to the Lord's Supper as a means whereby 'Christ transfuses his life to us'.[26]

What are the features that revelation and sacrament have in common?

Firstly, both the revelational and the sacramental mediate that which is personal. Writing in the context of the Holy Communion, J. R. Lucas states: 'If we, as theists, believe that the universe is fundamentally personal in character, it follows that our ultimate understanding will not be in terms of things, which occupy space and may or may not possess certain properties, but of persons, who characteristically *do* things.'[27]

Secondly, both revelation and sacrament, in order to disclose, paradoxically also hide. The most obvious case is the Incarnation and the *ensarkosis* of the second person of the Trinity. In order for this revelation to occur, some divine attributes were hidden. But far from the material hindering divine disclosure, it facilitates it.

Thirdly, what is mediated in both revelation and sacrament is apprehended by faith. Any personal relationship is based upon the notion of trust – belief in the promises made by one to another, founded upon the character of the one pledging himself. It was this faith in God's promise which was counted as 'righteousness' for Abraham (Gen. 15:6) and which Paul takes as a model for all believers (Rom. 4 and Gal. 4). This faith finds its proper focus in Holy Communion. Writing about the place of faith in Calvin's view of the Lord's Supper, Gerrish states:

> The proposition [the gift is to be received by faith] rests on the intimate connection of the sacraments with the word of God, and it is directed, above all, against the impersonalisation of sacramental efficacy in medieval scholasticism. The Schoolmen taught that the sacraments of the 'new law' confer grace provided only that no obstacle of mortal sin is in their way. Calvin detected in this 'pestilential' notion a superstitious attachment to the sacramental sign as a mere physical thing – and, indeed, an implicit denial of the cardinal Reformation doctrine of justification by faith. A sacrament received without faith cannot be a sacrament correctly understood as an appendage to the divine word or promise.... When the word accompanies the sacrament, it must retain its essential character as proclamation...the sacramental word is not an incantation, but a promise. The eucharistic gift therefore benefits those only who respond with the faith that the proclamation itself generates.[28]

This is parallel to what Jesus says about receiving the revelation of God in his person. Therefore the risen Lord says to Thomas: 'Because you have seen me you have believed, blessed are those who have not seen and yet have believed' (John 20:29).

The Character of the Lord's Supper

In light of the above discussion on the nature of the sacramental, it would be appropriate to use the term 'sacrament' to describe the Lord's Supper as a whole, rather than particular elements within it. This in part stems from the fact that it is a dynamic activity with the emphasis upon actions.

This point is well made by the Hansons[29] when writing about the excesses of the medieval mass: 'All these interpretations of the sacrament are distortions into a different key of the original rhythm of the eucharist, which was communal, dynamic and concerned with an event rather than a thing.' Similarly, P.T. Forsyth maintained that the Last Supper was not 'so much the bread as the breaking, not so much the elements as the actions that are symbolical'. [30] A similar claim for the centrality of actions in the Lord's Supper is made by Gregg.[31]

The Communion is not only dynamic in character, but is also multi-dimensional in that it engages at several sensory levels. The auditory, visual and tactile senses are all brought into play during Communion, providing a broader experience than the spoken word alone.

We now turn to the different temporal aspects signified by the Lord's Supper.

The Past

Central to the celebration is the retrospective temporal dimension, arising initially from its development out of the Passover meal, with its refocusing upon Christ's sacrificial death.

Two actions figure in the synoptic accounts of the Last Supper and the Lord's reinterpretation of the Passover in relation to his own impending death; the giving of the bread (together with the accompanying explanatory words, 'this is my body given for you'), and the giving of the cup (and accompanying interpretation, 'the blood of the new covenant'). Since the coppola 'is' would have been absent in the Aramaic or Hebrew utterance, it is taken that the actions are meant as significations; but of what? E. Schweizer suggests that the 'I' refers to the totality of the person – the giving of the complete self.[32] The phrase 'given for you' certainly appears to reflect Old Testament sacrificial terminology relating either to the making of a sacrifice or to the death of a martyr on behalf of others.[33] Jeremias posits the reference to Jesus as the eschatological Passover Lamb.[34] Marshall draws attention to the close similarity in language between the 'For many/you' in the 'cup saying' of Mark and Isaiah 53:1 1ff as being seminal to Jesus' self-understanding of his death and its subsequent reflection in his reinterpretation of the Passover meal. However, he goes on to point out that it is possible to combine all of the above suggestions, which would mean that Jesus saw himself as fulfilling several strands of Old Testament types simultaneously.[35]

Whatever the divergence over details between the Synoptists, there is unanimity that at the most significant moment the actions of Christ were in the following order: *(a)* he took the bread (or cup) into his hands; *(b)* he gave thanks; (c) he broke the bread; (*d*) he gave the bread and cup to his disciples; *(e)* he said 'This is my body', or (in some form) 'This is my blood of the covenant'. This is important for our understanding of the administration of the Communion and the nature of the sacramental act, as we shall see.

Gregg[36] pays attention to the meaning of the phrase *eis...anamnesin* (in remembrance) and seeks to determine the corresponding Hebrew root. He argues that this is to be sought in the *zkr* group and more specifically *zikkaron* in the sense of a commemorative *act*. It is proposed that in the *zikkaron* one is not simply engaging in the mental recollection of events, but an embracing of the totality of the event as a single whole, whereby the *zkr* involves revitalizing this total reality. 'There will be in every commemorative act, dynamic consequences, as both God and man grasp the whole act accordingly.'[37]

How the gap between the 'then' and the 'now' is bridged, according to Gregg is found in the term 'actualise' – quoting

Childs: 'A real event occurs as the moment of redemptive time from the past initiates a genuine encounter in the present.'[38]

Applied to the phrase *eis... anamnesin*, the following interpretation is suggested: 'Take, give thanks, break bread and say the interpretative words, at each weekly festival communal meal, as in the commemorative act you initiate a genuine encounter in the present by means of redemptive time from the past.'[39]

The term 'you initiate' may be considered rather unfortunate as it creates the impression that we have the power to bring something about in a quasi-mechanical way. However the emphasis on the manward aspect is surely right, that through the Lord's Supper, God's people benefit from Christ's work on the Cross. So Alan Stibbs writes:

> The Greek word *anamnesis* expresses the idea of a calling to mind, a recalling or recollection, exactly similar to the way in which the Jews at the celebration of the Passover recalled their deliverance from Egypt. To the Semitic mind thus to commemorate a past event was personally to realise and experience its present operative significance as one event with abiding consequences. So Canon W. M. F. Scott wrote: '"Do this in remembrance of me" can now be seen to mean that as we "eat this bread and drink this cup" our Lord's sacrifice becomes here and now operative in our lives.'[40]

The other aspect of the retrospective dimension of the Lord's Supper is that of proclamation: 'As often as you eat this bread and drink this cup you do show [proclaim] the Lord's death until he comes' (1 Cor. 11:26). This is not a showing to God, but to each other, to tell each other that he died for us.

The Future

This naturally leads to the second temporal aspect of the Lord's Supper as anticipatory and future, a looking forward to the Messianic meal. As Marshall writes: 'the Lord's Supper is linked to the Passover in that the Passover is a type of the heavenly banquet while the Lord's Supper is the anticipation of the heavenly banquet.'[41] This is particularly focused in Luke's account of the Last Supper with the idea of fulfilment in the Kingdom of God and Christ's followers 'eating and drinking at my table in the kingdom' (Luke 22:14-30). So the Eucharist is 'an ordinance for those who live between the cross and the End. It looks back to what Jesus did and said "on the night when he was betrayed" (1 Cor. 11:23) and recalls his death on behalf of all men. But it also looks forward to the Parousia.'[42]

What is evident from the above discussion is the dynamic nature of the sacramental act. The movement is primarily manward (corresponding to the movement of divine revelation itself) – the *giving* of the bread, the *giving* of the cup, all to be *received* by man. There are only two points at which there is any movement Godward and these lie either side of the sacramental act itself.

First, there is the giving of thanks to God for the bread and the wine. As we have noted this is clear in the ordering of the events in the synoptic accounts. What is important from a careful observation of the sequence is that at this stage the bread and the wine have not been given any sacramental significance. The interpretative words which give the bread and wine such significance are said during the manward administration. To conflate the two – thanksgiving with the interpretative words – tends to lead to an unscriptural understanding of consecration, so that the prayer 'changes' the bread and the wine, if not in terms of substance, then in significance (transignification). However, this is not the way the sequence operates in Scripture. The change in significance is brought about by the interpretative words and corresponding action, not the prayer. Although Cranmer has been criticised as having something of a blind spot at this point,[43] he may have been far more aware of this significance than some critics allow. Commenting on the changes made from the 1549 Communion service to that of 1552, MacCulloch observes that:

> the sequence of material was thoroughly rearranged, so that the prayers of intercession were completely removed from the former 'canon', and the narrative of the Saviour's words of institution was immediately followed (without even an 'Amen') by the distribution of bread and wine to the communicants, so that they would make their communion with these words still echoing in their minds. The gospel words were there to instruct, not to effect any change in the elements distributed.[44]

Secondly, there is the response of thanks and praise *after* Communion has taken place, when it is appropriate to offer *ourselves* as living sacrifices (Rom. 12:1). One may also include within this the sacrifice of praise, 'the fruit of lips that confess his name' (Heb. 13:15), but again this is something distinct from the sacramental actions themselves.

Given that both items of thanksgiving are a prelude and a consequence of the sacramental act, it follows that the term 'Eucharist' is really a misnomer when applied to the sacrament itself. The 'Lord's Supper' which emphasises the gracious provision of the Lord manward, or 'Holy Communion' indicating the personal, spiritual intercourse with the Risen Lord, are far more accurate indicators of the nature and purpose of the sacrament.

The Present

We must now discuss the third temporal aspect of the Lord's Supper – the present. Before we consider the question of the 'presence of Christ' and how this is to be conceived, brief mention will be made of the other present aspect, that of fellowship with other Christians through fellowship with Christ.

It has long been argued that one of the main expectations of the Messiah was that he would gather around him followers,[45] who in effect are the 'Church'.[46] This gathering and the intimacy and acceptance signified is particularly enhanced by a communal meal. At Sinai not only was the Word proclaimed as people were gathered (Exod. 19, cf Deut. 4), and the covenant ratified by the shedding of blood (Exod. 24:4-8), but a meal was held by Moses and Aaron and the seventy elders in the presence of God (Exod. 24:9-11). It is not surprising, therefore, that with the establishing of the eternal covenant through Christ, as he gathers a people to himself by the Word of the gospel, that the new-found relationship with God and consequent relationship between his people should be fostered through a fellowship meal which contains within it symbols, the means whereby that fellowship is secured.

So we find in 1 Corinthians 11 that it is as Christians 'come together' that they are 'church' (1 Cor. 11:20) and eat the Lord's Supper. This is the means whereby we 'participate in the body and blood of Christ' (1 Cor. 10: 16f) and cultivate unity as well as testify to it: 'Because there is one loaf, we, who are many, are one loaf, for we all partake of the one loaf' (1 Cor. 10:17).

We now turn to consider the related and often vexed question of realising Christ's presence at the Lord's Supper.

From what has been argued about the dynamic nature of the sacrament itself, with the focus on the actions and accompanying words, together with the parallels between the sacramental and revelational, it follows that the primary category within which we are to conceive of the nature of the Lord's Supper is a personal one, with the Lord being present not in the elements themselves but through the actions done with them.

A. M. Stibbs illustrates the force of this principle by referring to baptism:

> If the water which is to be used to baptise is previously consecrated this action is not part of the sacrament. Nor ought such water to become a focus of worship as a sphere of the localised presence of the regenerating Spirit. Rather the sacrament of baptism involves a dynamic movement. It only exists as the water is administered; that is, as the appointed deed is done, and the significant words said to accompany and explain it. This means the sacrament cannot be 'reserved'. Its essential character also makes undeniably plain that its movement is wholly manwards.[47]

> Similarly, in the other sacrament of the gospel, Christ's special presence, his promised and active movement towards us in grace, is not associated with static and lifeless elements which are 'changed' by consecration, but rather with the address to us of a movement of administration accompanied by significant words, which indicate its sacramental meaning, and thus confront the recipients with the present opportunity to have dealings with the Lord, and to appropriate by faith His proffered blessing.[48]

Stibbs then uses the illustration of a telephone conversation to a far away friend, and through that conversation the friend's 'presence' is experienced for a few minutes. He goes on to say:

In ways like this, but far more wonderfully and with no make-believe, when I attend an administration of the Lord's Supper, and see and hear the sacramental movement begun, and realise that it is personally and imperatively addressed to me, and to all there present with me, and that it demands corresponding action and response; then it is right to believe that in this movement Christ himself is present and active and offering afresh to give to me, through His death for me, His indwelling presence by His Spirit, and the outworked experience of all the benefits of his passion ... to speak of answering a telephone call is indeed an illustration utterly inadequate and unworthy. For this movement *is like the approach of the bridegroom to the bride. Its proper consummation like the giving and receiving of the ring in marriage. Indeed, it is like the crowning intercourse of love itself* (italics mine).[49]

It is these latter illustrations which are highly suggestive of what happens at Holy Communion and which most closely approximate the 'symbolic instrumentalism' of John Calvin. What will be explored below is the way in which we might more readily conceive the 'mediation of the divine' in the dynamic sacramental act by drawing upon what has already been outlined regarding performative utterances.

The Lord's Supper as Performative

It is proposed that the Lord's Supper (and the same would apply to baptism) can be conceived of in the same way as Austin's and Searle's speech acts, while recognising that the Supper itself is also composed of individual speech acts.

In the first place, as a whole, the Lord's Supper is equivalent to Austin's *locutionary act,* that is, it has a referential basis – the historic Cross-work of Christ and all the benefits that flow from that.

Secondly, Holy Communion in its entirety is also an illocutionary act, the Lord by his Spirit *does* things. In the *giving* of bread and wine and through the accompanying words, the correlated aspects of divine love, forgiveness and eschatological hope (all of a deeply personal nature) are not merely attested to but imparted. Stibbs' picture of the groom approaching the bride, or the evocative (even 'risque') picture of intercourse itself, underscores the performative, rather than merely informative nature of the event taking place. For just as the physical act of embracing or kissing someone is capable of conveying forgiveness and acceptance (as in the story of the Prodigal Son, Luke 15:20), so the physical act of the giving of bread and wine conveys the forgiveness and gracious acceptance of God. This is not to be thought of in a quasi-magical/mystical way, any more than we need think of an embrace in a quasi-magical way. Certainly, as with any speech act, for both the meaning and illocutionary force to operate, certain conventions have to be true (in this case the convention established by the Lord himself that the bread symbolises his body and the wine symbolises his blood). Similarly we may think of the illustration of the giving of a wedding ring: this does not simply signify love and commitment – its giving *in part brings it about,* establishing the wedding covenant; the same can be said of the sacramental act of the giving and receiving of bread and wine.

Thirdly, we may also consider the perlocutionary act of the sacrament, what is *achieved* by it. This is largely dependent upon the apprehension not only of the meaning of the sacramental action but the illocutionary force. For the promise to be grasped, assurance attained, unity achieved, loving obedience elicited, as Austin says, 'illocutionary uptake' must be secured.[50] What is required is not only an understanding of the meaning of the statement and the sacramental act, 'My body which is given for you, take and eat this in remembrance of me,' but the force with which the sacrament and statement is to be taken – that it *counts* as promise, persuasion, assurance and unification.

Searle[51] distinguishes the meaning (propositional content) – that which the act 'counts as' – by the formula $F(p)$. $F =$ the illocutionary force and $p =$ the meaning. What we argue is that the *sacramental* act enhances the F dimension, thus conveying *through* the giving of bread and wine together with the interpretative words something more than the mere saying of the words, 'Jesus loves you and died for you.'

As with a particular text, the illocutionary force of the Lord's

Supper results from a combination of the meaning and intentions of God and the form he 'incarnates', his authoritative voice and presence, which is the dynamic sacramental form itself.[52]

As Vanhoozer claims that 'while proponents of propositional revelation have cherished the (*p*) of the speech act F(p)',[53] so likewise the 'symbolic memorialist' understanding of the Lord's Supper underplays the F aspect of the sacramental.

In a similar way to Caird's classification of language according to function, John Searle maintains that we do five basic things with language: 'We tell people how things are, we try to get them to do things, we commit ourselves to doing things, we express our feelings and attitudes and we bring about changes through our utterances. Often we do more than one of these at once in the same utterance.'[54] We would contend *mutatis mutandis* that the same applies to the sacramental act of the Lord's Supper, with God achieving these five 'illocutionary points' manward. Truth is communicated regarding the death of Christ and his benefits, God seeks to get us to do things, to respond in loving Christian service and heartfelt praise, he conveys his feelings and attitudes towards us as well as bringing about the changes he seeks.

The question then arises: How is the 'illocutionary uptake' achieved in relation to the Lord's Supper? The answer is, by faith. That is, there is the element of *assentus,* recognising things to be true regarding the person and Cross-work of Christ and the meaning of Holy Communion, as well as *fiducia,* that personal trusting in the one who conveys his promises and presence through the sacramental act.

Would Calvin Agree?

It is proposed that the insights afforded into the nature and function of the sacramental by the application of speech act theory not only cohere with Calvin's theology of the sacraments in general and the Lord's Supper in particular, but that they provide the explanatory framework for which Calvin was striving.

Defining a sacrament Calvin writes: 'It is an external sign, by which the Lord seals on our consciences his promise of goodwill towards us, in order to sustain the weakness of our faith, and we in turn testify our piety towards him, both before himself, and before angels as well as men.'[55] Within this simple definition we observe the illocutionary nature of the sacrament: God *does* things, *'seals* our consciences', 'sustains the weakness of our faith' as well as the perlocutionary nature in what is brought about in our response; 'we in turn *testify* our piety towards him.'

Calvin also recognises the distinction between the (p) and the (F) of Searle's formula *F(p)* when he writes:

> [Some argue] we either know that the word of God which precedes the sacrament is the true will of God, or we do not know it. If we know it, we learn nothing new from the sacrament which succeeds. If we do not know it, we cannot learn it from the sacrament, whose whole efficacy depends on the word. Our brief reply is: the seals which are affixed to diplomas, and other public deeds, are nothing considered in themselves, and would be affixed to no purpose if nothing was written on the parchment, and yet this does not prevent them from sealing and confirming when they are appended to writings.[56]

Two points are worth observing.

Firstly, Calvin's use of this illustration of sealing diplomas underscores Austin's contention that such acts can only operate performatively given certain conventions – recognizing the function of imprinting a document with wax. They are as Calvin says 'nothing in themselves', as indeed neither are bread and wine anything in themselves in terms of signification (especially when one rejects the physical presence of Christ 'under' the form of the elements), unless one holds to the convention or language-game in which they operate within the setting of the Church.

Secondly, Calvin's whole argument turns upon the understanding that in terms of the propositional content of such documents, the seals add nothing. What is written is sufficient for communication in terms of the truth content about a certain state of affairs, e.g. a will that relates what has been bequeathed to whom. But what the seal *does* is to give a certain force to the document, making it a mandatory legal document having imperative power. The sealing of this *type* of document (and the

seal is integral to making it such a document) enables something
to be achieved that mere words would not. The same is true of the
sacraments. They are instrumental as performatives are
instrumental in bringing about that which is intended by the author.
Thus: 'We conclude, therefore, that the sacraments are truly termed
evidences of divine grace and, as it were, seals of the goodwill
which he entertains towards us. They, by sealing it to us, sustain,
nourish, confirm and increase our faith.'[57] The illocutionary and
perlocutionary aspects of the sacraments are all encapsulated in
this conclusion.

Finally, the need for faith as a necessary condition to achieve
the 'illocutionary uptake' of the sacraments is also stressed by
Calvin:

> Wherefore, let it be a fixed point, that the office of the sacraments
> does not differ from the word of God; and this is to hold forth and
> offer Christ to us, and in him, the treasures of heavenly grace. They
> confer nothing, and avail nothing, if not received in faith, just as
> wine and oil, or any other liquor, however large the quantity which
> you pour out, will run away and perish unless there be an open vessel
> to receive it... but the sacraments do not of themselves bestow any
> grace, but they announce and manifest it.[58]

By placing the sacraments in the same conceptual category as
God's word, the validity of our thesis, that strict parallels exist
between speech acts and sacramental acts, is strengthened all the
more. One has to pay attention to several factors regarding the
sacraments as one has to in approaching the Bible. Four such
factors are numerated by Vanhoozer: Proposition (what is being
communicated – meaning); Purpose (the function of the text/
speech act); Presence (the form of literature, its particular
'incarnation') – and the Power (the illocution).[59] It is the distinctive
form of the sacrament which contributes so decisively to its
illocutionary power.

It is clear that if the link forged between speech acts and
sacramental acts holds, Calvin was much closer to the nature and
purpose of the Lord's Supper as divinely instituted than either
Zwingli or indeed Cranmer, if the latter is to be classed as an

advocate of 'symbolic parallelism'.[60] Both undervalue the performative nature of the sacraments, Zwingli more so than Cranmer. Both create too great a separation between the sign and the thing signified, understandably so in wanting to avoid the error of transubstantiation. But, as we have seen, there is an alternative way of understanding the instrumentality of the sacraments which Calvin instinctively pursued, however dangerous the risk he ran of being misunderstood.

The Need for an Evangelical Rethink of the Lord's Supper?

When the idea of propositional revelation came under attack, especially in the nineteenth century, Evangelicals stressed in response the propositional nature of Scripture, possibly to the detriment of other aspects, especially the illocutionary force of the texts. Perhaps a parallel situation has occurred with regard to the sacraments. For fear of holding an unbiblical instrumentalist view, some Evangelicals have lapsed into a form of reductionism, with the Lord's Supper collapsing into an elaborate visual aid. As we have seen in the writings of Stibbs, this need not be the case. A deeper appreciation of Calvin's work on the subject, against the backdrop of the speech act theory, may provide what is necessary to recapture a richer appreciation of this central sacrament of the gospel.

NOTES

1. B A Gerrish, 'Sign and reality: The Lord's Supper in the reformed confessions', *The Old Protestantism and the New*, T&T Clark (1982), pp. 118-30.

2. J. Calvin, *Commentary on 1 Corinthians,* Eerdmans (1980), p. 203.

3. J. Calvin, *Institutes of Christian Religion* Book IV, Eerdmans (1983), p. 564.

4. B A Gerrish, *Grace and Gratitude: The Eucharistic Theology of John Calvin,* T&T Clark (1993), p 133

5. Calvin, *Institutes* IV ch XIV, p. 493

6. Calvin, *Institutes* IV ch XVII, p. 563

7. G. B. Caird, *The Language and Imagery of the Bible,* Duckworth (1980), pp. 7-36

8. J. L. Austin, *How To Do Things with Words,* Clarendon Press (1961).

9. J. R. Searle, *Speech Acts: An Essay in the Philosophy of Language,* CUP (1969).

10. J. L. Austin in *Truth,* G Pitcher ed, Prentice-Hall (1964), p 28. 'Can we be sure that stating truly is a different *class of assessment* from arguing soundly, advising well, judging fairly, and blaming justifiably? Do these not have something to do in complicated ways with facts?'

11. L. Wittgenstein, *Philosophical Investigations,* Blackball (1958).

12. J. L. Austin, *How to do things with Words,* p. 45 *et passim.*

13. J. Macquarrie, *God-Talk,* SCM (1967), p 196.

14. 1 Corinthians 5:7

15. Calvin, *Institutes,* Book IV, ch XVII, p. 558.

16. D. M. Baillie, *The Theology of the Sacraments,* p. 49.

17. S. S. Smalley, *John – Evangelist and Interpreter,* Paternoster (1978).

18. S. S. Smalley, pp. 204-5.

19. A phrase attributed to E. C. Hoskyns, *The Fourth Gospel,* F. N. Davey ed.

20. Gerrish, *Grace and Gratitude,* p. 209.

21. Karl Barth, *Church Dogmatics,* T&T Clark, 11:1, p. 55ff.

22. Barth, *Church Dogmatics,* 11:1, p. 54.

23. Barth, *Church Dogmatics* 1:2, p. 230.

24. Barth, *Church Dogmatics* 1:1, p. 52.

25. Calvin, *Institutes* Book IV ch XVII, p. 562.

26. Calvin, *Institutes* Book IV ch XVII, p. 563.

27. J. R. Lucas, *Freedom and Grace,* SPCK (1976), p. 111.

28. Gerrish, *Grace and Gratitude,* p. 139.

29. A. and R. Hanson, *Reasonable Belief,* Oxford (1981), pp. 232-3.

30. P. T .Forsyth, *The Church and the Sacraments,* Independent Press (1947), p. 234.

31. D. Gregg, *Anamnesis in the Eucharist,* Grove Liturgical Study No 5.

32. E. Schweizer, *The Lord's Supper According to the New Testament.*

33. I. H. Marshall, *Last Supper and Lord's Supper,* Paternoster

(1980), p. 89.

34. J. Jeremias, *The Eucharistic Words*, pp. 220-5.

35. Marshall, p. 89.

36. D. Gregg, *Anamnesis in the Eucharist*, p. 24.

37. Gregg, p. 24.

38. B. S. Childs, *Memory and Tradition in Israel*, p. 84.

39. Childs, p. 27.

40. A. M. Stibbs, *Sacrament, Sacrifice and Eucharist*, Tyndale Press (1961), p. 45.

41. I. H. Marshall, p. 80.

42. A. and R. Hanson, *Reasonable Belief*, p. 231.

43. Cf. The 1957 Memorandum of the Church of England Liturgical Commission on *Prayer Book Revision in the Church of England*, pp. 30ff.

44. D. MacCulloch, *Thomas Cranmer*, Yale (1996), p 507.

45. Cf Rainer Reisner, 'Judische Elementarbildung und Evangelienuberlieferung in *Gospel Perspectives*, Vol 1, R. T. France and D. Wenham, Eds, JSOT 98O).

46. Cf. M Tinker, 'Towards an Evangelical view of the Church', *The Anglican Evangelical Crisis*, M Tinker (ed), Christian Focus (1995).

47. A. M. Stibbs, pp. 73-4.

48. A. M. Stibbs, p. 75.

49. J. L. Austin, *How to do things with Words*, p. 117.

50. J. R. Searle, *Speech Acts*, p. 25ff.

51. Cf K. J. Vanhoozer, 'The Semantics of Biblical Literature' in *Hermeneutics, Authority and Canon*, D. A. Carson and J. D. Woodbridge (eds), IVP (1986).

52. K. J. Vanhoozer, *Hermeneutics, Authority and Canon*, p. 91.

53. J. R. Searle, *Expression and Meaning: Studies in the Theory of Speech Acts*, CUP (1979), p. 29.

54. Calvin, *Institutes*, Book IV, ch XIV, p. 492.

55. Calvin, *Institutes*, Book IV, ch XIV, p. 494.

56. Calvin, *Institutes*, Book IV, ch XIV, p. 496.

57. Calvin, *Institutes*, Book IV, ch XIV, p. 503.

58. K. J. Vanhoozer, *Hermeneutics, Authority and Canon*, p. 91.

59. D. MacCulloch, *Thomas Cranmer*, p. 614.

9

Reversal or Betrayal?
Evangelicals and Socio-political
Involvement in the Twentieth Century[1]

Introduction

Augustine prefaces his magnum opus, *The City of God,* with an explanation of its purpose, namely, 'the task of defending the glorious City of God against those who prefer their own gods to the Founder of that City'. Augustine presents the City of God 'both as it exists in this world of time, a stranger among the ungodly, living by faith, and as it stands in the security of its everlasting seat.'

Here is the tension between the City of God and its present opponents on the one hand, contrasted with its glorious future on the other. And it is this tension of living between the 'now and the not yet' which creates the problem of how Christians are to relate to society. What do the people of God owe to 'the ungodly'? How are Christians to live out the present in the light of the future?

In his *Issues Facing Christians Today,* Dr John Stott writes:

> It is exceedingly strange that any followers of Jesus Christ should ever need to ask whether social involvement was their concern, and that controversy should have blown up over the relationship between evangelism and social responsibility. For it is evident that in his public ministry Jesus both 'went about ... teaching ... and preaching' (Matt 4:23; 9:35) and 'went about doing good and healing' (Acts 10:38). In consequence Evangelism and social concern have been intimately related to one another throughout the history of the church... Christian people have often engaged in both activities quite unselfconsciously, without feeling the need to define what they were doing or why.[2]

However, controversy there certainly is, not so much over the question of *whether* Christians should engage in socio-political activity, but how that involvement should express itself and upon what theological basis it should proceed. Robert K. Johnstone rightly observes:

> *That* evangelicals should be involved socially has become a forgone conclusion ... but *how* and *why* evangelicals are to involve themselves in society have proven to be more vexing questions. That they are to be involved brings near unanimity; how that involvement takes shape and what is its Christian motivation bring only debate.[3]

What this chapter seeks to do is to trace some of the fundamental developments in twentieth-century evangelical thinking in this area in general, and to analyse more closely how we might properly view the relation between evangelism and social action.

At the risk of some oversimplification we shall argue that the debate hinges on two rival interpretations of history and two models of social involvement. The debate itself is related to other issues such as hermeneutics – how the Bible is to be used – as well as differing understandings of some key doctrinal concepts such as 'The Kingdom of God' and the nature and extent of the work of Christ on the Cross.

A Tale of Two Histories

Kathleen Heasman documents how evangelicals in the last century and the earlier part of this century were significantly involved in social action, and comments that they 'were all agreed upon salvation by faith and the infallibility and overriding importance of the Scriptures'.[4] William Wilberforce, Elizabeth Fry, George Muller, Henry Venn and Anthony Ashley-Cooper are just some of the more notable names which read like a 'Who's Who' of evangelical social activists who played an unquestioned part in securing anti-slavery legislation, penal reform, improving factory working conditions and the care of needy orphans in a society desperately requiring change.

In the United States, Charles Finney was not only vigorous in promoting his own brand of revivalism but in reforming work as well, so that in his twenty-third lecture on Revival he could write: 'The great business of the church is to reform the world. The

Church of Christ was originally organised to be a body of reformers. The very profession of Christianity implies the profession and virtually an oath to do all that can be done for the universal reformation of the world.' One of the followers of Finney who took this call to heart was Theodore Weld, who subsequently devoted his life to the struggle against slavery.

However, between about 1910 and the late 1930s, evangelicals seemed to be less concerned with social issues, in marked contrast to their evangelical forebears. At least in part this was a reaction (some would say over-reaction), to the liberal theological developments which were taking place at the time in the form of the so-called 'Social Gospel' espoused by Walter Rauschenbusch, a Baptist minister and Professor of Church History at Rochester Seminary. He defined the Kingdom of God as 'a reconstruction of society on a Christian basis', contrasting the 'old evangel of the saved soul' with the 'new evangel of the Kingdom of God', which was primarily a matter not of getting souls into heaven, but 'transforming life on earth into the harmony of heaven'. It was the reaction against this teaching that led many Evangelicals to distance themselves from anything which looked remotely like it. Such considerations, when combined with a growing pessimism about the ability of society to make moral progress (a pessimism exacerbated both by the experience of the First World War and premillenialist teaching), make the disengagement by many evangelicals from social involvement to some extent under-standable.

On the wider ecclesiastical scene the social gospel movement became firmly entrenched in the ecumenical movement as embodied in the World Council of Churches, from which evangelicals were becoming further and further removed.

However, the 1960s saw new developments amongst evangelicals which led to modifications in their views of mission, evangelism and social action, which some have argued now run parallel to those of the ecumenical movement itself.[5]

The congress on the Church's Worldwide Mission at Wheaton, Illinois in 1966 was called in a conscious reaction against the direction in which the WCC was moving. The paper on social responsibility, entitled 'Mission and Social Concern', offered the following four guidelines:

1. That any programme of social concern must point men to – not away from – the central message of redemption through the blood of Christ.

2. Expression of social concern must provide an opportunity for spoken witness to Christ, recognising the incompleteness of non-verbal witness.

3. Efforts must not arouse unrealistic and unscriptural expectations; the reality of sin and the Second Coming were not to be minimised.

4. The desire to do good in the name of Christ should not lead to wasteful competition with secular agencies.[6]

What can be considered to be a distinctive evangelical approach to social action, over and against the more liberal ecumenical approach, continued at the more ambitious Berlin World Congress of Evangelism later that year. The tone and general theological flavour of the conference is captured by the opening address given by Billy Graham, in which he firmly maintained that: 'If the church went back to its main task of proclaiming the gospel and getting people converted to Christ, it would have a far greater impact on the social, moral and psychological needs of men than it could achieve through any other thing it could possibly do'.[7]

We find the same outlook echoed at Berlin by John Stott:

> The commission of the Church is not to reform society, but to preach the gospel. Certainly Christ's disciples who have embraced the gospel, and who themselves are being transformed by the gospel, are intended to be salt of the earth and light of the world. That is, they are to influence the society in which they live and work by helping arrest its corruption and illumine its darkness. But the primary task of the members of Christ's Church is to be gospel heralds, not social reformers.[8]

As we shall see, Stott was later to move on from that position, but that was the stance taken by the majority of evangelicals in 1966.

However, it would seem that already at this conference seeds were sown which were later to germinate into an approach to socio-political involvement which would mark a significant change of direction for evangelicals. As Paul Rees said:

> If the mission of the Church is narrow, the witness of the believing community is broad. The evangelistic mission is to proclaim 'Christ crucified' as the 'one mediator' of our salvation. But the confirming witness of believers is one in which they stand related to the whole life and to the total fabric of society. Here they bear witness both to the mercy of God's forgiveness and the judgements of God's justice. Nothing human is alien to their interests and, so far as their testimony and influence are concerned, Jesus Christ is Lord of all.[9]

Internationally, the next major development was the Lausanne conference in 1974, which Rachel Tingle claims produced a 'paradigm shift' in evangelical thinking.[10] The 'shift' was toward what is called 'holistic mission', and the term 'social action' was exchanged for the phrase 'socio-political involvement'. We thus have article 5 of the Lausanne Covenant worded as follows:

> Evangelism and socio-political involvement are both part of our Christian duty.... The message of salvation implies also a message of judgement upon every form of alienation, oppression and discrimination... the salvation we claim should be transforming us in the totality of our personal and social responsibilities.[11]

A year later, John Stott's change in thinking as crystallised at Lausanne was openly admitted:

> Today... I would express myself differently. It is not just that the commission [i.e. the Great Commission] includes the duty to teach converts everything that Jesus had previously commanded (Matt 28:20), and that social responsibility is among the things which Jesus commanded. I see now more clearly that not only the consequences of the commission but the actual commission itself must be understood to include social as well as evangelistic responsibility, unless we are to be guilty of distorting the words of Jesus.[12]

Not surprisingly, parallel developments are to be traced within Anglican Evangelicalism, as can be observed in the successive National Evangelical Anglican Congresses in 1967, 1977 and 1988. Writing a preparatory paper for NEAC 1 entitled 'Christian Worldliness', Sir Norman Anderson said:

> It has sometimes been debated whether the social teaching of the Bible flows from the doctrines of the person and work of Christ – that is, from the facts of redemption – or not... From my own standpoint, I would simply say that the Bible seems to me to approach questions of social responsibility in terms of the doctrine of creation and of God's plan for the created order, and not primarily in terms of the doctrines of incarnation, redemption and God's plan for His Church...[13]

But by the time we come to NEAC 3 in 1988 we have one major platform speaker, the then Secretary to the General Synod's Board for Social Responsibility, John Gladwin, who offered an evangelicalised liberation theology when he said, amongst other things, that 'God broke the back of injustice at the cross'. Also, a leading workshop leader, Dr Chris Sugden stated: 'The *content* of the gospel is to be defined in terms of the physically and socially poor.'[14] It would be fair to say that these were representative of a significant number at NEAC 3, such that one observer could write: 'NEAC 3 revealed sharp tensions and unexpected polarisations. Where major platform speakers referred to social or political issues, the style and content of their biblical exegesis and contemporary application engendered heated debate in the chalets and caravans of Caister.'[15]

During the intervening years, many initiatives were taken in Britain to put into practice the purported rediscovered evangelical social conscience. In 1971 the National Festival of Light was launched. O. R. Johnston played a major part in this and was later to take up the position of the chief executive of what was to become the Care Trust's political arm, Care Campaigns. In 1975 he put forward a biblical case for such Christian social involvement at the Leicester Ministers' Conference, later to be published under the title 'Christianity in a Collapsing Culture'. In 1982 the London

Institute for Contemporary Christianity (LICC) was founded under the chairmanship of John Stott. This was a creative 'think tank' for evangelicals wrestling with a wide range of cultural and social matters. Earlier, in 1969, the Shaftesbury Project was formed under the umbrella of the IVF and was later to merge with the LICC to form Christian Impact, now known as the Institute for Contemporary Christianity based at St Peter's, Vere Street in London.

How are these developments to be assessed from the standpoint of history?

The Great Reversal

One approach has been to refer to these developments as 'The Great Reversal', a term initially coined by the American historian Timothy L. Smith and then popularised by the sociologist David Moberg in a book which incorporates the phrase in its title.[16] This assessment notes the social withdrawal of evangelicals due to the influences already mentioned: disillusionment with social progress, the fundamentalist-liberal controversy, pre-millennialism, together with the overwhelming complexity of modern industrial society for which evangelicals seemed ill-equipped. From this perspective the increased commitment by Evangelicals to social issues is hailed as a 'Great Reversal', a sentiment well captured by Stott writing in 1984:

> One of the most notable features of the worldwide evangelical movement during the last ten to fifteen years has been the recovery of our temporarily mislaid social conscience. For approximately fifty years (c 1920-1970) evangelicals were preoccupied with the task of defending the historical biblical faith against the attacks of liberalism, and reacting against its 'social gospel'. But we are convinced that God has given us social as well as evangelistic responsibilities in his world. Yet the half-century of neglect has put us far behind in this area. We have a long way to catch up.[17]

More recently Dr Stott has been at pains to stress that the consultation at Lausanne I endorsed the primacy of evangelism, a priority underscored at Lausanne II at Manila in 1989:

Evangelism is primary because our chief concern is with the gospel, that all people may have the opportunity to accept Jesus Christ as their Lord and Saviour. The Grand Rapids Consultation of 1982 sought to tease out the relationship between evangelism and social responsibility in the following way: First, social activity is a *consequence* of the gospel, so 'faith works through love'. But, the report goes on to say 'social responsibility is more than a consequence of evangelism; it is one of its principal *aims*'. Secondly, 'social activity is a *bridge* to evangelism'. And thirdly, 'social activity... accompanies [evangelism] as its *partner*. They are like the two blades of a pair of scissors or the two wings of a bird, as they were in the public ministry of Jesus.' The partnership is, in reality, a marriage.[18]

The Great Betrayal?

A different perspective on these developments asks whether the liberalism which evangelicals were busy defending themselves against in the 1930s has in fact entered into the mainstream of the evangelical movement by the back door. This verdict on history might be termed 'The Great Betrayal'.

Although this is not a designation adopted by any of those who are critical of developments in the evangelical movement during the last 30 years, it is the conclusion that some are moving towards. Arthur Johnstone of Trinity Evangelical Divinity School, in his analysis of trends in the theology of evangelism, expresses the concern that, far from evangelicals rediscovering their heritage, they are in danger of losing it.[19]

That concern is articulated by Peter Beyerhaus in his preface to Johnstone's *The Battle for World Evangelism:*

It is particularly one new element, widely hailed by others as a sign that the new Evangelicals have come of age, about which I – like my friend Arthur Johnstone – have argued with my other beloved friend John Stott. For, unlike some of our Latin American colleagues I consider this element incompatible with the concept of evangelism as normatively expounded by both the Fathers of the Reformation and of the Evangelical Awakening. I am referring to the theological co-ordination of evangelism and socio-political involvement as equally constitutive elements of our Christian duty, or even – which is not the same – of the mission which Christ gave to His Church.[20]

Johnstone is of the view that it was principally at Lausanne that the theology of evangelism became blunted because it lost the unique status it had previously held in evangelical thinking prior to Berlin 1966.[21]

Others who would also wholly identify with the call for evangelicals to engage in social involvement have expressed similar concerns. Thus Sir Fred Catherwood comments:

> In the sixties I wrote that we evangelicals should come out of our pietistic ghetto and take part in the social debate as Christian citizens... I and others in the movement won the argument. But we also lost a vital part of the case we were making. We did not allow for the 'zeitgeist'. We argued that it was the task of the Christian church to bring the trends in public opinion to the standards of eternal truth and judge them by God's word. But that was not what happened. The evangelicals joined the liberals in a concern for social issues, but it was the world and not the church which set the agenda.[22]

Is what has taken place a return to the kind of evangelical social involvement characterised by our forefathers and simply brought up to date in a way appropriate to new social and political contexts, or has a theological mutation occurred such that what is considered by some to be the basis of such action would hardly be recognised by the likes of Wilberforce as being evangelical at all?

A Comparison of Two Models
One way of determining the answer to this question is to consider what some of the great eighteenth and nineteenth century evangelical social Reformers taught about their theological and moral motivation, and then compare it with what the heirs of Lausanne are advocating. When we do this, we discover that the differences are not insignificant.

The Reforming Evangelicals
The social reforms of the nineteenth century took place in the wake of the revivals of the eighteenth century, which provided the moral context and spiritual impetus for the reforms. The relationship between the two has been carefully considered by J.

Wesley Bready in his *England Before and After Wesley*. What did Wesley teach about the gospel and social action? In his *Preface* to the first Methodist Hymn Book (1739) Wesley wrote: 'The gospel of Christ knows no religion but *social,* no holiness but *social* holiness. This command have we from Christ, that he who loves God loves his brother also.'

In the University sermon delivered in St Mary's, Oxford in 1774, Wesley pictures Christianity as 'beginning to exist in individuals', next as 'spreading from one to another', and finally 'as covering the earth'. He then asks his congregation to pause 'and survey this strange sight, a Christian world!' He proceeded to challenge those in leadership positions within the town as to whether they were of one mind with the love of God shed abroad in their hearts (i.e. converted). He then pleaded that the sure hope for a better age was a better man, and only Christ's new man can herald Christ's new world. So Henry Carter comments: 'To Wesley a scheme of reconstructing society which ignored the redemption of the individual was unthinkable.'[23]

Similarly, Bready writes of Wesley:

As a prophet of God and an ordained ambassador of Christ, he did not conceive it his task to formulate economic, political and social theories; nor did he judge himself competent so to do. His 'calling' he believed was far more sacred, and more thoroughgoing: it was to lead men into contact with spiritual reality, to enable them to possess their souls and enter the realms of abundant life. For if once men, in sufficient numbers, were endowed with an illumined conscience and spiritual insight they, collectively as well as individually, would become possessors of the 'wisdom that passeth knowledge'; and in that wisdom social problems gradually would be solved.[24]

Wesley saw his priority as preaching the gospel. Being a Christian also entailed good works, being a good citizen, indeed being a good neighbour. He was committed to the second great commandment: 'Love your neighbour as yourself.' But he saw that the second commandment could only substantially be fulfilled if the first commandment held pride of place: 'Hear O Israel, The Lord our God, the Lord is One. Love the Lord your God with all your heart and with all your soul and with all your mind and with all your strength' (Mark 12:29-31). How can men and women love God while they are in enmity with him?

How can people be addressed as 'Israel' unless they belong to 'Israel'? Reconciliation is first required and the means of that reconciliation is the gospel.

As Bready demonstrates, Wesley's impressive endeavours in promoting social action, working towards slavery abolition, ameliorating the effects of gambling and liquor abuse, promoting literacy and education amongst the poor, as well as his more conspicuous political comments regarding the American Revolution, arose from a Spirit-fired application of the following fundamental Christian doctrines: (1) our unity and responsibilities as creatures before the Creator, (2) the corruption of the will by sin, so that all social problems are fundamentally spiritual, (3) the principle of stewardship and the future judgement to come.[25] At no point did Wesley conceive of gospel proclamation as being of equal theological weight to social action, although the former entailed the latter.

When we turn to William Wilberforce we find the same principles at work.

Wilberforce is most widely known for his part in the abolition of the slave trade, but he also had another great aim. On Sunday, 28th of October, 1787, he wrote in his diary: 'God Almighty has set before me two great objects, the suppression of the Slave Trade and the Reformation of Manners', that is, the reform of the morals of Britain. In order to achieve this second goal, he devised a plan to form a new Society for the Reformation of Manners, with a view to raising the moral tone of the nation by clamping down on offences such as the publication of indecent or blasphemous literature and the desecration of the Lord's Day. Jonathan Bayes in his treatment of this campaign notes: 'His plan was that his Society for the Reformation of Manners should serve to restore England to its Protestant faith by standing against those moral offences which militated against Christianity. As a by-product, Wilberforce believed, there would follow a general moral improvement.'[26]

Being the shrewd politician that he was, he did not restrict the membership of the society to evangelicals. Initially he couched his campaign in purely moral terms. But then he went further to challenge the religious outlook of many by writing his book, *A Practical View of the Prevailing Religious System of Professed Christians in the Higher and Middle Classes in this Country Contrasted with Real Christianity.* This was published in 1797, having taken four years to write. Wilberforce's aim was to share his testimony and to lead members of his own class into vital Christianity by exposing the shallowness of nominal Christianity. The book, much to the surprise of the printer, went through five reprints within six months and just kept on selling.

Wilberforce argued that the general lack of concern with true Christianity could be traced back to two maxims: 'One is that it signifies little what a man believes; look to his practice. The other (of the same family) is that sincerity is all in all.' So he writes:

> The first of these maxims proceeds from the monstrous supposition that, although we are accountable creatures, we shall not be called upon to account before God for the exercise of our intellectual ... powers. The second ... proceeds on this groundless supposition: The Supreme Being has not afforded us sufficient means of discriminating truth from falsehood or right from wrong.

The ignorance of basic Christian truths was the result, argued Wilberforce, of a failure to recognise the depth and extent of man's moral depravity through original sin, and that although nominal religion may pay lip service to Christ, it lacked that which was required of authentic faith, a commitment of the totality of one's life so that everything is done to the glory of God.

Bayes suggests that in the medium and long term, the impact of both the Society and *A Practical View* was considerable. Bayes contends that the improved moral mood in society in the 1830s and the sense of being accountable to God which pervaded society at every level was, 'in no small measure due to Wilberforce'. However, as *A Practical View* shows, Wilberforce, like Wesley before him, saw conversion as being the main need, especially given his strong view of human corruption by original sin. In drawing out some of the implications for today, Bayes concludes: 'Like Wilberforce we need to be convinced of the primacy of conversion: until men and women are made new by the Holy Spirit, there will never be a genuine external reformation.'[27]

Of particular significance in shaping the Reforming Evangelicals' approach to social involvement was their view of eschatology and the reality of judgement. For example, Anthony Ashley-Cooper, the Earl of Shaftesbury, confessed: 'I do not think in the last forty years I have lived one conscious hour that was not influenced by the thought of our Lord's return.' Wilberforce, in his *A Practical View*, writes of the authentic believer:

> That he was created by God, redeemed from death, the consequence of original sin, by the incarnation of the Son of God, who had commanded him to be grateful and pious towards God, merciful and benevolent towards men; ... and that, as he neglected or obeyed these commands, he was to expect punishment or reward in a future life.

Such an understanding of the relation between gospel renewal and societal reformation is very similar to the position advocated at Wheaton and Berlin in 1966, but rests less easily with what some evangelicals have proposed since.

The model of the Reforming Evangelicals might be contrasted with that of the Radical Evangelicals whose spiritual pedigree can, as we shall argue, be traced directly back to Lausanne.[28]

The Radical Evangelicals

Ranald Macaulay observes that at Lausanne a rift occurred which centred on the meaning of the phrase 'Kingdom of God'.[29] This is key to understanding much of the debate that has ensued.

Back in 1967, in his paper for NEAC 1, Sir Norman Anderson argued:

> There is a sense in which that Kingdom is already a present reality, for the King is already on his throne, waiting till all things are put under his feet... But is there a wider sense in which one can think of the Kingdom as advanced wherever the will of the King is done, even by those who do not give Him personal allegiance? This, it

seems to me, is dangerous ground, for we cannot regard the Kingdom of God as having materialised in a factory for example, merely because social justice and harmony reign therein.... The Evangelical holds no brief for the so-called 'social gospel', for society, as such, cannot be 'redeemed' or 'baptised into Christ'.... But it can be reformed.[30]

Matters have moved on a long way since then, for the Radical Evangelical would contest almost everything in Anderson's statement. Rather ironically, in the first Sir Norman Anderson lecture delivered at the Salt and Light Conference at Swanwick, 1988, we find Graham Cray stating: 'Jesus' proclamation concerned the "reign of God" – God who is creator, upholder and consummator of all that is. We are not talking about one sector of human affairs ... we are talking about the reign and sovereignty of God over all that is.' Then in an attempt to substantiate the belief that the Kingdom of God is extended by the Spirit via non-Christians he said: 'Since Pentecost the Spirit has been poured out on *all* flesh, not just all Christians.' The same argument has been advanced more recently by Nigel Wright: 'All the earth is the Lord's and so we trace the Spirit at work beyond the Church, especially in movements that make for human dignity and liberation.'[31]

Dr Chris Sugden, also advocating the Kingdom of God as the basis for evangelical socio-political involvement, extends the redeeming work of Christ on the Cross to cover all positive social change in society, thus: 'Jesus' rule and action are cosmic. He disarmed the principalities and powers which create division in society. Where we see barriers broken down, can we divorce this from God's will seen in Christ's victory over the powers on the cross? (e.g. between Jew and Gentile, slave and free (Gal. 3:28))' and 'this understanding gives us a basis for seeing God at work in society beyond the church applying the effects of Christ's victory on the cross through social change'.[32]

Developing this point, Sugden and Samuel argue that *any* movement, Christian or not, which tries to establish social justice is to be interpreted as having the same character as Jesus' Kingdom acts of power and healing.[33] What is one to make of such a claim?

First of all, it is based upon a dubious understanding of the term 'Kingdom of God' which means far more than 'God rules'. In Scripture it is something to be entered into, sought, requiring poverty of spirit (Matt. 5:3; 7:21; 7:13). As Professor Don Carson correctly maintains, it is to be understood in terms of the sphere of salvation entered into through faith in Jesus Christ.[34] R. T. France similarly contends:

> It is as wrong to identify the Kingdom of God with social reform as it is with the church or heaven, and for the same reason: it is a category mistake.... To talk of men, even Christian men, bringing about God's kingdom is to usurp God's sovereignty. Yet this sort of language is increasingly being heard in evangelical circles. It is strangely reminiscent of the language of 19th century liberalism, which called upon men to create a just and caring society which was called the 'Kingdom of God'.[35]

Perhaps liberalism has entered via the back door after all!

Secondly, it must be said that Scripture is being handled in a way which is hermeneutically suspect from an evangelical point of view. Instead of Scripture being determinative, it is the *context* in which the Christian finds himself which shapes belief and biblical interpretation. In the NEAC 3 booklet, *Evangelical Roots,* Chris Sugden states: 'The Good News we love is defined in the Scripture as good news to the (physically and socially) poor; and that means that what the good news means to poor Christians (in Scripture and today) should set the criteria for focusing what the good news means to others.'[36]

Elsewhere he gives an example of how this contextualised exegesis works out in practice with a group of Christians operating amongst quarry workers in Bangalore. The team sought to 'affirm' the socially oppressed workers' desire for security 'in the light of the Bible'. Therefore, it is asked: 'Had not God provided Israel with land, a place to belong and access to resources?' So they began to work with the quarry workers towards their goal. A pay rise resulted and the workers attributed their good fortune to God. 'This,' it is claimed by Sugden, 'represented the starting-point for these people to enter the life of the Kingdom'.[37] Not only is this 'paradigmatic approach' to interpreting Scripture common to the proponents of liberation theology, it is reminiscent of the principles taught by the peddlers of prosperity healing. But we might well ask: why select these themes of Exodus and Blessing? Why not the prophetic call of Jeremiah that the oppressed people of God should not rebel against the tyrant Nebuchadnezzar?[38]

Also, when it is said by Sugden that *wherever* just relationships are established we are to take these as signs of God's Kingdom, and Galatians 3:28 is cited in support, it must be firmly pointed out that what Paul is referring to is what happens in the *church* as a result of people hearing the gospel, and not 'just relationships' in society at large.

Such a loose and selective approach to handling the Bible hardly accords with what is generally regarded as a hallmark of evangelicalism, namely, respecting the historical integrity of the text and how it functions within the overall canonical sweep of Scripture.

But thirdly, it is worth noting that the Kingdom approach of the Radical Evangelicals to social ethics is remarkably similar to that of Rauschenbusch, as Brian Stanley observes: 'This is extremely difficult to distinguish from the claim of Rauschenbusch that wherever corporations abandon monopoly capitalism for the "law of service" or undemocratic nations submit to real democracy "therewith they step out of the Kingdom of Evil into the Kingdom of God".'[39] It is evident too that it bears little, if any, relation to the Reforming Evangelicals of the eighteenth and nineteenth centuries. So Oliver Barclay comments: 'I can discover no signs of Kingdom thinking in the programmes of Wilberforce, the "Clapham Sect" and Shaftesbury.... They... used much more straightforward biblical themes.'[40] Elsewhere Dr Barclay writes:

Certainly we seem to be doing much less than our theologically less sophisticated nineteenth-century forebears did. There is no evidence that the nineteenth-century evangelicals were troubled by these theological questions. They accepted a straightforward responsibility to help the deprived, and therefore set to work to tackle some of the structures that upheld such deprivation.[41]

This is a sad indictment indeed.

It may be argued, however, that the departure of the Radical Evangelicals from the evangelical mainstream is an aberration and not a necessary result of the changes which took place at Lausanne I and II. After all, Stott himself would hardly endorse the 'Kingdom' approach outlined above. Indeed, in his response to another 'Kingdom' advocate, Ron Sider, he is so critical that he can write: 'I still want to insist that the kingdom of God in the New Testament is fundamentally a *Christological* concept, and that it may be said to exist only where Jesus Christ is consciously acknowledged as Lord.'[42]

But it may well be the case that the Radical Evangelicals were simply attempting to be consistent in drawing out the implications of the way of thinking that was developing at these conferences. The result is the emergence of two streams of thought: those represented by the likes of Catherwood and Anderson on the one hand that would be placed in the Reforming Evangelical category, and those represented by Sugden and Wright on the other, who would be identified with Radical Evangelicalism and its salient similarities with the old liberalism. If this is so, then the position of Dr Stott is most interesting, for it would appear that there is an internal inconsistency in his position which places him with a foot in both camps.

Therefore, going back to Dr Stott's treatment of the results of the Grand Rapids Consultation,[43] it may be granted that while the Reforming Evangelicals would have agreed that 'social activity is a *consequence* of evangelism', one would be hard pressed to find any evidence that they would have shared the view that it was one of its 'principal *aims*'. Where in the New Testament is this ever put forward as being the case if evangelism is taken as proclaiming the evangel? The evangel is (as presented by the apostle Paul in Romans 1:2-5, and indeed the rest of the epistle) an exposition of that gospel together with its implications. It is impossible to find any reference to social transformation being integral to its message, it is a spiritual transformation which is its focus. As people's relationship with God is changed, social change also takes place, which is primarily, although not exclusively, within the realm of the redeemed community – the church (Eph. 1:13: 'And you also became God's people when you heard the true message, the Good News that brought you salvation. You believed in Christ, and God put his stamp of ownership on you by giving you the Holy Spirit he promised' (GNB)).

Some, however, would question this definition of the evangel, like Paul Schrotenboer: 'I would see the term "holistic evangelism" as including both the telling of the Good News and the regal summons to convert to God and the call for social systemic reform in the name of Christ.'[44] But this is a tactical move, establishing a definition *a priori* which outmanoeuvres and displaces all others. Schrotenboer may define evangelism in this way, but does the Bible? The answer is surely 'no'.

Was Paul's aim as an evangelist to bring about social change? Not directly. His priestly duty of proclaiming the gospel of God was 'so that the Gentiles might become an offering acceptable to God, sanctified by the Holy Spirit' (Rom 15:16). That is, they become incorporated into the people of God by believing the message of repentance and forgiveness of sins through the Lord Jesus Christ.

But if social responsibility is put forward as a principal aim in evangelism, it is a small and logical step to conceiving social change as part of the evangel itself. To take that step is to produce 'another Gospel'.

Secondly, as we have seen, Dr Stott in elaborating the Grand Rapids document speaks of evangelism and social activity as a *partnership,* like two blades of a pair of scissors or two wings of a bird, while earlier on insisting that evangelism has a logical and theological priority.[45]

This position is untenable, for the very imagery used negates the claim that evangelism has priority. Can one say which blade in a pair of scissors is more important? Hardly, both are equally important, for without both blades the pair of scissors would simply cease to be scissors, let alone function. Similarly, can one speak of one bird's wing as having priority? Both are equally important, for without a *pair* of wings the bird would not be able to fly at all. Perhaps, unthinkingly, social action has been exalted to the same *status* as evangelism, and, as we have seen, neither Wesley nor Wilberforce would countenance such a notion. But this is an inconsistency, for elsewhere in the Grand Rapids report it is stated explicitly that:

> evangelism relates to people's eternal destiny [no mention here of social activity], and in bringing them the good news of salvation, Christians are doing what nobody else can do. Seldom if ever should we have to choose between healing bodies and saving souls... Nevertheless, if we must choose, then we have to say that the supreme and ultimate need of all humankind is the saving grace of Jesus Christ.[46]

But such a claim is undermined by talk of evangelism and social action being 'in reality a marriage'.

Dr John Woodhouse's comment on this point is very astute:

> The significant disagreement among evangelicals has to do with the motivation that has been advanced for our social concern. On the one side of the debate, a perceived neglect of social responsibilities is redressed by arguing that social action is *more significant* than evangelicals have hitherto acknowledged. It is a worthwhile question to ask whether in the proposed heyday of evangelical social action – last century – the kind of theological justification advanced today was present. My impression is that it was not on the other side of the debate, it is acknowledged that to love one's neighbour *is* a Christian duty.... And who would deny that we have neglected our duties. It is right that we should be called again and again to care. But when that obligation is given the theological undergirding that belongs properly to the task of evangelism, when the evangelistic task is no longer seen as unique in importance, when evangelistic responsibility is taken for granted, and our neglect of social action causes deeper remorse than our neglect of evangelism, then the cart has been put before the horse and is trying to grow legs.[47]

A cautionary tale is told by Professor Don Carson of an assessment made by a Mennonite leader of his own movement:

> One generation of Mennonites cherished the gospel and believed that the entailment of the gospel lay in certain social and political commitments. The next generation assumed the gospel and

emphasised the social and political commitments. The present generation identifies itself with the social and political commitments, while the gospel is variously confessed or disowned, it no longer lies at the heart of the belief system of some who call themselves Mennonites.

Carson comments: 'Whether or not this is a fair reading of the Mennonites, it is certainly a salutary warning for evangelicals at large.'[48]

Is there a better way of understanding the relationship between evangelism and social action? I would suggest that there is, and that it is based on a model proposed by Karl Barth. Barth argues that God's activity in the world has a centre and circumference.[49] The centre is the coming of God's kingdom in Jesus Christ, the circumference around this centre is God's gracious providential rule of all things.

When it is asked what activity of man reflects God's activity at the centre, the answer is service. Barth takes his cue from the action of Jesus Christ as the Servant, giving himself for the sake of the world and for the Father's glory, so Christians are called first to be servants. Our life of service is to be understood within the community of God's people – the church, whose life is geared to announcing God's kingdom in Christ to the world.

When asked what activity of man corresponds to God's overruling providence at the circumference, the answer is work. God in his fatherly providence sustains, directs and cares for his world. Therefore, our work is about sustaining, directing and caring for the world.

Just as God's providence surrounds and supports the centre of his action in the coming kingdom in Jesus Christ, so our human work should surround and support our service of the kingdom. Sometimes, of course, the two coincide, as in the case of a full-time Christian minister which would run parallel to the ministry of Christ whose work was service. Also, a point will come when the Kingdom of God and creation are at one, with the establishment of the new creation towards which salvation history is moving.

This model is extremely helpful in enabling us to grasp the relation between evangelism and social action. Intuitively, Stott recognises this relation, but in order to give social involvement a greater prominence in evangelical thinking than perhaps it has had at some points in its recent history, that which lies at the circumference has been drawn into the centre and the result is an unstable tension. The Radical Evangelicals extend the centre out to the circumference so that all of God's activity is viewed as kingdom activity. But the advantage of Barth's model is that while recognising that creation and redemption belong together, as does God's providential activity and his specific saving activity, they are nonetheless to be distinguished, such that God's providential work serves his saving work. Because evangelism is central to the extension of his kingdom, in a way that, say, a Christian politician forming political policy is not, evangelism has priority over social involvement in that it belongs to the centre of God's activity in the world.

Dr Marytn Lloyd-Jones and Social Involvement
Given his wide ranging influence it is appropriate to make one or two references to observations made by Dr Martyn Lloyd-Jones on the issues under discussion, for on these matters, as on so many others, he spoke prophetically.

As we have seen, there is a tendency for evangelicals to appeal for social involvement in the present by upholding as models the great Evangelical Reformers of the nineteenth century. But, as Dr Lloyd-Jones noted, this is a false comparison and doomed to lead to disappointment unless one at the same time recognises the part played by the eighteenth-century Awakening upon such a movement. Of course, herein lies the difference, for we do not live in the aftermath of a Revival. In a letter to Iain Murray concerning the wisdom of publishing an article by Raymond Johnston on Christian social involvement, Lloyd-Jones writes: 'He [Johnston] completely fails to see that the Wilberforces and the Shaftesburys can only succeed after times of Revival when there are many Christians.'[50] This does not mean that Dr Lloyd-Jones put all his eggs in the Revival basket, as it were, for elsewhere he writes:

If we give the impression that we have no concern about political and social matters we shall alienate people; and I suggest that we have done so, and so the masses are outside the church. On the other hand, if we think we are going to fill our churches and solve our problems by preaching politics and taking an interest in social matters we are harbouring a very great delusion.[51]

How, then, are Christians to proceed? In the same address Dr Lloyd-Jones essentially adopts the position of the Reforming Evangelicals. 'The New Testament', he argues, presents the Christian as 'salt in society and leaven and surely the whole point of those two comparisons is that Christian influence is to be a quiet influence and a slow process of influencing society'.[52] However, the eschatological dimension must not be minimised: 'The Christian's primary concern must always be the Kingdom of God, and then, because of that the salvation of men's souls.'[53] With Wesley and Wilberforce we find Dr Lloyd-Jones reiterating:

Men must be born again. How can they live the Christian life if they have not become Christians?... Nevertheless, government and law and order are essential because man is in sin; and the Christian should be the best citizen in the country. The Christian must act as a citizen and play his part in politics and other matters to get the best conditions possible... and be content with that which is less than Christian... [54]

However:

The Christian must of necessity have a profoundly pessimistic view of life in this world. Man is in sin and therefore you will never produce the perfect society. The coming of Christ alone is going to produce that. The consequence of this pessimism about the present and optimism regarding the ultimate future is that the preacher's primary duty is to exhort people to be ready to meet their judge.[55]

Conclusion

As we look at our nation, which in terms of its social problems, pagan superstitions and spiritual apathy, is not unlike that of the eighteenth century, the need for authentic evangelism, and some would say, Revival, is obvious to any but the most dewy-eyed romantic. Opportunities and responsibilities for social action also confront Christians simply to demonstrate Christian love and good stewardship as those who live in a democratic land, for 'to whom much is given, much will be required'. Also, as Sir Fred Catherwood comments in his autobiography, where churches have become involved in social care in the inner cities, it has given them a hearing for the gospel.[56] The danger to which we should be alerted by this paper is that because of some within the evangelical movement attempting to provide a theological basis for social involvement which is more akin to the social gospel, conservative evangelicals are in danger of repeating the same mistake as some of their forebears in the 1920s and 30s, namely, over-reacting and over-compensating by downgrading social involvement in order to preserve the priority of evangelism and the purity of the gospel.[57]

Is it not possible to recapture the simple spirit and evangelical convictions of the past which arise out of Scripture so that we can be effective in the present in the light of things to come? After all, the one who said 'Go and make disciples of all nations' is the same Lord who said 'Fill the earth and subdue it'; he is One Lord, Creator and Redeemer.[58]

It has recently been suggested that a biblical theory of ethics shaped by biblical theology might well provide a basis for such convictions.[59]

Michael Hill argues that the shape of biblical theology is always teleological, that is, moving towards a goal. He writes:

> The Bible story begins with an order in creation governed by the purpose of God. The story goes on to tell of the fracturing of that order and the neglect of the purposes of God. Wonderfully it tells of the one obedient man who upholds and fulfils the design of the Father. Knowledge of God's purposes is restored and the means of recovery established. Kinds and purposes find their true relationship in Jesus. The substance of morality is found in the value of kinds and the true nature of kinds is only detected in their goal or telos ... the goal of creation is the Kingdom of God. The nature of the kingdom is spelt out in terms of harmonious relationships.[60]

Hill maintains that strictly speaking Christian ethics is about applying biblical moral standards to those who have been made new creatures in Christ. But in the world where not all are committed to the Lordship of Christ, the goal of Christian ethics – a community of mutual love relationships – is not always achievable, so 'retrieval ethics' operates in situations less than ideal. The corollary of this would be that until the consummation of the Kingdom, society might well be reformed and brought closer into line with God's creative purposes, not least through Christian involvement as an expression of neighbourly love, but it cannot be said to have been redeemed, that is a term properly applied to the Christian community.

When we turn to Paul's letter to the Colossians with its distinctive emphasis on the unitary activity of God as Creator-Redeemer, we discover that many of the theological themes noted by Hill, and which shaped the thinking and action of the Reforming Evangelicals, are very much to the fore.

First, thanksgiving is offered to God the Father because of the Christians' faith and love which springs from their future hope which has broken into their lives through the message of the gospel (Col. 1:3-8). This in turn leads on to intercession that fruit 'in every good work' be borne so that the believers may live lives worthy of the Lord, given their new status as members of the Kingdom of God's Son (1:9-13). This Son is not only redeemer but the one through whom all things were created, he is the heir of the universe, the one for whom it was made. Those once alienated from God have been reconciled by his atoning death with a view to being presented to God as holy, a destiny guaranteed if they hold on to the gospel of hope (1:15-23). The commission given to Paul to present the Word of God in its fullness, which means presenting Christ, entails suffering. Christians are to resist being lured away by hollow philosophies, but to persist in Christ (1:24-2:23). In keeping with their new status in Christ, these believers are to be heavenly minded, which involves putting to death desires and practices which arise out of their fallen nature and to put on attitudes and practices which accord with their new nature (3:1-14). These are to work themselves out not only within the community of the redeemed, but also the wider spheres of social relationships in the home and work (3:15-4:1). What is more, there is to be an outflow into what we would call evangelism, so that Paul can ask that prayers be made on the apostles' behalf that God will open a door of opportunity for gospel proclamation and that the Colossian believers themselves might know how they might act towards outsiders, making the best of every opportunity with a view to sharing their faith verbally (4:1-6).

In other words, it is the priority of the gospel of redemption which, when rightly appropriated, leads to both evangelism and social action as naturally as a seed when planted produces both leaves and flowers (Col. 1:6). But given that evangelism is the planting of the gospel seed which gives rise to further evangelism and what might be broadly termed social action, there is a certain logical necessity, not to say theological necessity, for evangelism to be given pride of place within the life and purposes of the church. To confuse evangelism with social action will, in view of this survey, inevitably lead to the diminution of both.

NOTES

1. The substance of this paper formed the 1999 Evangelical Library Lecture.

2. John R. W. Stott, *Issues Facing Christians Today*, Marshall Morgan and Scott (1984), p. 3.

3. Robert K Johnstone, *Evangelicals at an Impasse: Biblical Authority in Practice,* John Knox (1979), p. 79

4. Kathleen Heasman, *Evangelicals in Action: An Appraisal of their Social Work in the Victorian Era*, London (1962), p. 13.

5. See Efiong S. Utuk, 'From Wheaton to Lausanne: The Road to Modification of Contemporary Evangelical Mission Theology', *Missiology: An International Review* 14/2 (19860, pp. 205-20.

6. Conference papers published in *The Church's Worldwide Mission*, Harold Lindsell (ed), Word Publishing (1966).

7. 'Why The Berlin Congress?', *Christianity Today*, 11 November 1966.

8. John R.W. Stott, 'The Great Commissions' in Henry and Mooneyham, *One Race, One Gospel, One Task*, World Congress on Evangelism, Berlin 1966, World Wide Publications (1967), vol 1 pp. 50-1..

9. Paul S Rees, 'Evangelism and Social Concern' in Henry and Mooneyham, *One Race, One Gospel, One Task*, vol 1 p. 308.

10. Rachel Tingle, 'Evangelical Social Action Today: Road to Recovery or Road to Ruin?', in *The Anglican Evangelical Crisis*, Melvin Tinker (ed), Christian Focus Publications (1995), p. 196.

11. Full text in *Let the Earth Hear His Voice*, J D Douglas (ed), Minneapolis: World Wide Publications (1975).

12. John R W Stott, *Christian Mission in the Modern World*, Falcon (1975), p. 23

13. J. N. D. Anderson, 'Christian Worldliness – the need and limits of Christian involvement,' *Guidelines*, J I Packer (ed), CPAS (1967), p. 216,

14. See Melvin Tinker; 'NEAC 3 – A Conference Too Far?', *Churchman* (1988), vol 102,

15. Vera Sinton, 'Evangelical Social Ethics: Has it Betrayed the Gospel?' in Melvin Tinker (ed), *Restoring the Vision*, Monarch (1990), p. 130.

16. David O Moberg, *The Great Reversal: Evangelism and Social Action*, J B Lippincott Company (1977).

17. John R. W. Stott, *Issues facing Christians Today*, p xi.

18. John R. W. Stott, 'Holistic Mission', *The Contemporary Christian*, IVP (1992), p. 340.

19. Arthur P Johnstone, *World Evangelism and the Word of God*, Bethany Fellowship (1974), and *The Battle for World Evangelism*, Tyndale House (1978).

20. Johnstone, *The Battle for World Evangelism*, p. 10.

21. Johnstone, *The Battle for World Evangelism*, pp. 329-30.

22. Sir Fred Catherwood, 'The Zeitgeist' *Transformation*, October/December (1986).

23. Cited in J. Wesley Bready, *England Before and After Wesley*, Hodder and Stoughton (1939), p. 203,

24. Bready, *England Before and After Weslev*, p. 257,

25. Bready, *England Before and After Wesley*, pp. 251-2,

26. Jonathan Bayes, 'William Wilberforce – His Impact on Nineteenth Century Society', *Churchman*, vol 2 (1994), p. 125.

27. Bready, *England Before and After Wesley*, p. 134.

28. For an exposition of what this term means and entails, see Nigel Wright, *The Radical Evangelical*, SPCK (1996).

29. Ranald Macaulay, 'The Great Commissions', *Cambridge Papers*, vol 7, no 2 (1998).

30. Anderson, 'Christian Worldliness' *Guidelines*, p. 231.

31. Wright, *Radical Evangelical*, p. 112.

32. Sugden, *Kingdom and Creation in Social Ethics*, Grove Ethical Studies, No 79, Sugden and Barclay (1990), p. 20.

33. See Vinay Samuel and Chris Sugden, 'God's Intention of the World; Tensions Between Eschatology and History' in Tom Sine (ed), *The Church in Response to Human Need*, Montrovia (1983), pp. 225-6,

34. D. A. Carson, *The Sermon on the Mount An Evangelical Exposition of Matthew 5-7*, Baker Book House (1982), pp. 11-15.

35. R. T. France, 'The Church and The Kingdom of God', D. A. Carson (ed) *Biblical Interpretation and the Church – Text and Context*, Paternoster (1984), p. 41.

36. Chris Sugden, 'Passage to India' in *Evangelical Roots*, Church of England Evangelical Council: 1988, p. 27.

37. Chris Sugden, 'The Impact of Conversion' Monica Hill (ed) *Entering the Kingdom*, Marc (1986), pp. 39-55.

38. See Melvin Tinker, 'Content, Context and Culture, Proclaiming the Gospel Today' in Melvin Tinker (ed), *Restoring the Vision*, Monarch (1990), p. 72.

39. B Stanley, 'Evangelical Social and Political Ethics: An Historical Perspective', *Evangelical Quarterly* 62:1 (1990), pp. 19-26.

40. Barclay, *Kingdom and Creation in Social Ethics*, Grove (1990), p. 23.

41. O. R. Barclay, *Evangelicalism In Britain*, 1935-1995, a Personal Sketch, IVP (1997), p. 111.

42. R. J. Sider, with a Response from J. R. W. Stott, *Evangelism, Salvation and Social Action*, Grove Books (1977).

43. John R. W. Stott, *The Contemporary Christian*, p. 340.

44. Paul G Schrotenboer, 'Response to the Article by Lesslie Newbigin, *International Bulletin of Missionary Research* 6/4 (1982), p. 152.

45. John R. W. Stott, *The Contemporary Christian*, pp. 339-40.

46. John R. W. Stott, *The Contemporary Christian*, p. 339.

47. John Woodhouse, 'Evangelism and Social Responsibility' in B G Webb (ed), *Christians in Society*, Exploration 3, Lancer (1988), pp. 19-20.

48. D. A. Carson, *The Cross in Christian Ministry*, Baker (1993), p.63.

49. Karl Barth, *Church Dogmatics* III 4 (56), T and T Clark (1978), pp. 565ff.

50. Dr Martyn Lloyd-Jones, *Letters 1919-1981*, Banner of Truth, (1994), p. 222.

51. Dr Martyn Lloyd-Jones, 'The Christian and the State in Revolutionary Times', *The Puritans Their Origins and Successors*, Banner of Truth (1987), pp. 342-43.

52. Dr Martyn Lloyd-Jones, *The Christian and the State*, p. 341.

53. Dr Martyn Lloyd-Jones, *The Christian and the State*, p 343.

54. Dr Martyn Lloyd-Jones, *The Christian and the State*, p 344.

55. Dr Martyn Lloyd-Jones, *The Christian and the State*, p 346.

56. Sir Fred Catherwood, *At The Cutting Edge*, Hodder & Stoughton (1995).

57. This concern is highlighted by Macaulay, in *The Great Commissions*.

58. For a discussion on how Christian ethics might be commended to society at large see, M Tinker, 'The Priority of Jesus: a look at the place of Jesus' teaching and example in Christian Ethics,' *Themelios*, vol 13, No 1, 1987.

59. Michael Hill, 'Biblical Theology and Ethics' in *Interpreting God's Plan – Biblical Theology and the Pastor*, R J Gibson (ed), Paternoster (1998), pp. 91-109.

60. Michael Hill, Biblical *Theology*, pp. 107-8.

10

The Phantom Menace:
Territorial Spirits and SLSW

Introduction
George Lucas's 'The Phantom Menace – Episode 1' of the great
Star Wars saga has broken all box office records – even 'Titanic'
has sunk without a trace by comparison! Increasingly, however,
within Christian circles there is developing a school of thought
which, in its own way, parallels the popularity and ideas of Lucas's
cinematic epic, which could conveniently be termed 'Spirit Wars'.
Here is a sample: 'The hypothesis I am suggesting... is that Satan
delegates high ranking members of the hierarchy of evil spirits to
control nations, regions, cities, tribes, people groups, neighbour-
hoods and other significant social networks of human beings
throughout the world. Their major assignment is to prevent God
from being glorified in their territory, which they do through
directing the activity of low ranking demons.' So writes Peter
Wagner in his book *Wrestling with Dark Angels*.[1]

To describe this type of spiritual engagement, Wagner has
coined the phrase 'Strategic-Level Spiritual Warfare' – SLSW.
This may be an example of theological art imitating life, since the
very term carries echoes of Ronald Reagan's 1980s dream to
defend America against the 'evil Empire' of his day by developing
the Strategic Defence Initiative (SDI) or 'Star Wars' programme.
Wagner is not alone in promoting this concept. There is now an
international group of Christian leaders forming the 'Spiritual
Warfare Network' which includes David Yonggi Cho, Cindy
Jacobs and George Otis Jnr.

What is SLSW?
There are three strands to this new brand of spiritual warfare.

First of all, as previously mentioned, there is the belief that there is a hierarchy of demonic spirits, with lower ranking fallen angels having power over specifically designated geographical areas. Wagner proposes that it is vital to learn the names and nature of the assignments of the demonic spirits as the first step to effective spiritual warfare. This, however, is not an absolutely necessary condition 'Effective spiritual warfare does not require knowing the names of the spirits, but experience has shown that when we are able to identity them specifically by name, we seem to have more authority over them, and therefore we can be more effective.'[2]

Others, like George Otis Jnr, advocate 'spiritual mapping'.[3] This involves extensive research on the religious history of an area – the prevailing folk religions, superstitions and practices. The assumption is that behind such beliefs and behaviour lie malevolent spiritual forces which use these as instruments to blind people to the gospel. As we become more informed about these things we can pray more effectively against their influence.

The second strand is that of dealing with the corporate and generational sin of a region. The leading name here is John Dawson.[4] The trick is to identify the sins of a town or city (including its past sins), confess them and repent for them on behalf of the inhabitants, allowing offended parties to 'release forgiveness', for 'Satan is terrified by reconciliation'.[5] Wagner gives this his 100% backing: 'No aspect of warfare is more important than identificational repentance' (the term given by Dawson to describe this process).[6] He also writes: 'Through accurate and sensitive spiritual mapping we can identify strongholds rooted in unremitted sins of past generations.'[7]

The third element of SLSW is 'in your face' prayer warfare (my term). Some, like Cindy Jacobs, draw attention to the way Jesus ended his temptations in the wilderness: 'Away with you, Satan'; here it is argued, is biblical warrant for this type of praying against territorial demons in an area.[8]

Just in case the more biblically conservative might be disposed to dismiss such ideas as belonging to the speculative Christian streams of North America, here I quote two publications relating to events and ideas in Hull and North Yorkshire. Here is the first: 'Hull isn't all bad or all good, it's a mixture just like you and me. There are good and bad things in its history and about it at present. There are signs of the Kingdom of God but also boulders in the path of the people of Hull coming to Jesus as Lord and saviour. There are roots in Hull's past that need to be brought to the cross and repented of; some of these were done to Hull, some are at least in part its own responsibility. By these processes and as we pray through this special year, we hope that the spirit, the "Angel of Hull", will be set free to fly, to be all that God intended it to be.'[9]

The second describes that 'On March 17 of this year (St Patrick's Day), a major reconciliation event was held at St Mary's Church, Whitby. At this event, two men (representing the ancient Celtic church and the later more dominant Roman church) asked for and received forgiveness for the divisions and hurts caused through the famous Synod of Whitby in 664 AD. From that date onwards, the church in Britain lost the rich, vibrant and aggressively missionary culture of the Celtic Christians to the more formalised and hierarchical Roman structure. The leaders of the three churches believe God has called them and their churches together to build on and "tap into" the breakthrough that took place that night.' [10]

Such beliefs are becoming increasingly pervasive. But is there sufficient biblical warrant for such views?

The Bible and Territorial Spirits

In a book entitled *Spiritual Warfare – What does the Bible really teach?*,[11] Dr Clinton Arnold reviewing the Biblical material repeatedly makes statements such as these:

'Turning to the Scriptures for insight about the so-called territorial spirits, we *will not find much, but* there are a few important passages that clearly affirm the reality of demonic spirits associated with territories.'[12]

'The New Testament gives us *little direct teaching* about

angelic patrons over cities, territories, regions or nations. Jesus says *nothing* about these higher-level spirits. Neither does the Book of Acts *contain explicit teaching* about them;'[13]

'Paul's references to the "principalities and powers" *says nothing* about regional or city spirits.'[14]

Then referring to Revelation 18:2: 'Fallen, Fallen is Babylon the Great! She has become a home for demons and a haunt for every evil spirit,' he writes. 'This passage *does not explicitly speak* of territorial spirits, but *could* include them. More important, Babylon is personified as a woman in Revelation 17 and is depicted as riding on a beast. This animal represents demonic power since it came up out of the Abyss (Rev. 17:8). The passage thus affirms and illustrates the close nexus between a city and a demonic power that influences the human rulers of the city.'[15] (italics mine)

What is Arnold's summary conclusion? 'The biblical and historical evidence supports the idea that there are territorial spirits. These are fallen angels that wield some kind of dominion over people groups, empires, countries or cities. They exercise their supernatural power not only to bring harm and misery but, most important, to keep people from coming to a knowledge of the one true God.' However, he is critical and cautious of some of the methods advocated by the SLSW approach: 'The evidence does not appear to suggest a strategy for dealing with territorial spirits similar to what some are proposing today.' [16]

Here we have an example of a scholar who wants to have his cake and eat it. It is openly admitted that the biblical data base for such beliefs is slender indeed and that no evidence exists at all which 'describes, or instructs us on how, or even whether, we are to engage these high-ranking territorial spirits'.[17] Yet, because of a prior commitment to the idea of territorial spirits, by a process of supposition, speculation and unwarranted extrapolation, an attempt is made to give credence to the notion.

There are primarily two biblical passages which form the basic point of reference for territorial spirit beliefs: Deuteronomy 32 and Daniel 10

In Deuteronomy 32:8 we read: 'When the Most High gave the nations their inheritance, when he divided all mankind, he set boundaries for the peoples according to the number of the *sons of Israel*.' It is generally agreed that the phrase 'sons of Israel' would be better rendered 'sons of God' as attested by the Septuagint and Qumran. This then carries the idea that as the imperial monarch rules his provinces through governors and satraps, so God governs nations through the members of his heavenly court (cf. Psalm 82.) However Israel is special in that God governs them directly: 'For the Lord's portion is his people, Jacob his allotted inheritance' (v.9). The question still remains whether some of these 'sons of God' are malevolent. Even if the answer is yes (and the 'judgement passages' of Psalm 82 seem to suggest this is so – vv. 1-2, 6-9), God remains sovereign over them, achieving his good and eternal purposes. This is particularly the theological emphasis of a book like Daniel.

In Daniel 10 we have more than an indication that behind the earthly struggle of God's people is an invisible 'heavenly one'. Thus an angel appears to Daniel and explains his delay: 'The prince of the Persian kingdom resisted me twenty-one days. Then Michael, one of the chief princes, came to help me, because I was detained there with the king of Persia' (Dan 10:13). Later Daniel is informed by the angel, 'Soon I will return to fight against the prince of Persia, and when I go, the prince of Greece will come.' Note how Michael is referred to as a 'prince', as are these other two entities. This would distinguish them from earthly kings and confirm the view that they were angelic beings. However, there are two important points to note.

Firstly, it would be a misnomer to speak of such beings as *'territorial* spirits', as if there is a specific link between angelic activity and a geographical entity. Such spirits are to be more associated with political and religious power and ideologies (here the political and religious cannot be separated). In 1 Corinthians 10:20 Paul tells us that when people worship idols (as did all these world powers), it is not idols that they worship but demons. Thus behind the national gods of Persia were supernatural and evil personalities, feeding and directing malice towards God's people. So, one is not denying demonic influence in the political/religious ideological spheres of life. But this is a long way from tying demons to specific areas. (One also wonders that if the territorial view is correct, then every time there is a boundary reorganisation or the break up of a country – like Yugoslavia – there is a political reshuffling of the demonic cabinet!)

Secondly, Daniel is not commanded or requested to offer prayers to 'bind' or 'oust' these 'princes'. And this is not surprising, given that one of the main theological motifs of the book is the sovereignty of God. Daniel simply gets on with the business of being a faithful witness in captivity and praying that God's purposes will be fulfilled. And where he does confess a nation's sin, as in chapter 9, it is not of the 'identificational repentance' variety as propounded by Dawson – Daniel prays on behalf of God's covenant people as a member of that covenant community. He does not 'repent' on behalf of, say, the Babylonian Empire. The equivalent today would be church leaders interceding for the church, confessing the sins of God's people and pleading for mercy and renewal. To quote Arnold: 'What the Book of Daniel does impress on our hearts and minds so clearly is the absolute sovereignty of God. He is in control of history. God knows and has predetermined the succession of empires. He is infinitely superior to the heavenly powers.'[18]

Even with these two 'proof texts' from Deuteronomy and Daniel no major theological doctrine or Christian practice is built on them in Scripture. Should we not follow the Bible's example in this regard?

Ephesians – a test case

It would not be unreasonable to suppose that if any credence at all is to be given to SLSW it would be found in Paul's letter to the Ephesians. The reason for this is that given the nature of idol worship in Ephesus itself, as we see from Acts 19 and the cult of Artemis, we would expect at least some indication of the sort of 'spiritual warfare' technique which is being advanced by the likes of Wagner. In fact we find no such thing. In his ministry in Acts, there is no evidence that Paul encouraged or engaged in prayers against territorial spirits. He simply preached the gospel and carried out apostolic ministry. Here is Arnold's comment (remembering he believes in territorial spirits): 'The silence of Scripture on the issue of strategy is quite evident. When we consider that the New Testament records the spread of the gospel into pagan lands where idols and occultism held sway, it is very surprising to find no mention of a strategy that stresses discerning, naming and praying down territorial spirits.'[19] And then, commenting specifically on the Ephesus mission, he writes: 'Neither is there any indication that Paul himself regarded "Artemis" as the high-ranking spirit over Ephesus and the west coast of Asia Minor, nor do we see Paul confronting or instructing his converts to engage the territorial spirit behind Artemis worship. What Luke stresses in his account of Paul's ministry in Ephesus is Paul's evangelistic teaching (in the synagogue and then in a lecture hall) and his deliverance work.'[20]

Not surprisingly, we find Paul's letter to the Ephesians to be of one piece with his ministry as recounted by Luke. There is no mention of praying down territorial spirits or mapping the spiritual territory. There was no need, for Paul teaches the supremacy and victory of Jesus over all authorities (visible and invisible) as won at the cross, the fruits of which are now being demonstrated to all and sundry in the arena of the church. Therefore, let us see what Ephesians actually teaches.

The location of the spiritual battle
The classic passage on 'spiritual warfare' which occurs in chapter 6 is the climax of all that has gone before and so must be understood within the context of the letter as a whole. In chapter 1 Paul has made it clear that Jesus Christ is the source of all spiritual blessings: we have redemption in him (v.7), we are God's possession, sealed by the Holy Spirit (v.13), having a power at work within us comparable to the power that raised Jesus from the dead (vv. 19-20). So who needs to tap into some other power by re-enacting and repenting for the collective sins of the past? Jesus is above every rule and dominion, i.e. he is Lord of all (v. 22). With what purpose in view? It is for the sake of his church, which is his body (v. 25). A key passage is 3:10: 'His intent was that now, through the church, the manifold wisdom of God should be made known

to the rulers and authorities in the heavenly realms.' Given that it is the church which is the manifestation of God's plan of redemption and the instrument through which he brings this plan about, it would follow that the main place where the devil will attack will be in the church itself. We might well expect the local church as the expression of the heavenly church to be the main spiritual battlefield. That is in fact what Paul teaches.

It is the power of the gospel message which has been made manifest in bringing into being a believing community. So in 2:1-3 it is men and women outside of Christ who are dead in trespasses and sins. In terms of their social and intellectual environment they follow the ways of the world's mind-set in opposition to God. There is also the effect of their natural fallen inclination, called the 'flesh', as well as the influence of a supernatural opponent, 'the prince of the power of the air.' Paul does not give priority of one over the other; all are involved in corrupting rebellious mankind.

The status and standing of Christians could not form a greater contrast. They are members of a supernatural community which God indwells by his Spirit (2:22). They are no longer slaves to evil forces, but 'through faith in Christ can approach God with freedom and confidence' (3: 12). As such they are 'to be strong in the Lord and his mighty power' (6: 10), all made available to us by Christ's victory on the cross, appropriated by simply believing the gospel message (2:8).

The nature of the battle
In 6:10 Paul writes: 'For our struggle is not against flesh and blood but against the rulers, against the authorities, against the powers of this dark world and against the spiritual forces of evil in the heavenly realms.' Demonic spirits certainly exist. But the term Paul uses to describe our contending with them is taken not from the military sphere, but the world of wrestling. He speaks of us 'struggling' – *pale* – a hand-to-hand struggle. How does this take place?

In 6:11 reference is made to the devils 'schemes', literally – 'stratagems'. What this involves is amplified in 4:14, where the same phrase occurs calling for Christians to grow in biblical knowledge so they might not be 'blown here and there by every wind of teaching and by the cunning and craftiness of men and their deceitful stratagems'. In other words, the devil will try and destabilise Christians and corrupt the church fellowship through false teaching (maybe through teaching which would have us looking for ways of countering Satan which are not legitimate because he does not operate in that way!).

The devil is also mentioned in 4:27: 'Do not give the devil a foothold.' How? The injunction comes in the middle of some practical teaching about the way Christians are to relate to the body of Christ – the church – because of their new life in Christ (vv. 25-32). More specifically it is through anger (v. 26) that such a foothold can be given to the devil. That is a foothold *within* the fellowship. What better way to bring into disrepute the church's claim that reconciliation and peace has been achieved through the cross (2:15-16) if there is bitter wrangling between believers! The spiritual battle is less glamorous, more personal and nearer to home than the SLSW programme would have us believe.

The means of conducting the spiritual battle

The call in 6:10 is to *collectively* put on the whole armour of God, an allusion to Isaiah 59:17. The trap Christians can fall into is to be mesmerised and led astray by the power of the metaphor Paul uses, thus providing more grist for the mill for the new spiritual warfare advocates. If, for one moment, we were to put to one side the components of the armour metaphor, what are we left with? It would be basic 'down to earth' Christian truths and practices which are far from romantic but far more demanding. Here they are:

Truth (v. 14). Holding on to right doctrine as well as speaking the truth and not lying to each other (4:25).

Evangelism – the gospel of peace (v. 15). That is how the church in Ephesus was established in the first place: 'And you also were included in Christ when you *heard the word of truth, the gospel of your salvation*' (1:13). No special prayer march or spiritual mapping here just arguing the gospel in the synagogue and lecture theatre for a period of two years. The result? People were converted. They repented of their magic arts – no extra special 'ministry' to deal with 'generational sin is recorded or required. The gospel is God's sufficient means of making us into God's workmanship (2:10). Certainly Paul prayed and asked for prayer. But not for spirits to be bound, but that he might be enabled to preach the gospel fearlessly (6:19).

Faith – that simple trust in God (v. 16). Trust is personally in God and not techniques, holding on to, and working out, the implications of our secure position in Christ which is our salvation (v. 17). We are put into a right relationship with God and accordingly are to live right lives before him (righteousness – v.14 – including our lives at home and at work, 5:22–6:9). How is that faith and knowledge fed? By the Scriptures, which is the Spirit's sword (v. 17).

Finally, there is *prayer* – which is integral to everything, praying *in* the Spirit *for* all the saints (v. 18). Not even a hint that we are to pray against territorial spirits.

The objective of the spiritual battle
The aim may seem so pedestrian. It is not to disarm principalities and powers; Christ has already done that (Col. 2:15). That is why he is seated above every rule and authority and why in principle Christians are seated with him and so are secure (Eph. 2:6). The objective is to 'stand'. Four times Paul speaks of this. By standing firm we testify to whatever principalities and powers there may be of Christ's victory on the cross. By standing and not being distracted into dubious 'ministries', we get on with evangelism and so see others drawn into his kingdom. By standing we engage in believing prayer, praying for the right things with correct understanding and so advance Christ's cause in the world.

Conclusion
One of the greatest successes of World War Two was Operation FORTITUDE. This was the invention on the part of the Allies of a fantasy invasion force directed at the Pas de Calais. Notionally under the larger than life General Patton, a fabricated '1 Army Group' was created in south -east England. Using a massive array

of dummy landing craft and a signals network, a phoney order -of-battle was established bigger than the actual 21 Army Group which landed in France. The deception was so effective that it kept many of Rommel's major Panzer divisions pinned down at Calais well after the D-day landings had taken place. Is there not a parallel to be drawn with what is happening in some church quarters today? As we have seen, no convincing Scriptural evidence exists for territorial spirits or the practices being advocated attendant upon such beliefs. What is being proposed by the proponents of SLSW is light years from the practice of the apostles. The result is that through a sad and bitter irony the devil is achieving his own *Operation Fortitude,* distracting Christians from the business they should be engaged in by getting them to focus their attention on what is in effect a 'phantom menace'. Surely, it is now time to abandon wild speculative ideas with equally bizarre and strange practices and get back to the clear worldview of the Bible and the old Evangelical belief in the power of the gospel. If not the deception will continue, and one can only shudder to think of the consequences.

NOTES

1. C. Peter Wagner and F. Douglas Pennoyer (eds), *Wrestling with Dark Angels: Towards a Deeper Understanding of the Supernatural Forces in Spiritual Warfare*, Regal Books (1990).

2. C. Peter Wagner, *Confronting the Powers: How the New Testament Church Experienced the Power of Strategic-Level Spiritual Warfare,* Regal Books (1996), p.200.

3. George Otis Jr., 'An Overview of Spiritual Mapping' in *Breaking Strongholds in your City,* ed. C. Peter Wagner; Regal (1993).

4. John Dawson, *Taking Our Cities for God: How to Break Spiritual Strongholds*, Creation House (1989).

5. John Dawson, *Healing America's Wounds*, Regal (1994), p. 276.

6. Wagner, *Confronting the Powers,* pp. 249-62.

7. Wagner, *Confronting the Powers*, pp. 158-59.

8. In C. Peter Wagner, *Warfare Prayer: How to Seek God's Power and Protection in the Battle to Build His Kingdom*, Regal (1992).

9. *Hull a City of Hope,* produced by 'The Angel Group' (1999).

10. 'The Good News', July, 1999.

11. Clinton Arnold, *Spiritual Warfare, What Does the Bible Really Teach?*, Marshalls (1999).

12. Arnold, p. 170.

13. Arnold, p. 177.

14. Arnold, p. 178.

15. Arnold, pp. 178-79.

16. Arnold, p. 181.

17. Arnold, p. 183.

18. Arnold, p. 176.

19. Arnold, pp. 183-4.

20. Arnold, p. 191.

11

The Priority of Jesus:
A Look at the Place of Jesus' Teaching
and Example in Christian Ethics

Introduction

It is not unusual to come across the rule-of-thumb advice: 'Do what Jesus would have done,' being given to a Christian facing a particular moral problem. Initially at least, this might appear as 'wise counsel'; after all, what could be better than to appeal directly to the example of the Master himself? Indeed, it is the apostle Peter who urges Christians to follow in Christ's footsteps (1 Pet. 2:21), and this means working out the Christ-pattern in the rough and tumble of day-to-day existence. But for all its immediate attractions, not least that of simplicity (and it is important that we do not complicate matters unnecessarily), such a recommendation requires more of the Christian than might appear at first sight.

Without wishing to deny the charismatic experience of direct guidance by the Holy Spirit on matters of morality (which even John Wimber admitted can sometimes be due more to indigestion than the Third Person of the Trinity!)[1] there is a tendency to respond to such advice simply by allowing the imagination to sketch rather hazy and romantic pictures of Jesus moving about in the situation within which we find ourselves, and almost magically handling the problem in question.[2] But as Os Guiness points out in another context,[3] which Jesus are we thinking of? Our picture of Jesus might be as far removed from the portrait of Christ in the Bible as was the 'Gentleman Jesus' of the Victorian drawing room. After all, we are well aware that both 'Jesus the pacifist' and 'Jesus the revolutionary' have their advocates. If all were to be left at the level of sanctified imagination, then the charge that where you get ten Christians together you will find eleven different opinions might not be wide of the mark.

In point of fact, far from short-circuiting ethical thinking, trying to discern 'what Jesus would have done' requires a good deal of careful application. It involves cultivating a familiarity with the sort of things Jesus said and did during his earthly ministry – the principles he enunciated, the way he responded to moral matters, the pattern of behaviour he established, and so on – all this providing some of the raw material out of which guiding principles might be forged. Even so, this is only the beginning, for there is one major fact which has to be faced, the glaringly self-evident one that there is an historical and cultural distance between the world of Jesus and our world today. Although this point may be deemed as 'self-evident', it is one which can surprisingly be passed over with remarkable ease in Christian ethical thinking. Jesus did pronounce on matters which *prima facie* have no direct relevance for us today (e.g. paying the temple tax, Matt. 17:24f.; walking the extra mile, Matt. 5:41f.). What is more, we have to face ethical dilemmas which the teaching of Jesus could not directly address because they arise out of recent technological developments (e.g. *in vitro* fertilisation, genetic engineering, nuclear warfare). Without lapsing into the irresolvable cultural relativism of the sort in which Nineham finds himself,[4] such factors should put us on our guard against assuming that with the teachings and example of Jesus we can, with the odd adjustment made for minor cultural differences, make a point-for-point direct transfer to our present situation without engaging in some of the rigorous hermeneutical groundwork of the sort suggested by Marshall.[5]

There are two important questions raised by the type of considerations outlined above which form the primary focus of this study: (1) To what extent is moral authority to be attached to the actions and teachings of Jesus for our guidance today? and (2) how are those actions and teachings to be appropriated in the service of ethics? In short, how are we to conceive of the priority of Jesus in Christian ethics? In an attempt to move towards answering these questions, five interrelated areas of thought will be explored:

1. The basic features of Christian ethics. This will provide the wider perspective against which the teachings and actions of Jesus can properly be considered, while at the same time not losing sight of the fact that the words and deeds of Jesus are themselves constitutive of that perspective.

2. The nature of Christ's ethical teaching and how it contrasts with legalism.

3. Christ as exemplar. What this means and an assessment of the peculiar epistemological problems it raises.

4. The extent of the moral obligation attached to the teachings of Jesus. This will be specifically linked to a moral decision-making process.

5. The relation between 'Creation ethics' and 'Kingdom ethics'.

Although in this study a wide range of discursive material will be considered, the main objective is a practical one, namely to determine how we might more effectively understand, and get to grips with, ethical problems in the light of Jesus' teaching and pattern of life, and so take up the call of the one who said, 'Come, follow me'.

Features of Christian ethics

Creational

It is proposed that the starting point for Christian ethics is God and his will for creation, and in this sense one may refer to Christian ethics as 'creational' in design and foundation, with their focus upon the moral ordering of the world, which in turn is related to the character of God and the nature of man. Such 'creation ethics' need to be distinguished from what is often referred to as 'natural law', the difference lying in the epistemology of the two approaches.[6] Natural law, which plays an important role in Catholic moral theology,[7] has a prestigious history with a lineage extending back through Thomas Aquinas to Aristotle. It takes as its basic premise the belief that God has so shaped human nature that it is only by leading a moral life that this nature can achieve satisfactory realisation. Following on from this, natural law theory claims that it is possible to read off from these 'givens' of human nature the sort of moral imperatives God may have set and which are necessary to follow if one is to move towards real human fulfilment.

Without denying natural law's fundamental premise, one is forced to question the extent of its usefulness and the validity of its epistemology. In the first place it falls foul of what G.E. Moore called the 'naturalistic fallacy'. This makes two complementary points. The first is that such a position assumes that it is possible to derive what man 'ought' to do from what man 'is'. But as David Hume aptly demonstrated, this simply cannot be done without having already built into the situation moral assumptions from the start. Thus what 'ought' to be done is brought to a factual situation (what 'is') and is not deduced from it. The second point involves taking the step of defining 'good' in terms other than of itself, e.g. 'the pursuit of happiness' or 'the realisation of man's God-given potential'. But as Moore went on to show,[8] while what is 'good' may *also* be something else (happiness, fulfilment, etc.), it cannot be defined by that something else, i.e. placed within the *same* category of meaning (such that good *means* happiness). The fallacy is revealed by a simple test. If it is being claimed that one should follow a particular course of action because, say, it 'maximises human happiness', one can ask, 'Why?' What reasons can be given to convince me that I should do this? Although a variety of subsidiary reasons may be adduced to support the original contention, such as that 'social stability will be secured', eventually an appeal will be made to the belief that we should do it because it is 'good'. If by this the person is maintaining that good *means* the particular goal envisaged, then it is reduced to the level of trivial tautology. For example, if good means human happiness, on purely linguistic grounds this amounts to saying no more than that human happiness is human happiness. But if not, then it has to be conceded that what is 'good' is irreducibly something other than 'human happiness', although related to it, having its own moral category of meaning.

In the second place, even if one were to grant that a phenomenal approach to morality, rather than a largely philosophical one, could be harnessed in the service of natural law,[9] establishing that moral experience is universal (man *does* have a moral sense) and that there is a certain amount of agreement between different cultures over what actions are right and which qualities are good, giving moral content to form,[10] one is still left with what are at best broad generalisations as well as a fair degree of cultural diversity; and one is forced to ask with Paul Ramsey,[11] what is particularly *Christian* about the results?

The alternative approach being advocated here begins with God and his revelation, together with a consideration of moral experience (itself validated by Scripture, the *locus classicus* being Romans 2:14-16), and then moves towards moral imperatives which are grounded in and proceed from the Divine Creator. This is not to suggest that ethics cannot in the first instance exist independently of theology: quite clearly they can and do for many people,[12] but rather that Christian theism provides ethics with a 'metaphysical home' and substantial coherence when related conceptually to other elements within the Christian framework.[13]

However, it could be objected at this point that by opting for an ethic which is creational, established by special revelation, one has left unresolved a dilemma classically formulated in Plato's *Euthyphro,* viz: 'Does God will a thing because it is good, or is a thing good because God wills it to be so?' To opt for the former would mean surrendering the 'Godness of God', for it would be to admit another principle outside of God to which he must conform ('Goodness'). But to go for the second horn of the dilemma would mean that in principle 'right' and 'wrong' are merely products of arbitrary will. David Brown argues that it is by adopting a naturalist position, rooted in natural law theory, that a resolution of this problem is possible.[14] He maintains that God, by ordaining man's natural capacities in such a way that only by leading a moral life can they be fulfilled, has made it possible to ascertain what is right or wrong without direct reference to his will, and so they cannot be considered arbitrary. On the other hand, there is an ultimate connection with God's will in a way which is not arbitrary, because human nature and morality are linked to God's loving concern for man. But it is difficult to see how this solves the problem. What it does is to push it further back, for one can ask whether God willed the fulfilment of human nature and ordered it in such a way because it is good, or whether it is good because he willed it? The dilemma remains but in a different form. A much more satisfactory answer has been proposed independently by White[15] and Ward,[16] who in different ways postulate that what is good (Ward's 'realm of values') is *also* what God wills and what God wills is also good, the two ultimately residing in the being of God as two aspects of the same reality. Thus, far from creation ethics being arbitrary, they are consistent with the loving purposes of God and the nature of man as he intended.

Taking the link between a moral universe and the Moral Creator a stage further, one can suggest that God is *the Good,* not in some abstract Platonic sense, but as the personal, revealing God who is the ground of all goodness (cf. Mark 10: 18f.). Consequently what are perceived as moral imperatives, instances of goodness in obligatory form, are different aspects of this one unitary reality - the Good. It follows that those attitudes and modes of behaviour which are considered 'virtuous' amount to the correct and appropriate responses of man not only to the way things really are, but also to the God in whom the perceived values of goodness and rightness reside and find complete resolution.

Covenantal

Central to both the Old Testament's and the New Testament's understanding of the relation between God and his people is the concept of 'covenant'. Some, like Karl Barth, would go further in claiming that covenant is central to the understanding of the *whole* of God's dealing with creation, in that 'Covenant is the internal basis of creation and Creation is the external basis of covenant'. In establishing his covenant God does so in an act of gracious freedom as classically formulated in Deuteronomy 7:7-8: 'It was not because you were more in number than any other people that the LORD set his love upon you... it is because the LORD loves you.' Running throughout his covenant *(berit)* with his people, and establishing it, is the gracious love of Yahweh *(hesed)*. Although God's covenant in promissory form is to be found in his dealings with Abraham (Gen. 15:18) and David (2 Sam. 23:5), it is particularly in the book of Deuteronomy that the concept takes on a role of tremendous theological significance,[17] encompassing in both form and content the mutual *obligation* of those involved. The actual stipulations of the covenant which were binding upon Israel are set out in the form of a written 'law' *(torah)* (see Deut. 4:44). In fact so close was the connection in the minds of the people between law and covenant, that to obey the law was to obey the covenant (cf. Jer. 11:1ff). What is more, the implications of such a relationship established by covenant were to penetrate every area of life, as is evidenced by the Holiness Code of Leviticus 19 – any sacred/secular division with which we are only too familiar was ruled out on the basis of the *berit* (something of which the prophets had to continually remind the people, cf. Isa. 1:10-26).

It was with the Deuteronomic covenant in mind that Jeremiah, in the midst of national apostasy and defeat, made the innovatory declaration that a new covenant would be made, with the law written upon the people's hearts (31:31ff.), a promise also taken up by Ezekiel (36:26). However, it was in the person and work of Christ that this promise was to become a reality, establishing a *kaine diatheke* (Luke 22:20), a new *kind* of covenant of the type envisaged at a distance by Jeremiah. To those under the freedom of the 'law of Christ' comes the obligation to fulfil it in neighbourly concern (Gal. 6:2) and to exhibit a life characteristic of the people of God called to be holy (1 Pet. 2:9ff.). To modify Barth's phrase it becomes clear that covenant is the internal basis for Christian ethics (its motivating principle and frame of reference), and ethics is the external manifestation of, and response to, God's covenant.

Objectivity

Another important claim of Christian ethics is that morality is objective, not only insofar as there is a phenomenon called moral experience, but that matters of right and wrong have an existence and meaning independent of our evaluation of them. This is indicated by the fact that such matters are the subject of discussion with reasons being given for why we think a particular action to be right or wrong, something we don't do when things are solely a matter of subjective preference (e.g. taste). This is what Baelz calls the 'logical impartiality of ethics'.[18] All of this accords with what has gone before – that goodness and rightness are expressions of the nature and character of God, distinct from the created order and yet manifest in and through it.

Teleological

By using the term teleological it is being claimed that Christian ethics are primarily purposive, ordered towards a goal. What is good for man *is* related to the type of creature he is and the purpose for which he was made, and it is here that the premise of natural law finds its place, not as a means of determining moral imperatives without reference to God, but as an indication that true fulfilment lies outside of man in relation to God. The naturalist approach of Brown is in grave error of giving the impression that the final end of man is to be found within man (the fulfilment of his nature by living the moral life), thus opening the door for a new form of Pelagianism. Rather, the final end of man, as witnessed to by moral experience and special revelation, is that it is something which is over and above him, which makes its claim upon him, and this is God himself, the 'summum bonum'. Ward puts it well: 'For theism, God is the purpose and inner nature of all being; he is the ontological base of reality; and to respond to him is to respond to being's real nature.[19]

It is this goal and the eternal context in which it is framed that determines much of the content, rationale and direction of Christian ethics, and which marks it out from many other ethical frameworks. This should put the Christian on his guard against making superficial comparisons with other ethical beliefs and cause him to delve a little deeper into what is being proposed. For example, the utilitarian principle of 'the greatest good of the greatest number' might at first sight seem attractive and compatible with Christian ethics, but the Christian would want to ask: (a) How is the 'greatest good' to be understood? (b) How does it relate to the goal of developing man's relationship with God? and (c) What difference in perception is made when the claim is placed within an eternal context?[20] What is more, the view that the primary end of the moral life is not to be found solely within the nature of man *qua* man, but in responding appropriately to the Creator (which itself is part of being true to our nature), means that however much in practice theology is separated from ethics (and vice versa!), it is a division which is not warranted by the biblical witness and which, if pursued, will always result in an inadequate ethic, one which leaves a major part of reality out of its reckoning (in fact the *grounds* for reality – God).

Attitudinal

The final mark of Christian ethics is that they are attitudinal, having a concern for character and attitudes and not simply with the observance of external moral rules, which can become ends in themselves (cf. Matt. 23:23). Christian ethics go deeper than this in that they are to do with man's response to God and his attitude toward his fellow men and creation. The upshot of this is that Christian ethics are more 'open-ended' than legalism or casuistry, going beyond fixed points (cf. Matt. 5:21-22*)*.

The above is not meant to be an exhaustive or even a comprehensive list of the components of Christian ethics, but an indication of those features which are central to its composition and which form a backdrop against which the teachings and example of Jesus can be properly viewed and understood and against which a moral decision-making process can be developed.

Jesus and ethics – the teaching

In turning to Jesus' ethical teaching three preliminary points need to be made. The first is that Jesus' view of ethics is firmly rooted in the Old Testament. The disparity between Jesus' ethical teaching and that enshrined in the 'law and the prophets' is, as we shall see, more apparent than real. Indeed, for Jesus the whole of the law was summed up *in nuce* in the dual requirement of loving God and loving one's neighbour (Matt. 22:37-39), which itself comes from the torah (Deut. 6:5; Lev. 19:18). This is also a clear indication of the theocentricity of Jesus' ethics and eschatology.[21]

This is particularly related to the central message of Jesus' proclamation concerning the kingdom of God. In the person and work of Christ this reign had begun and carried with it its own ethical demands (Luke 3:10ff.). Yet although the kingdom had been inaugurated by Christ, its consummation lies at some point in the future, the nature of which should have a determining effect upon the way the members of the kingdom act in the 'mid-time' (Matt. 6:19; 25:31ff.). Far from Jesus presenting an 'interim ethic' as suggested by Schweitzer,[22] it is an authentic and lasting ethic appropriate to the reality and demands of the kingdom.

Finally, arising out of the last point, the ethics of Jesus is an ethic of the Spirit.[23] Although it is mainly in the epistles of Paul that the work of the Holy Spirit and Christian behaviour are firmly linked, there is a drawing together of the two in the gospels, albeit in an indirect manner. Luke especially relates the Spirit, kingdom and prayer to decisive moments in the ministry of Jesus.[24] In this connection it is interesting to note that the parable of the Good Samaritan (Luke 10:25-37) is placed between the story of the sending of the seventy to announce the coming of the kingdom, in which Jesus rejoices 'in the Spirit', and Jesus' teaching on prayer and the need to ask for the gift of the Holy Spirit. However, it is in the Gospel of John that the centrality of the Spirit in the Christian life is stressed. He is the one who will enable Christ's followers to bear fruit and so glorify him (John 14–16).

Central to any understanding of Jesus' attitude towards ethics is a group of sayings that are to be found in Matthew 5:17-18, although originally they may have been independent of each other.[25] First of all there is the statement: 'Think not that I have come to abolish the law and the prophets; I have not come to abolish but to fulfil.' This is then followed by another statement reaffirming the abiding significance of the law: 'For truly I say to you, till heaven and earth pass away, not an iota, not a dot will pass from the law until all is accomplished.'

It should be pointed out that the texts do not say anything about the law *per se*. A distinction is not made between ceremonial, moral or civil law, as some Christians do today; rather, Jesus is concerned with the law in its entirety. Clearly the key to the interpretation of these verses is to be found in the meanings of the verbs 'abolish' and 'fulfil'.

In saying that he came not to abolish the law *(katalusai* = 'nullify' – doubly stressed in verse 17), it could appear that Jesus is enjoining continual adherence to the law. However, Jesus goes on to say positively that he has come to 'fulfil' the law (*plerosai*), and this verb suggests more than simple adherence. It is something which has to be understood from the standpoint of the whole of Jesus' ministry, and the thought is not so much that Jesus came to keep the law right down to the last detail, but rather that he gives to the law and the prophets a deeper and richer understanding, expressing their inner intention and purpose; thus they are 'fulfilled completely'. R. J. Banks summarises the relation between Jesus and the law as follows: 'It therefore becomes apparent that it is not so much *Jesus'* stance towards the law that Matthew is concerned to depict: it is how the *Law* stands with

> regard to him, as the one who brings it to fulfilment and to whom all attention must now be directed.... The true solution lay in understanding "fulfilment" in terms of an affirmation of the whole law, yet only through its transformation into the teaching of Christ was there something new and unique in comparison.'[26]

Perhaps one should further add that it was also by the law's realisation in the life of Christ that something new and unique occurred.

Such an understanding would go a long way towards explaining Matthew's concern for 'righteousness', with the noun *dikaiosune* occurring some five times in the Sermon on the Mount. In the Old Testament the primary meaning of 'righteousness' *(tsedeq)* is that which meets with approval in the heavenly court. The man who is declared 'righteous' is the one who is pronounced as standing in a right relationship to God. As Steve Motyer has shown,[27] this is intrinsically bound up with God's salvific purposes in that he is concerned with establishing righteousness (doing and seen to be doing what is right) by acting on behalf of the outcast and the needy. It is in Christ that this is decisively achieved, the one in whom the will of God is realised, the covenant completely kept and through whom salvation has been wrought. The ethical implications for Christ's followers then become clear: they too are to seek God's kingdom and his righteousness – his rule and saving action – and are to reflect the same character of righteousness in their lives. It is by acting on behalf of those who cannot help themselves that they are to exceed the 'righteousness of the Scribes and Pharisees' (cf. Matt. 5:20; 25:31). Thus, far from the law and the prophets being dissolved by Christ, they are in fact completed and transcended by him. What is more, their inner intention, which is the outworking of God's saving rule, is in turn to be recapitulated by members of the kingdom both individually and corporately.

One implication of such an interpretation is that for the Christian, Old Testament ethics cannot be viewed in isolation from Christ who is their full expression and exposition. Love is the fulfilling of the law (Rom. 13:8), and in a deep sense Christ's love did just that (thus he is the 'end of the law', Rom. 10:4). But what we see completed by him and in him is to be reworked in the lives of his followers. Although from the standpoint of Old Testament exegesis one can consider the ethical precepts without reference to Christ, from the standpoint of trying to determine their application for the Christian such findings need to be 'filled out' by placing them in the light of Christ's teaching and example.

A second implication of this position is that as law and grace become integrated under the over-arching concept of 'righteousness' fulfilled in Christ, Christian ethics proceed from the starting point of forgiveness and acceptance. This in fact is a pattern already established in the Old Testament but which is often missed because of the Reformed preconception of law being prior to grace. It was after the event of the Exodus, itself an act of grace, that the law was given. Indeed one may see the giving of the law as an expression of grace, a means of drawing the covenant relationship into a state of maturity. Paul also works to the same pattern, the ethical exhortations following developed doctrine of the saving acts of God (cf. Gal. 5). Theologically this is in effect to reverse Matthew's ordering of the Sermon on the Mount, placing the demand of 5:48 first, 'Be perfect', and the resolution of 5:17ff., 'I came to fulfil', last.

We now turn to the way Jesus handled the so-called 'traditions of the elders'. Scholars have differed in their views as to whether the Sermon on the Mount was intended by Jesus or Matthew as in any sense a new law. It is certainly not a law-code of the sort found in the Old Testament, e.g. in the Book of the Covenant (Ex. 20:21-21:23). John Robinson describes much of this material as 'shocking injunctions',[28] designed to jolt a person out of moral complacency, enabling them to 'see' things in a new way and so respond in a manner which is appropriate to the coming of the kingdom of God. Dodd[29] prefers to speak of them as 'parables of the moral life', disclosing to a person the sort of things which might be required of anyone who is a member of the kingdom. Both these descriptions have their validity, but one should be wary of reducing the moral force of Jesus' sayings by over-generalisation. What we see are a number of 'rules' quoted by Jesus, some of which are to be found in the Old Testament, others being the 'traditions' of the elders, all of which have been treated in a legalistic and casuistic manner (e.g. Matt. 5:21-48). On each issue – swearing, adultery, divorce, etc. – Jesus goes back to some underlying principle of truth which is concretely expressed as an imperative. Far from weakening the requirements of the law, Jesus' treatment gives them greater force and a wider field of application, going well beyond the restraints of legalism. According to Dick France, the effect is 'to make a far more searching ethical demand. In all of this, there is a sovereign freedom in Jesus' willingness to penetrate to the true will of God which lies behind the law's regulations.'[30]

It is this internalisation of the law which underscores the point made earlier that ethics also embrace attitudes (Matt. 5:2 ff.). Of course this is not to imply that 'thought' and 'deed' are to be given equal moral weighting, so that 'one might as well be hung for a sheep as a goat'. It does mean that when speaking of moral action, one must give the concept of 'action' a much wider interpretation than the mere physical act and its consequences. In considering the moral value of a particular action three constituent elements should be evaluated: intentions, consequences and event.

To take *intentions* first. As far as one is able, one should try and assess whether they are good rather than selfish. The problem of course is that there is usually a mixture of motives, desires and intentions; some are good, others less so. Invariably our 'wants' also contaminate to some degree our understanding of what is right, creating a distorted 'moral vision'. However, there are instances where a sharp dichotomy does exist between what we want (e.g. to preserve our life) and what we should do (rescue the drowning man). One of the errors of situationism as advocated by Joseph Fletcher[31] is that too much weight is given to intentions, such that if a person is convinced that his intentions are right, the act becomes morally acceptable. But this is too individualistic, and while psychologically securing a person from blame, does not ensure that an action is morally right. This is why intentions need to be taken together with the other two components of moral action as well as the moral imperatives which stand over and above the situation.

While situationism gives a prominent place to intentions, it is utilitarianism which gives pride of place to *consequences*. But this too proves to be an inadequate criterion for determining the 'rightness' of a course of action. To say that one should take the course which promotes 'the greatest happiness for the greatest number' begs the question of what constitutes 'happiness'. This is far too general a concept to be of any use. What is more, it requires that the moral agent should be in a position to determine what consequences his action will bring. But this again is asking too much, for we are all painfully aware of the many unwanted effects that our 'well-intentioned' actions have thrown up in the past. Finally, this position fails to take into account the complex relationship between events and consequences. To speak of an action as 'a means to an end' is in itself an abstraction, for that 'means' is an 'end' of an earlier 'means'. The web of cause and effect is far more mysterious than this position allows for. However, possible consequences do have to be taken into account as we wrestle with the options open to us in a moral situation, and the Christian will also be humbled by the fact that consequences of eternal significance have to be placed in the balance.[32]

In addition to intentions and consequences, *the act itself* will need to be taken into the reckoning. It is questionable whether one can legitimately speak of 'an act-in-itself', as if the act could be divorced from its wider context of intentions and consequences. However, one may make a working distinction (rather than a formal one) between an 'event' – which is neutral in description, and an 'action' – which is related to intentions and consequences. Such a distinction might enable one to discern more effectively the moral relevance of a factor which can easily be overlooked while solely operating with the notion of 'moral action'. For example, on the basis of intention and consequence a case could be made for sex outside of marriage (intention = I wish to share my love with my partner; consequence = no unwanted pregnancy due to contraception and we are happy). But if after considering the sex act as 'event' it is concluded that this in itself is expressive of promise and commitment, then this brings into question the morality of the situation, for what is being expressed by intercourse is denied by the overall situation, including the intentions of those involved. (A similar exposure of the disparity between actions, intentions and consequences is to be found in Jesus' treatment of the tradition about 'Corban' in Mark 7:5-13.)

As we have seen, Jesus' approach to ethics is far more 'open-ended' than legalism. It is also deeper in that it takes into account motives and intentions, and wider in that a decisive eschatological perspective is envisaged. As we shall see later, it is this 'dynamic' interaction between principles, intentions, actions and consequences which form the heart of Christian moral decision-making.

Jesus and ethics – the example

In speaking of Jesus as 'God incarnate' (and thus the 'Good' incarnate), one is making a double point. The first is that it is *God* who does that which man cannot do and refuses to do, namely the fulfilling of the law and the perfect expression of the moral life. The second is that it is God as *man* in whom these things happen, thus what man *ought* to be actually *is* in Christ. As W. F. Lofthouse put it, 'If we could tolerate the paradox, we might say that he was man because he was what no man had ever been before... Christ did not become what men were; he became what they were meant to be.'[33] Therefore, not only would the Christian wish to point to the teaching of Jesus to illuminate morality, but also to his acts as providing a model or paradigm for true moral behaviour. This is particularly important if one is to make use of the vast wealth of ethical material in the gospels which goes beyond specific moral teaching. This is especially true in a gospel such as John where, as John Robinson notes,[34] very little moral teaching is given didactically, but a considerable amount is conveyed through action. Indeed this is the Johannine emphasis upon living as Jesus lived and not merely as he taught (John 13:34; 1 John 2:6; 3:16). For John, Jesus is the exemplar *par excellence*.

The concept of Jesus as moral paradigm also gathers up much of what was said earlier about the fulfilment of 'righteousness'. As it is in Jesus that God's righteousness is shown, especially in the cross where God declares himself both just (*dikaion*) and the justifier (*dikaiounta*) of him who has faith (Rom. 3:26), we are given tremendous insight into what true righteousness means in action. This is well summarised by Motyer: 'The basis of the whole life of the people of God is his righteousness – his outreaching, saving mercy which rescues creation for himself. This righteousness has now been supremely expressed in Christ. But as men are grasped by it, "justified" and made acceptable to God, so they are stamped with the image of the righteous Saviour, and summoned to live in imitation of him as his people.'[35]

Without doubt, as Luther stressed, it is possible to hold to a slavish literalism of the notion of 'imitation of Christ' so as to turn it into a new form of legalism, and yet one should beware of so overreacting to this danger that one robs it of any ethical content. It is an idea which is firmly embedded in the New Testament, with its roots grounded in the Old with Israel's call by God to be 'holy for I am holy' (Lev. 11:44; 19:2; 20:26). Within the context of the master/slave relationship Peter writes: 'Christ also suffered for you, leaving you an example [*hupogrammon* – to 'trace' or 'copy'], that you should follow in his steps' (1 Pet. 2:21). Here it is the cross which provides the primary reference point at which the imitation is to be followed (cf. Eph. 5:21ff.). The same focus is to be found elsewhere. On the question of humility, it is the divine condescension which is appealed to (Phil. 2:5ff.), as it is in the case of charitable giving (2 Cor. 8:9). Certainly for Paul it was the realisation that God had done something of such magnitude for the Christian in the life, death and resurrection of Jesus that provided the nerve cord for Christian morality – cf. Galatians 2:20ff.: 'I have been crucified with Christ... it is no longer I that live but Christ.... I live by faith in the Son of God who loved me and gave himself for me.' In addition there is room for growth and development of the moral life, hence the call to 'put on the mind of Christ' and to 'bear fruit' (Gal. 5:22).

Rather than a detailed example to follow, Christ's life, and the culmination of that life in his sacrificial death, provides a pattern to be copied. But it is at this point that a particular epistemological problem is raised which can be formulated as follows: 'To recognise a person as a good example to follow presupposes that one already has a set of moral criteria by which to judge the example, therefore one may ask what, if anything, does the example add to our understanding of morality? Is it not superfluous?' It was Kant who put the problem in its starkest form: 'Even the Holy One of the Gospels must first be compared with our ideal of moral perfection before we can recognise him as such' (Grundlegung). However, the fallacy of this objection has been clearly set forth by Basil Mitchell.[36]

While agreeing that it is true that in order to recognise someone as a good example to follow we must have some notion of what 'goodness' is, Mitchell maintains that it does not follow that we should be able to describe in detail beforehand the actual features of a good example. He illustrates this point from the game of rugby. If a person recognises Fred Smith to be a good rugby player, and thus a good example to imitate, then he must have some idea of the game of rugby, the basic rules, the sort of moves involved, and so on. But this does not mean that the observer would be able to describe beforehand the moves Fred Smith was going to make. The rugby enthusiast has, as it were, a 'form' in his mind of the game 'rugby', and seeing Fred Smith in action gives new 'content' to that form. The same can be said when it comes to recognising a moral example. Man having a moral sense, as well as having specific moral content, can have that enriched as he looks to Christ, perceiving that here we do have an example to emulate. As Mitchell himself puts it: 'It does not, fortunately, take a saint to recognise a saint, a genius to recognise a genius, a master of a trade to recognise a master, a phronimos (wise man) to recognise a phronimos.'[37]

Jesus and ethics – relevance and application

It transpires from the discussion so far that, within the context of Christian ethics, it is Christ who is the focus of morality, the synthesis of the 'ought' and 'is'. As with any moral fact (and the Christian would wish to add that here is *the* moral fact incarnate) there is the necessity of obligation. Certainly a distinction has to be made between someone recognising something as a moral fact, which carries with it the notion of obligation, i.e. x is good therefore I ought to do x; and discussing whether something is a moral fact, in which case no decision has been made. Of course there is also the possibility that someone may recognise a moral fact and yet choose to ignore or reject it. This equally applies to Christ as ethical teacher and exemplar as to any principle or rule. Even so, if Jesus is the archetypal moral man, the Ideal, and is recognised as such, then this carries with it a sense of obligation that we too ought to imitate this pattern which, in turn, has to be translated into our own situation. But the question arises as to how this translation is to take place and to what extent the teachings and example of Jesus are binding.

So far it has been claimed that Jesus is the personification of the Good, the Universal which has been revealed in a specific historical-cultural situation. The fact that Jesus' teaching was clothed in the language of his day, and that his lifestyle and mode of behaviour were appropriate to his contemporary culture, means that a certain amount of relativity is introduced into Jesus' ethics. Indeed, this is a phenomenon which is inevitable with any use of language. The moment specific content is given to a principle it is also given a limited range of meaning relative to the culture and circumstances. Thus, 'Do not steal' will create a certain 'resonance' in the minds of the people who hear that injunction, conditioned by the sort of things which constitute 'stealing' in their particular culture. However, the specific principle enunciated is still an articulation of something which is universal; it does not undergo a thorough relativisation. This also applies to the idea of Jesus as 'example'. The pattern of humble service and sacrificial self-giving is expressed relative to Jesus' specific historical circumstances, the universal pattern being given concrete expression so that we can 'see' what this pattern involves, rather than allowing it to remain at the level of general abstraction. Having considered the historical acts and attitudes of Jesus as they are worked out in the first century context, we then have to translate them into our own. This means that there will be discontinuity, due to the loss of that which is culturally relative (e.g. feet washing), but also continuity in that beneath the specific expression there is a universal quality or 'core' which can be transferred and applied regardless of time and culture. Keith Ward gives an example of how such a translation of the 'imitation of Christ' might apply to a Christian who is a scientist. He writes: '... the man who feels that it is his vocation to pursue intellectual studies may allow the pursuit of truth to be the predominating value of his life; and in so doing he will not, of course, be "imitating Christ" in any direct sense, since Christ was not a scientist. But, at the same time, an acknowledgement of the Christian ideal of life will temper the scientist's attitude to his own vocation. It will prevent him from erecting an ideal of intellectual superiority, from despising the ignorant, and from supposing that the pursuit of truth is the only value which should be acknowledged by all men.'[38]

Allowing for both the universality of the life and sayings of Jesus for ethics and yet at the same time their relativity, what sort of process is involved in the moral decision-making which a Christian individual or community might engage in? What is offered below is one way of answering this question. In part it is descriptive in nature, formalising the sort of approaches Christians often adopt in reaching moral decisions, but it is also prescriptive in suggesting a particular approach which builds upon some of the considerations outlined above.

Taking the application of moral principles first. It is proposed that in considering a moral context, that is, either a particular moral problem to solve or a pattern of behaviour to follow, a dynamic interaction exists between the principles based upon Scripture and the overall situation. Thus one would need to take into account the various 'background factors' which make up the situation (e.g. what the needs are, the constraints of the situation, the ability of the moral agents, etc.) and in the light of these consider the relevant biblical principles. Identifying and interpreting the biblical principles is a supremely important task, since Scripture is the normative authority in Christian ethical decision-making. But attention should also be given to 'moral tradition', that is, other relevant ethical thinking which has been undertaken in the past. It is out of an interaction between these ethical resources and the actual situation, under the guidance of the Holy Spirit, that a moral decision is derived. This 'moral dialectic' can be summarised in diagrammatic form (see Figure 1 below).

Fig. 1

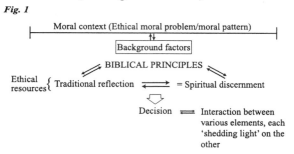

Many moral situations are complex, and the interactionist approach as outlined above allows for such complexity. It applies universal moral principles which are grounded in Scripture and elucidated by the same hermeneutical procedure adopted by Christ, viz. pinpointing the underlying truth and principle beneath a moral injunction or story and reapplying it to present circumstances. It also takes seriously the particularity of the actual situation, thus avoiding bland generalisations, yet it refuses to allow circumstances wholly to determine the principles employed (as with situationism) because of the belief in absolute values and a recognition of a wider, eternal context. There is also a place for traditional moral reflection, drawing upon the wisdom of those in the Body of Christ (past and present) whom God has gifted in ethical thinking. But also, it incorporates a strong charismatic element, realising that such a process is not a mere cerebral exercise, but an openness to the guiding hand of the Holy Spirit.

However, as it stands this process is incomplete, for a Christian would also want to appeal to the example of Christ himself. In coming to a decision about a particular moral situation, the Christian will not only take into account ethical principles but also patterns of behaviour, especially the pattern set forth by Christ. In other words, various 'paradigm acts' (lived-out examples) which related to a specific moral problem will also be incorporated into the moral decision-making process. For example, supposing that we are faced with a situation where we are being asked to give advice on whether a friend's unmarried daughter should have an abortion. This may be described as a 'neighbour situation' -there is a moral need arising in the life of a neighbour (in the broadest sense) and the immediate requirement is advice. Initially, the moral agent will have an immediate perception of the moral difficulty, considering the various 'background factors' which comprise the needy situation (e.g. the girl's age, the circumstances of the pregnancy, the attitudes of the girl and her parents, etc.), as well as having a primary moral response in being willing (hopefully) to listen and give appropriate advice, and having some ideas, however vague, on the issue in question. This primary stage can be represented as shown in Figure 2 (below).

Fig 2, Stage A

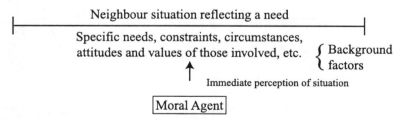

The one who has been sought for advice will then broaden and enrich his moral perception by drawing upon the ethical resources mentioned earlier. The biblical principles which will be determinative in our attitude will include the fifth commandment,

'You shall not kill', as endorsed by Jesus, and the whole biblical concern for the sanctity and quality of all human life. They will include also, and supremely, the importance of compassion, especially compassion for the weak and needy. It is at this point that the paradigm acts of Christ provide a focus for the moral agent in indicating what this compassion will involve. To be sure, the way Jesus approached needy situations will mean that two important qualities will be looked for. The first is that compassion be real, not sentimental, or a cover for some ulterior motive (e.g. seeking an abortion to get around the embarrassment of having to face one's friends with an unwanted pregnancy). It is clear that Jesus' compassion ran deep (cf. Mark 1:41) and was far from superficial; indeed, it was sacrificial. Furthermore, not only is this compassion to be real, it also has to be radical; not necessarily going for the 'easy option', which may not deal with the root of the predicament at all. Jesus had compassion for the rich young ruler, but its radical nature meant that it would not compromise with half-baked 'immediate' solutions (Mark 10: 17ff.). A further part of the process will be the evaluation of other people's thinking on the moral question in hand, this taking place within the wider context of the church as the Body of Christ, and under the prayerful guidance of the Holy Spirit (see Figure 3 below).

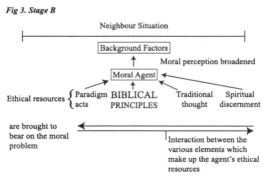

Fig 3. Stage B

Arising out of this moral dialectic, a decision is reached and informed advice may be given. However, it should be stressed that although the primary objective in the situation envisaged above was to give advice, clearly the moral process is much wider, calling upon the moral agent to realise in practice the second great commandment to 'love your neighbour as yourself.' This will mean extending a loving heart, and engaging in sacrificial empathy where required as well as offering wise words. Furthermore, the whole moral encounter should extend the moral repertoire of the agent and itself become a moral paradigm for future reference (see Figure 4 below).

Fig 4, Stage C: Action Taken (individual or corporate)

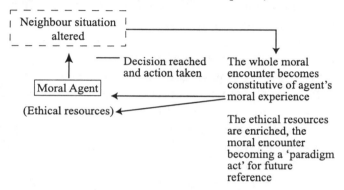

The extent to which the above model will be both acceptable and applicable will largely be determined by a person's stance viz-a-viz the Christian faith and biblical authority. If a person places himself firmly within the Christian fold, appeal to the Bible, tradition and the illumination of the Spirit will be both natural and acceptable. But what of the person who would place himself squarely outside Christianity? To what extent will the ethical teaching and example of Jesus be binding upon him?

Two preliminary points need to be made in this regard. The first is that the moral authority of Jesus is integrally related to his person – the 'What' is decisively linked to the 'Who'. That is, what Jesus says is both determined by who he is (the eternal Son of God) as well as being evidence of who he is. This is clearly brought out by Jesus' distinctive form of address, prefacing his words with 'amen', thus identifying God in advance with what he is about to say (Matt. 5:18, 26; 6:2; etc.). In addition to the fact that Jesus did not appeal to the 'traditions', this will account for the astonished reaction of the crowds as recorded in Matthew 7:28-29: 'When Jesus had finished saying these things, the crowds were amazed at his teaching, because he taught as one who had authority, and not as their teachers of the law.' But what is more, the authoritative pronouncements of Christ were of a piece with his actions. Not only did Jesus declare forgiveness of sins, he authenticated his words by healing (e.g. Mark 2:1-12), both word and deed thus being expressive of his being as unique bearer of the divine nature. The moral authority of Jesus is therefore both unique and supreme because it is not derived 'second-hand' but is proclaimed directly, stamped with the very authority of God.

The second point is that strictly speaking *Christian* ethics is for Christians, those who acknowledge the Lordship of Christ, who are members of the kingdom and who are empowered by the Spirit to bring about a substantial realisation of that kingdom in their lives. There is considerable weight behind the contention that the Sermon on the Mount is directed to those who are already, or potentially, followers of Christ (cf Matt. 5: l, 2 – it is the disciples who are addressed).

Even so, these two considerations do not carry the corollary that Jesus' teachings and life only have moral force for those allied to the cause of the kingdom. In both principle and practice this is clearly not the case. If, as has already been argued, morality is both objective and universal, part of the warp and woof of reality, then in principle it should be possible for such universals to be recognised, together with their binding nature, regardless of their source or the particular framework of beliefs held by the observer. This means that whether the source be Christ or Socrates, provided that it is to the true nature of moral reality they refer, acknowledgement should be possible by the person who in general does not subscribe either to the Christian faith or the philosophy of Socrates. To adapt Mitchell's example of the rugby player, it should be possible to recognise Fred Smith as a good rugby player even if one is not a supporter of his team or an active player oneself.

But not only is it possible in principle for those outside the Christian faith to recognise the validity of Jesus' ethical teaching, it is also the case in practice. It appears that Gandhi was able to accept much of Jesus' ethic, but not other elements of his teaching. One of the great dangers of nineteenth-century liberal theology was the reduction of theology to mere morality, with Christ being presented simply and solely as the Ideal Man pointing the way to the authentic moral life. This was a movement whose roots lay in Kant's contention that Jesus was the 'personified idea of the good principle'. However, given that Jesus is at the very least the focus of the Good (although much more than that), then it is eminently reasonable to expect that some perception of that 'Good' should occur on a universal scale. While it is true that one may wish to question the logical consistency (or lack of it) of those who would want to take on board the moral claims of Jesus while rejecting his religious claims, one is still left with the fact that those moral claims are recognised well beyond the bounds of the redeemed community; indeed such a recognition may be but the first step of a journey towards the full acceptance of the Lordship of Christ.[39]

Concluding remarks – creation ethics and kingdom ethics

At first sight, it might appear that a firm and irrevocable division has been made between creation ethics and kingdom ethics, but this is more apparent than real and dissolves under close analysis. We should be wary of stressing the discontinuity between creation and kingdom ethics at the expense of the continuity. The point of continuity is that God is the author, and relationships the subject, of both ethics as they are grounded in the loving grace (*hesed*) of God. The line of discontinuity is drawn around the fact that it is in Jesus Christ as representative Man that God's requirements of righteousness are met, a new covenant established, and relationships transformed by the eschatological Spirit which he dispenses. Indeed, it is Christ's redemptive work which provides the proper vantage point from which to view God's purposes in creation.

Even within the perspective of the Old Testament, any attempt to separate off creation ethics from the wider context of redemption is doomed to failure. As Von Rad has shown[40] not only are Israel's beliefs about creation inseparable from her beliefs about redemption, in many respects they are secondary. Therefore Chris Wright is quite correct in maintaining that: 'At every point this creation theology was linked to the fact that the Creator God was also their, Israel's, Redeemer God. This means that the "creation ordinances" can only be fully understood and appreciated when they are illumined by the light of Israel's redemptive faith and traditions, and not merely taken as "universal" and somewhat abstract propositions.'[41] If the word 'Christian' were to be substituted for the term 'Israel' in Wright's statement, then it would provide a succinct summary of what is being maintained here, namely that it is in the light of the New Testament, and especially of Christ's teaching and example, that Old Testament ethics can be appreciated and appropriated.

However, it is when a Christocentric approach is adopted, one which is in line with the New Testament's varied testimony that Christ is the integration point of all the works and purposes of God, that any hard-and-fast distinction between creation ethics and kingdom ethics has to give way to a more unified concept. We have already seen how Christ fulfils the inner intention of the law and the prophets; but it could equally be claimed that he also fulfils the inner purpose of creation as he brings about God's kingdom – viz. that the Creator and creature should live in harmony (the goal of covenant). For in Jesus, God's will is done, the kingdom has come and the Father's name is hallowed. But furthermore, what was achieved in the life, death and resurrection of this one Man, Jesus, will be universalised at the end of time, as the whole of creation becomes caught up in God's creative-redeeming action through this same person (cf Rom. 5:2 1ff.; 8:18ff.). Or to put it another way, in Jesus there is an actualisation of man's true potential as God intended (God's image); the ought becomes an historical reality. At the end of time the same image will be realised in other men, of whom Christ is the first fruits (1 Cor. 15:23). It is then that creation will be brought to true completion. The unity between creation and kingdom as found in Christ can be represented in Figure 5 (on following page).

This same emphasis upon the unitary activity of God uniting both the work and goal of creation and the kingdom is to be found in Barth.[42] He draws attention to what he sees as the *conditio sine qua non* of Christian ethics, the command and will of God, who in Jesus Christ is man's Creator, Reconciler and Redeemer. What

Fig. 5

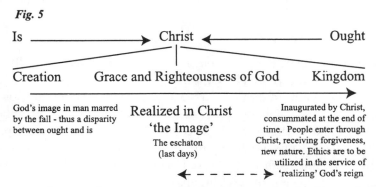

we perceive as three successive moments in God's activity (Creation, Reconciliation, Redemption, to use Barth's own terminology) are in reality one in the eternal movement of God (Creation – Reconciliation – Redemption). Thus from the overall standpoint of the God who 'sees the end from the beginning', any attempt to draw a division between creation/kingdom in absolute terms would be as erroneous as attempting to divide the Godhead.

The drawing together of creation and the kingdom to such a point that they more or less overlap is to be found in Colossians 1:15ff. In this great 'hymn' to the supremacy of Christ, Jesus is portrayed as the one by whom and for whom all things were created (v.15). This is paralleled by the fact that he is also the one in whom and by whom all things are reconciled, establishing God's rule (kingdom) throughout the created order (vv. 18-20). It follows that if the creation/ kingdom division is finally overcome in Christ, then so is the creation/kingdom ethics divide, with the latter being the transposition of the former. The Colossian hymn is shot through with praise to the Creator-Redeemer Christ, and it is as his pattern and teaching is worked out in the lives of his people, the members of his kingdom, that the same song will be heard - the song of the priority of Jesus.

NOTES

1. John Wimber, *Power Evangelism. Signs and Wonders Today*, Hodder and Stoughton (1985), p.70.

2. This is almost turning the Ignatius method of Bible study on its head. This method invites the reader to think himself into the biblical passage and so engage in an 'encounter' with Christ. To attempt to 'do what Christ would do' by the imagination is to try and envisage Christ stepping out of the text into our situation. In both cases hermeneutical controls are singularly absent.

3. Os Guiness, *Doubt Faith in Two Minds*, Lion (1976), p.91.

4. Cf D. E. Nineham, *New Testament Interpretation in an Historical Age*, Athlone Press (1976). For a critique of Nineham's views see Anthony Thiselton, *The Two Horizons*, Paternoster (1980, pp. 52-56.

5. I.H. Marshall, *Biblical Inspiration*, Hodder (1982), pp.99-113.

6. David Cook, in *The Moral Maze*, SPCK (1983), includes 'natural law' under the category of creation ethics, but he uses the term in a much broader sense, consonant with what is being suggested here, avoiding the excessive claims associated with strict natural law theory.

7. D. Brown, *Choices*, Blackwells (1983), pp.28-35.

8. G. E. Moore, *Principia Ethica*, Cambridge (1903), chapters ii, iii and iv.

9. Cf Greg Forster's *Cultural Patterns and Moral Laws*, Grove (1977).

10. Cf C. S. Lewis, *The Abolition of Man*, Fount, (1978), p.48.

11. Paul Ramsey, *Basic Christian Ethics.*

12. Some, like Don Cupitt, argue that ethics have to be autonomous and must be severed from religion for man 'come of age'; for a reply see Keith Ward, *Holding Fast to God*, SPCK (1982), pp. 50-62.

13. Cf V. White, *Honest to Goodness*, Grove (1981), and O.R. Barclay, 'The Nature of Christian Morality', in *Law, Morality and the Bible*, IVP (1978).

14. *Op. cit.*, pp.33-34.

15. *Op cit.*, pp.21-22.

16. Keith Ward, *Ethics and Christianity*, Allen and Unwin (1970), pp. 89ff.

17. R. E. Clements, *Old Testament Theology – A Fresh Approach*,

Marshalls (1978), p.96.

18. Baelz himself prefers to avoid the term 'objective' in relation to morals because of misunderstandings which could arise when placed in opposition to 'subjective', itself an emotive term. Hence his preference for the term 'logical impartiality' – *Ethics and Belief*, Sheldon Press (1977).

19. K. Ward, *The Divine Image*, SPCK (1976), p.41.

20. A point made forcefully and with his usual lucidity by C. S. Lewis in his essay 'Man or Rabbit', *God in the Dock*, Fount (1979), pp. 68-69), who in contrasting the beliefs of a materialist with those of a Christian shows how those differences will inevitably manifest themselves at the most practical levels of social policy.

21. Cf A. N. Wilder, *Eschatology and the Ethics of the Kingdom*, Harper Bros (1950).

22. A. Schweitzer, *The Mystery of the Kingdom*, Black, (1914).

23. Cf H. Thielicke, *Theological Ethics*, Fortress (1966), pp. 648-667.

24. An observation made by S. S. Smalley, 'Spirit, Kingdom and Prayer in Luke-Acts', *Novt* 15 (1973).

25. James Dunn, *Unity and Diversity in the New Testament*, SCM (1977), p.246.

26. R. J. Banks, Jesus and the Law in the Synoptic Tradition, *SNTS* Monograph 28, CUP (1975), pp.226, 234.

27. S. Motyer, 'Righteousness by Faith in the NT', in *Here we Stand*, ed. J.I. Packer, Hodder (1986), p.35.

28. J. A. T. Robinson, *The Priority of John*, SCM (1985), p.322.

29. C. H. Dodd, *Gospel and Law*, Cambridge (1951).

30. R. T. France, *Matthew*, IVP (1986), p.50.

31. J. Fletcher, *Situation Ethics*, SCM (1966).

32. Cf Matthew 5:27ff. gives the negative eternal consequences of failing to take the 'right' course of action and Matthew 6:1ff. the positive eternal consequences of true righteousness.

33. W. F. Lofthouse, *The Father and the Son* (1934), quoted by Pollard in *Fullness of Humanity*, Sheffield (1982), p.86.

34. *Op cit*, p.336.

35. *Op cit.*, p.53.

36. B Mitchell, *Morality, Religious and Secular*, Oxford (1980), pp 147 150.

37. Ibid p.149.

38. *Ethics and Christianity*, p.146.

39. Cf White, *op. cit.*

40. G Von Rad, 'The Theological Problem of the OT Doctrine of Creation' in *The Problem of the Hexateuch and other essays*, Oliver & Boyd (1966), pp.131-143.

41. Chris Wright, 'Ethics and the OT', in *Third Way*, Vol.1 No.9 (1977), pp.7-9.

42. Karl Barth, *Church Dogmatics* III, 4, T. & T. Clark (1961), pp.24-31.

12

The Suffering of Man and the Sovereignty of God: An Examination of the Relationship between the Problem of Evil and the Purposes of God

Introduction

On 1 November 1755 Lisbon was devastated by an earthquake. Being All Saints' Day, the churches were packed to capacity and thirty of them were destroyed. Within six minutes 15,000 people had died and 15,000 more lay dying. This was the eighteenth century equivalent to a nuclear holocaust, but one not caused by the perversity of man.

One of the many thinkers stunned and horrified by this event was the French philosopher Voltaire. His cry was quite simply: 'How could anyone believe in a benevolent and omnipotent God after this?' What else could he do, but treat with scorn Pope's lines in his *Essay on Man,* written from a comfortable villa in Twickenham:

> And, spite of pride, in erring reason's spite,
> One truth is clear, Whatever is, is right.

This, for Voltaire, was the crass poetic expression of the philosophy of Optimism – a philosophy which in a different guise just over 150 years later was itself to be cut to ribbons in the form of the bodies of those young men who died on the battle fields of the Somme and Paschendale. In protest Voltaire railed against such optimism in his *Poem on the Disaster of Lisbon,* which asked why, if God is free, just and benevolent, do we suffer under his rule? Later, similar thoughts were to find expression in the satirical novel *Candide,* whose teacher Dr Pangloss, a professor of Optimism, blandly assures him that 'All is for the best in the best of all possible worlds'. Later, after many more disasters, not least the hanging of Dr Pangloss by the Inquisition, Voltaire writes 'Candide, terrified, speechless, bleeding, palpitating said to himself: "If this is the best of all possible worlds, what can the rest be?" '

While neither the Bible nor any Christian theology founded upon the Bible ever claims that this is the best of all possible worlds, one must at least sympathise with the sentiments to which Voltaire is giving voice, namely, that at the very least there is an *apparent* contradiction between belief in an all powerful, loving God and the fact of suffering which is deemed evil. Therefore, it is common to speak of the 'problem' of evil or the 'problem' of suffering. However, at the outset it ought to be said that for the atheist, or the thorough-going materialist, there is not a problem of evil in the sense that evil and suffering do not apparently count against his beliefs. For the atheist/materialist suffering is a mere fact of existence, a datum of experience, like the redness of red or the wetness of water. It may be a problem for the atheist in that he, like the rest of us, has to cope with the unpleasantness of suffering as he struggles against its threat of annihilation so rendering all his efforts ultimately meaningless (if death really is the end), but as far as it goes his belief system is not significantly brought into question by suffering *per se*.

The dilemma formulated
But for the Christian, suffering and evil do pose a problem because of what he or she believes. So McClosky writes:

> Evil is a problem for the theist in that a contradiction is involved in the fact of evil on the one hand, and the belief in the omnipotence of God on the other.[1]

That is precisely what Voltaire was getting at. Or the problem may be put in the form of a dilemma as formulated by John Hick:

> If God is perfectly loving and good he must wish to abolish evil; if God is all powerful he must be able to abolish evil. But evil exists therefore God cannot be both perfectly good and almighty.[2]

Even if some of the terms Hick uses here were to be qualified so that 'good' were to be distinguished from sentimental indulgence and were to incorporate, as the Bible insists must be the case, God's righteous anger towards wrong, and 'omnipotence' were to be defined in a way that did not involve the ability to do that which was self-contradictory, as distinct from *antinomi* (the old chestnut, 'can God make a boulder so large that he cannot move it?') we have honestly to admit that *prima facie* there is a dilemma which needs to be addressed.

Therefore, let us focus on this particular formulation of the dilemma: if God is good he must wish to want to abolish evil, if he is omnipotent he must be able, but evil exists and so he cannot be both. A moment's reflection upon this conundrum soon reveals two things which this dilemma presupposes for it to be effective. The first presupposition is that if God is good and all powerful he must wish to abolish evil *now,* or at least it raises the questions of why he did not remove it earlier or why he allowed it to come into being in the first place. The second presupposition is that he must do it in an immediate and total way, presumably by divine *fiat.* In other words there is both a temporal and a means condition built into the formulation.

But what if it could be demonstrated, however tentatively, that God will not only deal with evil at some point in the *future,* but that he will as it were 'redeem' it by a means we would not think of, in a way that will transfigure it into that which is good? Then some, but by no means all, of the force is taken out of the dilemma. The tension would be relieved but not entirely removed. A perspective would be provided which would enable us to view the issue in a manner which is significantly different from the way it is generally perceived. It is this different perspective, which is provided by the Bible, that will be explored below.

Simple solutions
There are, of course, some simple solutions to the dilemma which essentially involve the removal of one or more elements of belief so that it ceases to be a dilemma at all. One could deny the existence of evil or suffering, viewing them as 'illusory' – Theravada

Buddhism or Christian Science might qualify as examples here. Alternatively, one could deny that God is all-powerful, as does the process theologian David Griffin, who states quite unashamedly that his solution is found by 'denying the doctrine of omnipotence fundamental to it'.[3] Or thirdly, one could deny the goodness of God, a view well captured by Archibald MacLeish in his play *JB,* an updated presentation of the story of Job in which one finds the haunting refrain, 'if he is God he is not good, if he is good he is not God'.

The traditional Christian claim, however, is that God is good, that he is almighty, and that evil and suffering are realities to be reckoned with. The 'problem', therefore, turns on how to relate these two articles of faith (the goodness and omnipotence of God) to the fact of suffering, without compromising either of these tenets of belief or trivialising human suffering.

The moral status of pain

In turning to consider the question, 'What makes suffering morally unacceptable?', a prior question needs to be addressed: 'Is all suffering evil or is it so only in certain contexts?' While psychologically most pain might be considered to be objectionable, it is not necessarily the case that it is morally so, especially if the pain endured is part of means to a recognised good. For example, biologically pain serves as part of the body's defence mechanism, preventing further injury by means of, say, a reflex action. Certainly it could be objected that this simply pushes the 'problem' one stage back, for one could ask, why the more serious injury? Even so, the point still remains that pain in itself is not necessarily evil. In some contexts it is morally neutral, like the 'healthy' pain after long exercise, or morally good, as in the case of corrective punishment.

Surely, what makes suffering so morally objectionable is its occurrence in a form that is wholly negative and irrational, apparently devoid of any significance. It is this which lies at the root of so many tormented human cries: 'Why should my ten day old baby die?' 'Why should such a gifted man be reduced to a mere shell through cancer?' It is this seeming lack of purpose, what is often referred to as dysteliological suffering, that provides the twist which calls for such pain to be viewed as evil. And so we might put the matter like this: suffering 'becomes' morally unacceptable when, within our own limited temporal context, it exhibits those features commonly recognised as standing in direct opposition to that which is good – e.g. disintegration, meaninglessness.

The why of suffering

When one asks the question, 'why is there suffering?' one could be straining towards one of two things. First, one could be looking for a cause: 'What is the cause of suffering?' – both in terms of an ultimate cause – 'where did it come from in the first place?' or in the more immediate sense, a proximal cause – 'what is the cause of this particular suffering?' (this question bearing a metaphysical, rather than biological, sense). This general line of approach to the question of evil has many distinguished writers to commend it – Augustine, C. S. Lewis and Alvin Plantinga to name but three. Here explanations are sought in terms of the defence of free will, the Fall, the activity of fallen angels and so on. Each of these has some part to play in moving towards an overall Christian understanding of suffering and evil in the world. However, it is the teaching about the Fall which is particularly significant and foundational.[4] The basic outline of the biblical plot is that the sovereign and totally good God created a good universe. We human beings rebelled and that rebellion is now such a part of our make up that we are enmeshed in it. All the suffering we now face turns on this fact, and is in some way related to 'sin', but not all suffering is related to sin in the same way. The Bible centres on how God takes action to reverse these terrible effects and their root cause, which is sin itself. Furthermore, the one who is a believer sees on the broader canvas the future dimension of a new heaven and earth where neither sin nor sorrow will ever be experienced again.

This means that there is a fundamental recognition by the Christian that the world in which we live is thrown out of joint at every level: it is not now the best of all possible worlds, the price of sin is great, and suffering in this life is in some measure a consequence of it. Perhaps the cry of our post-Enlightenment generation, echoing the cry of a man like Voltaire is, 'How can God be so cruel?', whereas the cry of earlier generations was one with a man like Martin Luther, namely, 'How can God be so merciful?' The reason why we find it difficult to say the latter (but not the former) is because we fail to appreciate the seriousness of sin and the pure character of a God who stands in opposition to sin.

Nevertheless, this is not to say that every item of suffering is the immediate result of sin. Jesus clearly corrects that idea, for it is patently obvious that many 'good people' suffer, and Christians of all people should certainly not expect a trouble free life; they have their 'losses and crosses' as the Puritans quaintly put it. However, some suffering can be the result of a specific sin (e.g. the man in John 5:1-15). This is a possibility but not a necessity. Sometimes the consequences of human sin can be more broadly distributed on the human scene in a way that does not appear very discriminating – war, plague, congenital defects, for instance. Therefore, to use the categories of retribution and punishment solely to understand specific sins is unacceptable and insufficient.

The biblical writers have a realistic estimation of both the human condition and the character of God. Unlike us, they are not so taken by surprise at human wickedness, nor by the suffering it occasions. What is more, with such an understanding comes the overwhelming sense of the kindness of God as his blessings (which we take for granted) come to us daily. This sense of amazement at such grace is reinforced by the fact that in spite of our ingratitude and the way we treat each other and God, he still goes on being kind when perhaps we should expect more signs of his displeasure. We tend to reverse this perception: we expect that no matter what, without qualification, life should go along quite nicely for us. When trouble comes our way we are taken aback to the point of resentment. The biblical perspective is a much needed corrective.

It is at this point that an objection is raised which goes something like this: ' If God does care about us and is so opposed to sin, which is the cause of so much suffering in the world, why does he not intervene to do something about it?'

Apart from this raising the question of the means and temporal conditions mentioned earlier, there are more sobering implications which we do not often think about, but which have been well put by the writer, herself no mean lay theologian, Dorothy L Sayers:

> 'Why doesn't God smite this dictator dead?' is a question a little remote from us. Why, madam, did he not strike you dumb and imbecile before you uttered that baseless and unkind slander the day before yesterday? Or me, before I behaved with such a cruel lack of consideration to that well meaning friend? And why sir, did he not cause your hand to rot off at the wrist before you signed your name to that dirty bit of financial trickery? You did not quite mean that? But why not? Your misdeeds and mine are none the less repellent because our opportunities for doing damage are less spectacular than those of some other people. Do you suggest that your doings and mine are too trivial for God to bother about? That cuts both ways; for in that case, it would make precious little difference to his creation if he wiped us both out tomorrow.[5]

In other words if we want strict and immediate justice, then what we are asking for is literally hell, for that is precisely what it would be.

However, as well as looking backward for an answer to the question, 'Why suffering?', one could also be looking forward, so that what one is really asking is: 'What is the *purpose* of suffering?' 'What possible good, if any, could there be in it?' This way of looking at the question was in fact taken up by a certain school of psychoanalysis called logotherapy, headed by Victor Frankel, who himself experienced the horrors of a Nazi concentration camp. It was there of all places that he noticed the positive way in which some people approached their situation. This observation in turn led him to quote Nietzche with approval when he said that 'Men and women can endure any amount of suffering so long as they know the why to their existence'. In other words, if that suffering can be placed within some wider context of meaning and purpose, much, but no means all, of the sting is taken out.

Pain with a purpose?

There is a story in John 9 which illustrates this point well: the healing of the man born blind. As Jesus and his disciples came across this man, it was the disciples who raised the question: 'Who sinned, this man or his parents?' They were looking for an answer to this tragic state of affairs in terms of causation linked to specific sinful action. But Jesus replied, 'Neither, but this happened so that (*hina*) the work of God may be displayed in his life.' Jesus alters the perspective by focusing upon the divine purpose behind the situation, linking it to the creative-redeeming activity of God. Accordingly the man is healed. This would appear to be where the theological centre of gravity lies in the New Testament, bearing in mind that the major concern of the writers is the practical one of enabling God's people to see that the suffering and persecution which they may be undergoing or are likely to face, when considered against the backcloth of God's eternal purpose, have creative significance. This comes out in several places: as specific instances we may think of Romans 5:1-5, and later 8:28ff: 'And we know that in all things God works for the good of those who love him, who have been called according to his purpose,' a statement set within the context of Christian suffering. But we may want to ask: 'Upon what grounds could Paul or anyone else make such a startling claim that God can and will work "all things for good"?' This, in fact, brings us to the heart of the Christian faith, namely the death and bodily resurrection of Jesus Christ.

If a decisive insight into the mystery of suffering is to be found anywhere, then it is to be found at the Cross where we come face to face with 'the God who is hidden in suffering', to use the term of Martin Luther. Here the foundational Christian belief is that the one who was known as Jesus of Nazareth was none other than the God who became man, the God who took to himself the sin of the world, bearing the penalty for sin which is rightly ours, absorbing evil, disarming principalities and powers and acting re-creatively to bring about the greater good. That is, it is seen as the means whereby people can be put in a right relationship with God, be forgiven and receive eternal life (2 Cor 5:19-21; 1 Pet 2:24), and God's kingdom established.

The perfect paradox

It is at the Cross that we are presented with the paradox running throughout the mysterious relationship between the evil of suffering and God's good purposes. From one point of view, the Cross was the worst thing that could have happened (the murder of the divine Son, so pinpointing forcefully our rebellious attitude towards God). Yet at *the same time* it was the best thing that ever happened (the divine means of rescuing us). Here we see God taking sin and suffering seriously because he tasted it first hand in his Son, suffering physical and spiritual of a magnitude beyond our comprehension. It was this that shaped the New Testament writers' attitude towards suffering. They not only looked to Jesus and the Cross as an example to follow (1 Pet 3:17; Heb 12:2), but as the theological centrepiece of the belief that the outworkings of what God had achieved by Jesus' death and resurrection *in time* would be brought to completion at *the end of time,* ushering in the new heaven and the new earth.

Wherever we look in the New Testament we cannot fail to be struck by the wonderful truth that the God whom we see in Jesus Christ is no remote God. For he was willing not only to get his hands dirty, he was willing to get them pierced for the sake of those who did it. Listen again to Dorothy L Sayers and the way in which she drives this point home in her play, *The Man Born To Be King:*

> For whatever reason God chose to make man as he is – limited and suffering and subject to sorrows and death – He had the honesty and the courage to take His own medicine. Whatever game He is playing with His creation, He has kept His own rules and played fair. He has Himself gone through the whole of human experience, from the trivial irritations of family life and lack of money to the worst horrors, pain, humiliation, defeat, despair and death. He was born in poverty and died in disgrace and felt it was all worthwhile.

Some of the good which can be brought out of evil can be glimpsed in this life. For example, through suffering we may become more caring, sympathetic and in a deeper way more whole people. We are reminded, quite rightly, that we are not gods but contingent beings, and it is no bad thing to have our minds focused on eternal matters through pain, so coming to the realisation that this life is not the whole story. Suffering can be a means into a deeper, more intimate relationship with the God for whom we were made. One person who has testified to this truth is Mary Craig, who describes how two of her four sons were born with severe abnormalities, one with Hohler's Syndrome and the other with Down's Syndrome. Interestingly enough she speaks of 'redemptive suffering'. So she writes:

> In the teeth of the evidence I do not believe that any suffering is ultimately pointless or absurd, although it is often difficult to go on convincing oneself of this. At first we react with incredulity, anger and despair. Yet the value of suffering does not lie in the pain of it but in what the sufferer makes of it. It is in sorrow that we discover the things that really matter; in sorrow that we discover ourselves.[6]

A similar perspective to that of Mary Craig is shared by Professor Sir Norman Anderson, whose son, Hugh, after a brilliant career at Cambridge, died of cancer at the age of twenty-one. With a father's heavy heart Professor Anderson wrote:

> People used continually to ask us why a young man of such promise, and with such a zest for life, should be allowed to die so young. To this the only reply, we both feel, is that we do not, cannot know. The vital question to ask God in such cases is not "Why did you allow this?" (to which he seldom, I think, vouchsafes an answer), but "What do you want to teach me through this?"[7]

How we respond is an important element in, as it were, creating the appropriate conditions for some good to be produced, but such a response requires a foundation. Neither Mary Craig nor Norman Anderson knew the particular answer to the question, 'Why?', but they did know why they trusted God who knew why, and that trust was based upon the solid foundation of God's revelation of himself in Jesus Christ.

However, it is important to stress that not all good will be seen in this life, and here the eternal perspective is crucial.[8] What is being suggested is that from the eternal perspective of God – the author of the drama – who 'sees the end from the beginning', all creaturely decisions and responses are woven in with all other events to serve his purpose. Individual actions do have significance in that they go towards making up patterns of lasting importance within the drama, but they do not exert an ultimate significance; that is provided by the sovereign God who places the decisions and actions of his creatures in an eternal context which alone affords ultimate meaning.

An illustration which might give us some 'feel' of how this might be so is the well known one of the weaving of Persian carpets. It is said that Persian carpets are made on a large frame. On one side of the frame stands the family placing threads into the framework, sometimes randomly, sometimes thoughtfully. On the other side of the frame stands the father, the master weaver, who takes all these threads and weaves them into a rich pattern of his design. When the carpet is completed the frame is then turned around for all to see. With certain qualifications, God may be likened to the master weaver in this respect: that he takes each 'thread' (events and actions) and weaves them into a pattern which gives the 'threads' their significance. However, unlike the master weaver, God 'from the beginning' not only knows what those 'threads' are and where they will be placed on this side of the frame (a consequence of his omniscience), but he also decrees the events and actions themselves according to the eternal counsel of his will (a consequence of his omnipotence and wisdom).[9] Some of the patterns and configurations can be discerned in this life (our side of the frame); however, it is only the other side of the frame (God's eternal purpose) which provides the lasting context from which ultimate significance is derived. The central point in that framework through which all of these threads are related and integrated is the life, death, resurrection, ascension and return of Jesus Christ.

The eternal perspective

Let us now tie this in with our earlier discussion about the nature of evil. Within our temporal context of experience some events are evil, including certain forms of suffering. But this is not the whole context, for another perspective is available. It is when the evil event is related to the wider context of God's eternal purposes that the evil is transfigured; within this broader God-given context evil events can be seen to contain good *ends*. This does not take the evil out of evil, but it does mean that evil has a real but temporary hold on reality. Let us focus on how this might be so by thinking about the events surrounding the crucifixion. In terms of the betrayal, the trial, the scourging and the torture of the Cross, the configuration of events is formed. Within this context such events are deemed evil, not least because man's wickedness is involved, the rebellion mentioned earlier. But this is not the final, nor even the primary, context from which these events derive their full significance (1 Cor 2:7ff); that is provided by God's action of redemption in which each event is a constituent part. Here one is not saying that the event of the Cross is being transposed *into* something good by virtue of the resurrection, as if the resurrection were a divine salvaging job; rather, the good (man's rescue from bondage to sin, the defeat of death etc.) is already being wrought *in and through* the event of the Cross itself, with the resurrection being but one vital aspect of the divine activity whereby evil is conquered. The resurrection of Christ is also a revelation, on our side of the frame, of the significance which is to be fully revealed at the end of time (Acts 2:23).

'If God is good and almighty, then why does he not do something about the fact of evil in general and suffering in particular?' The Christian's reply is that he has and he will. The goodness of God is maintained by relating each event to an intended good by placing it within the context of his own design, to be revealed at the end of time. The omnipotence of God is upheld by his weaving of all events into his eternal purpose, leaving nothing outside his ultimate control. Both the goodness and omnipotence of God in his dealing with evil find their expression in a way that we could never have contemplated left to ourselves, and that is in the Cross of Christ, the 'crucified God', to borrow the phrase of Moltmann.

No simple solution

And so we have come full circle to the point where we began, namely the relationship between evil, God's goodness and power. The scriptural testimony is that evil, sin and suffering are too deeply intertwined and all pervasive in the fabric of human existence to lend themselves to any simple solution. Furthermore, God's goodness embraces not only his undeserved love towards us but also his justice, his implacable opposition to all that is antithetical to his moral character. If it is simply justice we want, then that would mark the end of all of us. If it is simply undeserved love – forgiveness – we ask for, that would mark the end of a moral universe and God ceasing to be God. Simple justice – God denies us; simple forgiveness – God denies himself. But what we see in the person and work of Jesus Christ on the Cross is God's justice and God's love meeting in such a way that his omnipotence is paradoxically wrought in weakness. 'This is love,' says the apostle John, 'not that we loved God, but that he loved us and sent his Son as an atoning sacrifice for our sins' (1 John 4:10). And what that means is this: God's justice demands that sin (the root cause of all suffering in some way) is dealt with and punished. God's love is shown in that he took the punishment to himself in his Son on the Cross, so that, in the words of Barth, 'The Judge (Jesus) was judged in our place.' What we deserve – judgement and death – he willingly received; what we do not deserve – pardon and eternal life – he freely gives. And what was achieved there in veiled form and declared by the resurrection, will be declared before the whole universe at the end of time when the veil is finally lifted.

Focus on the cross

We end with a quote from P. T. Forsyth who, like Karl Barth after him, discovered the theological bankruptcy of the optimistic liberal theology upon which he had been raised, and turned to the deep theology of the Bible with the Cross of Christ at the centre. In the midst of the carnage of the First World War, when optimistic self-reliant evolutionism was reaping its own rewards, he wrote his great *Justification of God* in which he states:

If the greatest act in the world, and the greatest crime there, became by the moral, holy victory of the Son of God, the source of not only endless blessing to man, but perfect satisfaction and delight to a holy God (cross), then there is no crime, no war, which is outside his control or impossible for his purpose. There is none that should destroy the Christian faith which has as its object, source and sustenance that cross and its victory, in which the prince of this world has in principle been judged and doomed for ever. In that cross we learn that faith which brings things not willed by God are yet worked up by God. In a divine irony, man's greatest crime turns God's greatest boon. The riddle is insoluble but the fact sure.[10]

NOTES

1. N, Pike, ed, *God and Evil*, Prentice Hall (1964).

2. John Hick, 'An Irenean Theodicy', in *Encountering Evil*, S. T. Davies ed, T. and T. Clark (1981), pp. 38-52.

3. David Griffin, 'Creation out of Chaos and the Problem of Evil' in *Encountering Evil*, pp. 100-119.

4. For one of the most biblically penetrating and pastorally helpful books which deals with this issue see D. A. Carson, *How Long O Lord?*, IVP (1990). See also Melvin Tinker, *Why do Bad Things Happen to Good People*, Christian Focus (1997).

5. Dorothy L Sayers, 'The Triumph of Easter', *Creed or Chaos*, Methuen (1954).

6. Mary Craig, *Blessings*, Hodder and Stoughton (1979).

7. Norman Anderson, *An Adopted Son*, IVP (1985).

8. This thesis is explored in some detail by V P White, *The Fall of a Sparrow*, Paternoster (1985).

9. For a first rate discussion of the relationship between the providence of God and evil from a 'no risk' compatibilist point of view see Paul Helm, *The Providence of God*, IVP (1993).

10. P.T. Forsyth, *The Justification of God*, Duckworth (1916).

13

Towards an Evangelical View of the Church

Evangelicals and ecclesiology

In his address at N.E.A.C 3 in 1988, the then Archbishop of Canterbury, Robert Runcie, extended a challenge to Anglican evangelicals to do some serious thinking about ecclesiology and said:

> If the current evangelical renewal in the Church of England is to have a lasting impact then there must be more explicit attention given to the doctrine of the church.

Twenty years earlier in 1968, Professor Klaas Runia commented that

> There is an erroneous doctrine of the church, which is so often found among evangelicals. Many of them tend to regard the visible organised church as relatively unimportant, primarily because in it one finds many who have little faith, if any at all.

He then went on to urge evangelicals to

> give special attention to the biblical doctrine of the church ... If ever we want to solve the present problems of the church, we must first know what the church really is according to Scripture.[1]

In all honesty we have to admit that generally speaking there is some substance in what is implied by these two statements, namely, that there is a certain weakness in the way many evangelicals think about the church. If an evangelical were to be asked to say what he believed about the death of Christ or the inspiration of Holy Scripture, then in most cases he would be able to do so with relative ease. But if that same evangelical were to be asked to relate the essentials of his beliefs about the church, that might prove to be a little more difficult. As a result of this lack of clarity in thinking about the church, evangelicals become all the more prone to accept views about the church which are far from Scriptural, and certainly in the Church of England that means quasi-Catholic views of the church, this happening almost by default.

However, from another standpoint, evangelicals have been giving a great deal of time to thinking about the church in the last twenty years from a more practical point of view. Much of the discussion concerning the work of the Holy Spirit in the sixties and seventies was often ecclesiological, concerning 'every member ministry' for instance. Who is more concerned with evangelism and church growth than the evangelical? That is why it is not that wide of the mark to say that an evangelical's view of the Church of England is captured by the saying that it is 'the best boat to fish from'. This encapsulates, perhaps in a crude form admittedly, a deep scriptural truth. When evangelicals are patronisingly dismissed by some as having no ecclesiology, what critics often mean is that they do not like the ecclesiology that evangelicals have. As we shall see, evangelicals do have the richest, most authentic ecclesiology there is, because it is rooted in, and arises from, Scripture.[2]

The nature of the church

According to Paul Minear[3], the Bible uses over eighty figures and symbols to depict the church's nature, but we shall focus only upon one, namely, the church as the people of God.[4]

The apostle Peter takes the Old Testament term 'people of God' and applies it to the New Testament church (1 Peter 2:9) and so, as with many ideas and themes in the Old Testament, this finds its fulfilment in Christ and the age of the New Covenant. The actual word for church *ekklēsia*, which is the Greek rendering of the Hebrew *qahal,* basically means 'assembly' or 'gathering'. It is a term which describes the covenant-making assembly at Sinai (Deut. 9:10), as well as Israel gathered before God for covenant renewal (Deut. 29:1). In the New Testament this term is taken and almost exclusively applied to young Christian communities after Pentecost, in contrast with the term 'synagogue' used to refer to the Jews – the two exceptions being Acts 7:38, where Luke uses the term *ekklēsia* to describe Israel in the wilderness, and James 2:2 where he uses the term 'synagogue' to refer to the Christian congregation. So in what sense was the term *ekklēsia* used in the New Testament to depict the people of the New Covenant?

It is interesting to note that in the New Testament epistles the plural is used when more than one church is in view: 'the churches of God' (2 Thess. 1:4) and the 'churches of God in Judea' (1 Thess. 2:14, cf. 1 Cor. 7:17; Rom. 16:4; Gal. 1:2). It therefore appears that the term was only applied to an *actual gathering of people*.

Theologically we therefore need to ask: What is the relationship between 'the Church' and 'the churches'? This is a question that has been explored to great effect by Peter O'Brien[5], who points out that the 'assembly'/'congregation' is theologically construed in the sort of thinking expressed in Hebrews 12:22-24:

> But you have come to Mount Zion, to the heavenly Jerusalem, the city of the living God. You have come to thousands upon thousands of angels in joyful assembly, to the church (singular) of the first born, whose names are written in heaven. You have come to God, the judge of all men, to the spirits of righteous men made perfect, to Jesus the mediator of a new covenant, and to the sprinkled blood that speaks a better word than the blood of Abel.

Christians thus participate in the heavenly, eschatological church of Jesus Christ. This is what Paul primarily has in mind when he speaks of Jesus as being the 'head of the church' (Col. 1:18). Therefore, each local church is not to be seen as one member parallel to lots of other members which together make up Christ's body, the church. Nor is each church 'the body of Christ' as if Christ has many bodies. Rather each congregation is the full visible expression in that place of the one true heavenly church – an outcrop or colony of heaven – reflecting the eschatological gathering of God's people around God's throne. In the words of O'Brien:

> Paul consistently refers to the church which meets in a particular place. Even when there are several gatherings in a single city (e.g. at

Corinth) the individual assemblies are not understood as part of the
church in that place, but as one of the churches that meet there. This
suggests that each of the various local churches are manifestations
of that heavenly church, tangible expressions in time and space of
what is heavenly and eternal.[6]

In parenthesis we might want to ask: Where does this leave us *viz
a viz* our denominations? Does it mean that we become
independents or congregationalists? The answer is no, such a
conclusion does not follow from the premise. There are plenty of
reasons, theological and practical, why congregations should be
associated with each other. But it does mean that a denomination
is not a church, it is an association or federation of churches, which
in fact is the classic Anglican position. So long as the denomination
sees that, with its role as serving the local churches, and the
diocesan structures functioning more like a 'parachurch', all will
be well. But, as is increasingly happening, when the denomination
or diocese is seen as the main unit, with the local churches there
to serve them, then we are not only being unbiblical, but we are in
danger of having the gospel life blood sapped away. For example,
is it in accord with what has been said so far, that for the sake of
'fair distribution' evangelical curates are not being allowed to be
placed in evangelical parishes? Should the local churches have
increasing financial burdens placed upon them to finance
non-gospel activities or personnel in the diocese? What the local
churches should be saying is, 'No we don't want this, this is not
why we belong to this federation which is meant to serve our
interests – gospel interests – and we do not want men or money
being detracted from this.'

What many Anglican evangelicals have done is to adopt an
ecclesiology which is not biblical. The unbiblical ecclesiology is
the one which sees the denomination as primary and its structures
the place to be, so that occupying a diocesan post, being an
archdeacon, bishop, or archbishop, is seen as 'promotion' or, to
use that awful term, 'preferment'. It may not always be voiced in
that way, but sadly that is the unspoken feeling of many. This
does not mean, of course, that we should not seek to have
evangelicals in these positions if we can afford the manpower,

but let us see these positions for what they are, namely, posts in a servicing industry, ideally servicing the local congregation which is Christ's church. We have deliberately given a fair amount of space to discussing this idea of the church as the assembled people of God because it is fundamental to the New Testament and in practice far removed from the present outlook predominant in the Church of England.

Aspects of the church

On the basis of the biblical emphasis upon the *spiritual* nature of the church, the Reformers saw quite clearly that the church had two aspects: what we can call the invisible church and the visible church, or the church eternal and the church temporal. In saying this the Reformers were not claiming that there are two churches, one real, the other apparent, but rather that there are two aspects of the one reality which is the church. Thus the members of the invisible church (invisible to us, that is why we say we *believe* in one holy, catholic and apostolic church) are also members of the visible church, but exactly who they are is only known to God. Ultimately it is only the elect who constitute the church of Christ; and one day, when Christ returns, the invisible will become visible. In other words, it is made up of those whose names are written in the Lamb's book of life (Rev. 21:27). But let us not think that the Reformers, in reaction to Rome, which equated the visible mediaeval church with the true church, took flight in the invisible church, because they did not. Calvin in particular placed great store on the visible aspect of the church. He saw the church as being an earthly community where God's Word was preached and the sacraments administered:

> Wherever we see the Word of God purely preached and heard, and the sacraments administered according to Christ's institution, there, it is not to be doubted, a church of God exists.[7]

The same thought is expressed in Article 19 of the Thirty Nine Articles. The visible churches are only provisional; they will always be in error. So to state as the Archbishop of Canterbury did at N.E.A.C.3 that 'If it is the Body of Christ, the church too demands our belief, trust and faith', betrays an abuse of the metaphor between the visible and invisible church. What is more he was extolling an essentially Roman Catholic view of the church as found in the Pope's *Mystici Corporis Christi.*

Attributes of the church
The Nicene Creed confesses 'One holy, catholic and apostolic church' – the four essential attributes of the church.

Firstly, the church of Christ is *one.* This as we have already seen is essentially a spiritual unity, as indicated in the oft misquoted prayer of our Lord in John 17:21 – a favourite of the ecumenists: 'May they all be one; as thou, Father, art in me and I in thee, so also may they be in us, that the world may believe that thou didst send me' (New English Bible). This does not describe an external organisation – a church as some multinational ecclesiastical company – but a church of a deeply personal and spiritual nature, as is the mystery of the Trinity itself. The fact is, all true believers *are* one (we are back to the invisible or heavenly church again), and so are to express that oneness in action.

Secondly, we believe the church to be *holy,* set apart from the world for God, something increasingly being brought into question by the flagrant disregard of plain biblical teaching on morality. How can the holiness of the church be taken seriously when we have bishops and reports extolling homosexuality as a perfectly valid lifestyle?[8] We are to be in the world, but not of it; and this is something we desperately need to recapture if we are going to make an impact in our society today – holiness without which no man shall see God.

Thirdly, the church is *catholic,* which means universal and non-sectarian. If ever there has been a term which has been abused, it is this. For all the Church of England's claims to be catholic, it is really sectarian in practice; for example, in not recognising the orders of a non-episcopally ordained man whose rule is the Word of God. We must recapture its true meaning, namely the universality of the church; indeed the first time the term was used in Christian literature by Ignatius of Antioch, it referred to the heavenly church (Smyrna 8). What is the true test of catholicity?

It is that which the early church had: submission to the Word of God, the teaching of Christ and the apostles.

And so we come to the fourth attribute of the church, that it is *apostolic*. Again we must stress the negative, that this has nothing to do with so-called apostolic succession by the laying on of hands. This is an idea that was largely introduced into the Church of England in the last century by the Tractarians, and has nothing to do with historic Anglicanism. Rather it is that the church is founded upon the teaching of the apostles; it is in the succession of the apostles' teaching that the church is truly apostolic (2 Tim. 2:2). Such a view was common to both the English and Continental Reformers, as is summarised by Paul Avis, in his excellent treatment of the subject:

> By making the gospel alone the power at work in the church through the Holy Spirit, the Reformers did away with the necessity of a doctrine of apostolic succession, replacing it with the notion of a succession of truth. Correspondingly, the gospel of truth was held to be sufficient to serve the catholicity of the church.[9]

It is possible, as history sadly testifies, to have an unbroken line in bishops but for that 'church' not to be apostolic but apostate in perverting the apostles' teaching.

The marks of the church

We have already touched upon this when we looked at the question of the visible church. The church has certain distinguishing features, just as a living body has certain features which indicate that it is alive, like respiration, movement, etc. We refer to Article 19:

> The visible church of Christ is a congregation of faithful men, in which the pure Word of God is preached, and the sacraments be duly ministered according to Christ's ordinance in all those things that of necessity are requisite to the same.

Three marks are to be found there: The preaching of the Word of God in pure form, that is unadulterated by human speculation, whether by tradition or, as is more the case today, by liberal theology. Then there is the due administration of sacraments ('due' – 'proper') in which the ministry of the visible Word is to be linked to the audible word. This would seem to rule out any *ex opere operate* view of the sacraments which works regardless of belief on the part of the recipient.

Also it has been suggested by some that contained within this is discipline as a mark of the church, for here we have a congregation of *faithful* men. Here there is no question of judging who is and who is not finally saved – only God can do that – but there is the call to discern whether a person professes faith, a faith which is credible, one which shows itself in day-to-day living.

Even if we were to agree with the later Calvin (his definitive *Institutes* of 1559) that discipline does not constitute one of the marks of the church, it is surely nonetheless vital for the church's spiritual health and well-being.

The purpose of the church – distinguishing AD from BC

If we were to get the emphasis right on the *local* church, there is yet another attendant danger which in practice leads to a faulty ecclesiology and that is a failure to distinguish AD from BC, that is, failing to take seriously how Old Testament promise is met by New Testament fulfilment and is therefore abrogated. Instead, what tends to happen is that practices and models are lifted straight from the Old Testament and applied with one or two adjustments to the church today. So we have the localisation of God either in the reserved sacrament or in the 'hallowed' building. With this there is a ministry of priestcraft, with robes to match. What is more, we are often being told that the most important activity for Christians to engage in when they meet is 'worship', with the primary movement from man to God, which may either be in the form of a eucharistic celebration or a celebration of praise and prayer. But what we have to think through and translate into practice, is the difference Christ's person and death makes to the people of God. If in Jesus we have God's final work and God's final word (Heb. 1:1-4), then this has an earth shattering significance, not only for our view of the nature of the church, but for what the church's primary purposes are: what the church is meant to be doing.

What then is to happen when God's people gather together? As we have seen from Hebrews 12, that gathering is an expression on earth of the heavenly gathering around the throne of Christ. Following this imagery through (which is taken by the writer from Deuteronomy 10 and transformed through the filter of Christ), first and foremost we must submit to the one who rules through his Word. In other words, the primary movement is one of grace from God to man. Architecturally, let the building reflect this: let the pulpit occupy a central position. More importantly, let it be expressed ministerially, with the minister functioning and looking not like a sacrificing priest but a teaching presbyter. Let everything communicate not barriers but access, which has been achieved by Christ's sacrificial death.

This leads us to the next element of what is meant to happen when God's people assemble; they are to edify and encourage each other:

> Let us consider how we may spur one another on towards love and good deeds. Let us not give up meeting together, as some are in the habit of doing, but let us exhort one another – and all the more as you see the Day approaching (Heb. 10: 24-25).

The reason why God has given apostles, prophets, evangelists, pastor-teachers is so that God's people might be prepared for works of service for the building up (*eis oikodomen*) of the body of Christ (Eph. 4:11ff.). Note again the downward movement from God – his gift of ministries to the church; then the outward movement amongst his people – works of service – so that they might grow upwards in Christ. When we use the term 'edify' (*oikodomeō*) we tend to think of it individualistically and pietistically. That is not the way it is used in Ephesians 4. On this subject David Peterson[10] writes:

> Perfection is not an ideal to be attained but a reality to be met in Christ. Put another way we may say that the purpose of Christian ministry is to prepare the saints to meet their Lord. All ministry should have an eschatological focus and perspective.

He later adds:

> Edification occurs when Christians minister to one another in word
> and deed, seeking to express and encourage a Christ-centred faith,
> hope and love.

What should we be doing when we meet? 'Edifying,' and that of
course is the test Paul applies in 1 Corinthians 14 as to whether
certain things should be done and how they should be done.

From what has been said so far, we must not make the mistake
of thinking that church-gathering is synonymous with introversion
and exclusivism. Certainly in a very profound sense the church is
exclusive, but theologically it is necessary to coordinate the notion
of 'gathering' with 'dispersion' – 'calling' with 'sending' – so
that we may, to use the language of 1 Peter 2:9, 'declare the
wonderful excellencies of him who called you out of darkness
into his marvellous light.' One of the criticisms of the idea of the
church we have been exploring is that it 'may lead in practice to a
lack of a Christian face towards the world, and with it social
introversion'.[11] Although this may be the case, it is not necessarily
so.

How, then, are the ideas of being 'called together' and being
'sent out' with a view to evangelism and acting as salt and light in
the world to be understood? Maybe in the following way: It is the
church which, by definition, is called together. While it is
assembled the gospel may be presented and some unbelievers
present might be converted. But, by and large, the notion of
'sending out' with a view to proclaiming the gospel is not the task
of the church *qua* the church (i.e. as a gathering or institution),
but the task of individuals or groups of individuals. Apostles are
sent. Evangelists are sent. In one sense all Christians are sent (John
20:21), but the church-assembly is not sent. The purpose of the
sending is to gather in people by the proclamation of the gospel.
The goal is the church, its upbuilding and completion.

Let us follow through the implications of this biblical
ecclesiology as it impinges upon two major areas of present
concern for Anglicans, the questions of episcopacy and church
unity.

Episcopacy

There is little doubt that evangelicals in particular within the Church of England are giving a fair amount of time and attention to the question of episcopacy. The Anglican Evangelical Assembly of 1990 devoted a whole conference to the subject, and this is all part of a wider concern to grapple with the issue of ecclesiology. But why focus on episcopacy? For two main reasons. The first is a very practical and immediate one. There are now a number of evangelical bishops in the Church of England and they are asking for help to think through their role and their position within the church structures. Secondly, as the failed Methodist-Anglican reunion scheme has shown, the question of episcopacy is one which is central (as far as many Anglicans are concerned) to ecumenical relations: to what extent is it legitimate to view episcopacy as being essential to the being of the church?

Of course in putting the question in this form one has in mind a certain view of episcopacy, the view which came to the fore in Anglican circles with Newman's first *Tract for the Times,* which saw the threefold institution of bishops, presbyters and deacons as being divinely ordained, stemming from the apostles and secured by an unbroken line of ordinations. In 1946, the book *The Apostolic Ministry*[12] was published, which made a distinction between those ministries which were essential (that is, having an unbroken link with the apostles) and those which were dependent. So the question revolves not so much around episcopacy *per se* – after all Free Churches have oversight and eldership – but rather apostolicity understood in terms of succession being maintained by the laying on of episcopal hands, which is a different concept altogether.

It really is quite astounding that within such a relatively short space of time such a view should become so widely accepted as if it were mainline, historic Anglican teaching – let alone biblical teaching! More recently Carey and Hind have spoken of apostolic succession as precisely the 'recognition that the special ministry is a gift of God to, in and through the church and the continuity in office and responsibility is one of the signs of the continuity of the whole church in the faith and witness of the apostles ... one of the symbols [i.e. both signs and instruments] of the universality of the church.... [The] historic and distinctive ministry is one of the constitutive elements of the church of Jesus Christ: one of the means by which he himself exercises his own headship of his body and by which the Holy Spirit reminds Christians now of what Jesus taught his disciples and leads them into all truth.'[13]

But how can such a statement be taken at all seriously when we have had popes making declarations about infallibility, the immaculate conception and the like? Are we seriously to believe that here the 'Holy Spirit is reminding Christians now of what Jesus taught his disciples and leads them into all truth'? What of duly ordained bishops who deny the fundamentals of the faith? Is it really through such as these that 'Christ is exercising his headship'? One only has to ask such questions to reveal how vacuous and dangerously romantic such thinking is. What are we to say to such claims?

First of all, from a biblical standpoint, such a view of apostolic succession cannot be demonstrated. There is no indication that a congregation had to wait for an apostle to come along to authorise it. There certainly were ministries in Rome and Antioch long before an apostle visited these places. Why, if such succession is essential to the church, is no mention of it to be found, especially in the Pastoral epistles? The silence is deafening. As we have seen, there is an apostolic succession but it is the concern to ensure the continuity of apostolic doctrine (2 Tim. 2:2).

Secondly, from an historical standpoint this view leaves much to be desired. The one who placed great emphasis upon bishops as a means of ensuring unity in the church was Ignatius of Antioch in the second century, but even here we find no mention of manual transmission of apostolic authority. In a concern to fend off heresy, Ignatius urged Christians to conform to the mind of Christ, which, he argued, meant conforming to the mind of the bishop, even to the extent that the congregation was not to do anything without the express permission of the bishop (understood in terms of area oversight). For some this would be enough to provide some support for the present view of bishops prevalent in the Anglican communion – but is it? Professor Geoffrey Bromiley has this astute comment to make:

Ignatius' programme could not work out historically because it rested upon a naive and unsupported assumption, viz, a supposedly self-evident equation of the mind of the bishop with the mind of God... God did indeed choose apostles, and through them pastors and teachers... but he also laid upon them a responsibility of faithfulness to the spoken and written tradition. Far from enjoying a direct identity with the mind of God and a consequent infallibility, they had thus to be subject to God's own word in the apostolic testimony.[14]

In other words, if we were to take the principle that Ignatius is promoting, 'unity by conformity to the mind of Christ', and translate that into contemporary thought, it would be that a ministry which is truly apostolic is one which renounces self-opinion and humbly tunes itself to the mind of God as expressed in the apostolic, Biblical teaching.

Thirdly, from the standpoint of Anglican teaching, is it acceptable? Again the answer must be 'No'. According to Article 6, we are required only to believe those things demonstrable from Scripture. As we saw in Article 19, succession is not offered as one of the marks of the church. Richard Hooker, who although he prized episcopacy, did not consider it necessary and said that 'The church hath power by universal consent to take it away.' But not only in accordance with traditional Anglican teaching is episcopacy not of the *esse* (essence-being) of the church, neither is it absolutely vital for its *bene esse* (well-being) – we are merely told that it is something which has been received from ancient times and is continuing; it is something which is not contrary to Scripture. So as far as traditional historic Anglicanism is concerned, episcopacy is a matter of indifference.

We should, therefore, not be enticed into accepting a view of episcopacy which is scripturally and theologically deficient. We are not to allow this innovative doctrine to hinder fellowship and work with fellow believers who have a different ministerial structure, so that they cannot enter our pulpits or celebrate around the Lord's table – that is a scandal and must be overcome.

Even one such as Professor Geoffrey Lampe has written that we should be increasingly reluctant to be committed as Anglicans to a position in which our church too often seems to the rest of the world to be concerned with a gospel which is no gospel, a gospel of the grace of God in bishops[15] – how true!

Turning to the present situation, many Anglican evangelicals are tending to approach the question of episcopacy from the standpoint of accepted historical-sociological convention (the Anglican episcopate as we have it), and then try and read into it the roles and functions of episcopacy as we find it in the New Testament (teaching, pastoral care, mission etc.), with the resulting call for more bishops with more power and smaller dioceses to enable such roles to be fulfilled in today's society.

However, such a procedure needs to be stood on its head for it to be truly evangelical (sola Scriptura). We need to apply the principle of the 'dynamic equivalent' in our Biblical interpretation and application, and ask: who are the 'dynamic equivalents' to the presbyters/overseers in the New Testament? The answer, of course, is the pastor-teachers of the congregations, the vicars and curates.

Therefore, in order for New Testament oversight to be translated into a living reality today, we do not need to multiply the number of existing Anglican Bishops, but to increase and facilitate the number of pastor/teachers in our congregations, seeking people whose rule is God's Word, and whose 'focus of unity' is the gospel.

If the present Anglican episcopate structure is to be retained (although it may help if a term other than 'bishop' could be adopted), it could be reformed in a direction away from the monarchical model towards a truly servant role, whereby as area spiritual advisers and enablers, they commit themselves to encouraging, training and resourcing the true bishops of congregations to fulfil their calling: to teach the faithful and reach out to the unevangelized. Instead of the diocese being seen as the primary reality of which the congregation is but a small part, the situation would be reversed so that the concern of such 'area enablers' would be to make every resource available to foster the work of Christ where he is present, in the midst of his people, the congregation.

This would not only have the advantage of removing the

delusory 'career ladder' which exists, but bring us back into line with the Scriptural emphasis upon the local congregations as the primary *loci* of God's activity and objects of his concern. It may also be a great step forward for such 'area advisers/bishops' to be elected by the diocese itself and for a shorter fixed period of time so that he may return, at a future period, back to a congregation (if he were to leave one at all). In any event, more radical thinking in the light of Scripture is surely required.

Ecumenism

As we saw earlier, the unity of the church is one of the essential aspects of the doctrine of the church. The very term *ekklēsia* means 'gathering' – the people of God gathered around the Messiah. This too is linked to the 'catholic' dimension, so that there is one shepherd and one flock (John 10:16) – a favourite text of the Reformers – and there are others who are to be gathered in by the teaching of the apostles as we read in John 17:20-21. There is no doubt that this prayer of Jesus, 'that they may be as one even as the Father and the Son are one', was fulfilled at Pentecost: the spiritual unity was brought about by the Holy Spirit, a unity which was made manifest in terms of fellowship and submission to apostolic teaching. So it is not surprising to find that in the New Testament the proclamation of the fact of Christian unity is followed by a call to be 'eager to maintain the unity of the Spirit in the bond of peace' (Eph. 4:3).

The unity that the New Testament speaks of and urges is never uniformity, nor is it seen as some multinational conglomerate. It is a unity 'in Christ', emphasising its spiritual and personal nature; and a unity in truth, emphasising its doctrinal nature: after all it is possible to be united in error, a point once graphically brought home by Jewel: 'There was the greatest consent that might be amongst them that worshipped the golden calf and among them who with one voice jointly cried "Crucify Him!" '[16] Also Latimer was to remark, 'We ought never to regard unity so much that we would or should forsake God's Word for her sake.'[17] The New Testament never sees 'unity' as an end in itself: it is something which arises out of God's gracious movement towards us in Jesus

Christ and which we are to work out, in dependence upon him.

This means that there will be limits to unity. Where the apostolic truth is rejected, no unity exists. Paul pronounces a curse upon those who promote error (Gal. 1:8). John goes so far as to say that those who promote such heretical teaching never belonged in the first place (1 John 2:18ff; 4:1ff.). So not all so-called disunity is wrong. Indeed it would seem that in the New Testament there are two motives for disunity, one which is unacceptable, the other necessary.[18] The first is what can be called the 'Apollos' motive as we find it in 1 Corinthians 1 and 2, where the local church is being split on purely personal grounds – for non-theological reasons – and that is condemned. The second is what can be termed the 'Anti-christ' motive, as we find in John's letters, where one must separate oneself from those who are teaching serious error. So the first cause for disunity is lack of love, and this must be overcome; the second is lack of truth and the promotion of error, and this too, where possible, must be corrected, but if necessary, separation must occur.

Let us now work out some of the implications that this teaching has in two directions: what we can call 'external ecumenism' – the way churches of one denomination or none relate to others; and 'internal ecumenism' – how we might view churches within our own denominational structure.

The modern ecumenical movement as represented by the World Council of Churches and the new Inter-Church Process has as its focus external ecumenism, the bringing together of denominations and affiliations of churches: and it is with visible unity that it is primarily concerned. But as we have seen, the unity which exists is spiritual and it is the invisible church which is truly one, although it is within the local church that that unity should be expressed visibly.

However, it would seem that one of the reasons why there is much confusion and frustration in modern ecumenism is because it is mistakenly thought that a denomination is a church. We believe in the church – both local and universal, but as we have seen, it is seriously wide of the mark to say that we believe in the church denominational. A denomination is more of a para-church organisation, ideally organised to facilitate and encourage the work of the local church. As such it is not contrary to Scripture (as indeed other groups like the Church Pastoral Aid Society and Universities' and Colleges' Christian Fellowship are not). But to speak of a denomination as a 'church', as we do, is as misleading as to speak of a building as a 'church', which we also do. It is theoretically possible to have a 'unity' of denominations or only have one 'superstructure', and yet be far removed from the unity of which the New Testament speaks – unity in Christ and in truth. This is not to say that where possible one should not seek a greater understanding between such organisations, and where appropriate a sharing of resources – but is this really biblical ecumenism? Would it not be more in line with the New Testament view of the church to seek closer fellowship, a recognition of ministries, a coming together between local churches which do confess and have that oneness in Christ and truth? That is what would commonly be called evangelical ecumenism. Should this not be the prayer of evangelical believers, as it was that of the great Richard Baxter? Is it right that for the sake of a para-church affiliation, fellowship in the gospel should be hindered? Our survey so far would suggest not.

So what of 'internal ecumenism', which since the Keele congress of 1967 has seemed to be the main concern of Anglican evangelicals?

Again we need to raise one or two questions. Is it perhaps the case that just as a confusion has arisen because of the mistake of identifying the church with denomination, so there is confusion because there has been the tendency uncritically to accept a congregation as being a 'church' simply because it belongs to a denomination? Supposing, without being harsh or judgmental, that there is a congregation called St. Swithin's. But as far as one can tell, the pure Word of God is not being preached, nor the sacraments duly administered, and discipline not exercised. If these marks of the church are absent, then can it be called a church? This does not mean to say, of course, that those amongst the number there do not belong to the universal church – the church invisible; but it does raise a serious question mark about the congregation's validity or at the very least its health. Now we obviously have to be very careful at this point. We are not saying that a congregation which contains error, or where immorality is to be found, is not a church – look at Corinth. But we surely do have to ask whether a gathering where the gospel is repudiated in both word and symbol can in all honesty be conceived as a church, even though it belongs to a denomination. Such questions are not purely theoretical either: they have very practical and pastoral implications. For instance, one of your congregation is to move to a new town. Do you recommend that he finds the nearest church which belongs to your denomination or do you encourage him to find fellowship where the marks of the church are exhibited? Are members of the Church of England, or any other grouping for that matter, to put denominational loyalties above gospel loyalties in working with other congregations? We have to face these questions honestly if we are going to understand our ecclesiology in practice.

Conclusion

It is time for evangelicals and Anglican evangelicals in particular to get back to their biblical roots on the matter of ecclesiology. This will entail amongst other things:

(1) Affirming the priority of the local church;

(2) The implementation of biblical priorities and principles for the life of the local congregation;

(3) The promotion of evangelical cooperation for the spread of the gospel and

(4) Taking steps to prevent the undermining of gospel ministry presently being caused by the gradual slide of the denomination into a dead centralisation of power upheld by bogus theology.

NOTES

1. Klaas Runia, *Reformation Today,* Banner of Truth (1968), pp. 44f

2. For a detailed but disappointing response to the Archbishop's call see Tim Bradshaw, *The Olive Branch. An evangelical Anglican doctrine of the church,* Paternoster (1992). I say disappointing in that as an evangelical exploration of the doctrine of the church it is

an amazing omission that Stibbs is not even given a mention, nor the 'Robinson/Knox' position. It is decidedly weak in its biblical analysis.

3. Paul Minear, *Images of the Church in the New Testament,* Philadelphia (1960).

4. See E. Clowney's article 'Church', in *New Dictionary of Theology*, eds. Sinclair B. Ferguson and David Wright, Inter-Varsity Press (1988), p.140.

5. P.T. O'Brien, 'The church as the Heavenly and Eschatological Entity' in *The Church in the Bible and the World,* Paternoster (1987), ed. D.A. Carson.

6. P.T. O'Brien, *Colossians and Philemon, The Word Commentary Series,* Word (1982), p. 61.

7. *Institutes,* IV 1.9.

8. E.g. *Homosexual Relationships – a contribution to discussion,* Church Information Office, London (1979).

9. Paul Avis, *The Church in the Theology of the Reformers,* MMS (1970), p.28.

10. David Peterson, 'The Biblical Context of Edification' in 'Church, Worship and the Local Congregation', *Explorations* 2, Ed. BAG. Webb, Lancer Books (1987).

11. Graham Cole, The Doctrine of the Church: 'Towards Conceptual Clarification', *Explorations* 2,

12. *The Apostolic Ministry,* Ed. K. Kirk, London: Hodder & Stoughton.

13. Carey and Hind, 'Ministry, Ministries and Ministry' in *Stepping Stones*, ed. C. Baxter, London: Hodder & Stoughton (1987), p.59. The same outlook is expressed in *Episcopal Ministry,* Church House Publishing (1990). For a helpful critique of this see C. Green, *An Oversight? What Bishops' think about Bishops and how Evangelicals reply,* REFORM booklet (1993).

14. G. Bromiley, *Historical Theology,* Edinburgh: T. & T. Clark (1978), pp.53-54.

15. G. Lampe, 'Episcopacy and Reunion', in *Churchman.* Vol. 75 (1961), p.16.

16. Jewel, Parker Society, 3.69.

17. Latimer, Parker Society 1.487.

18. See Klaas Runia, *Reformation Today,* Banner of Truth (1968), p. 61.

14

Truth, Myth and Incarnation

Introduction

It is now several years since the controversial volume *The Myth of God Incarnate*[1] entered the theological scene, creating something of a major storm, the likes of which had not been seen since *Honest to God* in the early 1960s. In the wake of the furore which followed, a wealth of literature was generated, the subject matter of which tended to revolve around some of the key issues raised by Wiles, Hick, Cupitt *et al*. Hard on the heels of *Myth* came another collection of essays entitled *The Truth of God Incarnate*.[2] This was followed by *Incarnation and Myth The Debate Continued*[3] which formed the substance of a colloquy between some of the authors of *Myth* and others of a more orthodox persuasion. In the meantime a steady stream of articles and books have flowed from the pens of scholars showing that the Christological/Incarnational debate is still very much on the theological agenda.[4]

Of course, during the time which has elapsed since the writing of *The Myth of God Incarnate*, many of the original contributors have moved on in their positions. John Hick no longer sees 'Christianity at the Centre' (the title of an earlier book), but prefers to speak of the 'Centre of Christianity',[5] with the Christian religion being viewed as just one amongst many lying on the edge of a universe of faiths. Michael Goulder, feeling the tension between his personal convictions and those formally held by the Church of England in which he was an ordained priest, decided to resign his Anglican orders. Perhaps the most significant shift has been in the thinking of Don Cupitt, who has taken leave of God altogether, at least in so far as God has been traditionally conceived by Christians down the ages, so much so that on one television programme the renowned atheist A. J. Ayer claimed Cupitt as one of his own!

Such developments in themselves provide a clear indication of the central place incarnation doctrine has in Christian belief, such that a reinterpretation of this necessitates a thoroughgoing revision of all the other major strands of the faith if some sort of coherence and consistency is to be achieved.

For example, it has long been recognised [6] in Christian theology that questions concerning the 'who' of Jesus are integrally related to questions about the 'what' of Jesus, i.e. what he has achieved by way of the cross (function) cannot be divorced from who he is in his person (identity). Accordingly, a shift in one's conception of Christology will mean a necessary shift in one's understanding of soteriology, and vice versa. But it does not end there, for there will be other knock-on effects in the related areas of revelation, hamartiology (nature of sin), and the uniqueness or otherwise of the Christian faith in relation to other religions.

The purpose of this chapter is not to retrace old ground, but to stand back and take another look at some of the claims of the mythographers to see just how viable their case really is. Instead of approaching the subject head on, we shall take a more indirect route via a consideration of a trilogy of concepts which lie at the heart of the debate, namely those of truth, myth and incarnation. Having examined each of these in turn, we shall then try and assess one major attempt at bringing the three together as made by one of the representatives of the *Myth* school, John Hick.

Truth

We begin with the notion of 'truth'. What do we in fact mean when we say that such and such a thing is true? Even a moment's reflection will reveal that no clear-cut universal answer can be given, for whatever answer might be proposed, it will largely depend upon what it is we are referring to and the given context in which it occurs. For example, we might want to make the claim that 'this man is true', by which we mean that he is an honest and reliable fellow and can be counted on without question. This obviously carries a different sense to the claim that '2 + 2 = 4 is true'. Here it is being maintained that given the basic axioms of mathematics, the relation between the numbers 2 and 2 are such that when added together they always yield the answer '4'. Following this through, even a cursory consideration of the way the notion of truth functions within different disciplines underscores the fact that the sense of the term varies. A literary critic may claim that certain of Shelley's poems are 'true', a claim which has quite a different resonance to the physicist's contention that Einstein's theory of relativity is 'true'. Therefore J. R. Lucas is quite correct when he writes, 'There is no single criterion of truth. Different disciplines have different criteria, often unspecified, sometimes where specified, liable to conflict.'[7]

The plurality involved in establishing criteria for assessing a truth claim can be illustrated by way of three simple examples. The proposition that 'all bachelors are male' is of the order of an analytical statement and as such is necessarily true since the idea of 'bachelorhood' by definition entails the notion of 'maleness', and to deny the latter would involve a logical contradiction. Here the veracity of such claims can be determined by formally examining the relation between the concepts involved.

By way of contrast, the claim that 'it is raining' requires a different approach. Unlike the former example, this statement is not *necessarily* true, but is dependent upon its correspondence with certain facts. As such it is known as a 'synthetic statement'. In this case it is relatively easy to establish the veracity of the truth claim – one simply goes outside to look, and the coincidence of dark clouds and falling water droplets should convince any reasonable person of its truth status.

Our third example is the claim 'my wife loves me', which although belonging to the same class as the previous statement is a little more tricky to handle. The husband who makes the claim might feel justified in doing so on the grounds of a cumulation of evidence – e.g. the display of loving actions, faithfulness, verbal reassurances and so on. But someone might wish to tighten up this whole approach by introducing an element of 'falsification', by asking what circumstances would count *against* the original claim, thus rendering it false? Supposing, for instance, that the wife walks out on her husband, would this mean that the husband's original claim was untrue? Not necessarily, for supposing that the husband had not been paying enough attention to his wife recently, such action might be a calculated means of jolting him into mending his ways, and so far from falsifying the husband's earlier claim, it would become supporting evidence in its favour.

This brief discussion of different truth claims highlights for us a very important principle, namely, that when it comes to human affairs and interaction between persons, determining what is 'true' can often be a complex, intuitive and subtle business. Indeed, there is every reason to suppose that this equally applies to scientific, historical and metaphysical pursuits. Thus going beyond Lucas, it might be more appropriate to view language as an interconnecting network with a wide range of truth claims aligned along a spectrum, with those of a formal analytical nature at one end, and those open to empirical sense verification at the other, with the majority of others lying somewhere in between, the truth value of which is ascertained by a mixture of reason, observation and inference. Within the personal sphere of activity, all of these factors come into play in determining what is the case, and yet it is important that allowance is made for that which is inherent in all human interaction, namely a degree of 'opacity' or 'mystery'. Even when we disclose something of ourselves to another person, we at the same time hide something of ourselves. The mysterious (although not irrational) element, and all the ambiguities that it can produce, is vital for personal interaction since it elicits and establishes that which is integral to such interaction, namely trust.

All of this has direct bearing upon our present discussion, for it should sound a note of caution to those who would dismiss such talk about incarnation as 'meaningless' on the basis of applying too narrowly defined, and thus inappropriate, criteria. If the basic analogy of God's relation to the world and his activity in that world is that of interaction between persons, then just as allowance is made for ambiguity and imprecision in the human domain, one would expect at least a similar degree of tolerance in the divine. Far from this being a plea for a new form of obscurantism, it is a passionate enjoinder that we take seriously the personal analogy between divine and human activity, and recognise the useful insights it can yield in matters of doctrine as well as setting definite limits. This is not to say, of course, that one begins with the human and works towards an understanding of the divine (the weakness of natural theology), but that this is something which is *given* in God's special revelation in Scripture and so should be taken seriously.

To summarise what has been said so far: the notion of truth is as varied as are the means of establishing it. As well as paying close attention to the context in which the concept functions, we also need to note the way the concept is used. Here we may borrow a term from Wittgenstein and say that the notion of truth cannot be considered in isolation from the particular 'language game' in which it operates. Accordingly, some philosophers have designated the concept of truth as being 'polymorphous'. Anthony Thiselton ably demonstrates that the biblical data itself bear this out in identifying at least six different senses associated with the word according to context and function.[8]

Although it is possible with some qualification to speak of truths varying according to context or language game, there must be certain features or 'family resemblances' between them which provide some sort of universal point of reference, otherwise it would not be possible to associate 'truth' in one field with that in another. At least four such features will be suggested here. In the first place, to claim that we know the truth amounts to maintaining that we can see things as they really are without *substantial* distortion or concealment. One may go so far as to claim that one has grasped the essence of a thing, and so come close to the Greek etymological root for truth *aletheia* – a state of unhiddenness. In the second place, truth is contextual in that no truth claim can be considered independently of the wider framework of ideas of which it is a part. Thus the claim that 'God is love' by itself means very little. It begs the immediate question, 'Which God are we speaking of?' Is it that of Hinduism, Islam or the Judaeo-Christian tradition? What is more, whatever meaning is thought to be conveyed by this statement will in part be dependent upon purported divine *action,* for the notion of 'love' cannot be conceived of in the abstract, but only in relation to events. Thus straight away one is drawn into a consideration of a constellation of other beliefs arising out of a desire to assess the truth status of one statement. Thirdly, we would propose that although contextual, truth is universal. This means that if Jesus is both God and man, he remains so regardless of culture or background beliefs. Finally, the actual perception of truth inevitably contains a personal element and as such it is something which makes its claim upon us for recognition. Although personal, truth is not subjective, the product of whim or fancy. In this way truth stands over and above us (being objective), sometimes coming home to us with considerable force such that we exclaim 'it hit me between the eyes' or 'the penny dropped'.

These four features of truth converge in the traditional Christian claim that in the person of Jesus and the events surrounding his life, death and resurrection, God's truth has been fully and finally manifest (John 14:6; Heb. 1:2). The doctrine of the incarnation is in part an attempt to express that conviction conceptually – not simply that in Christ we have an expression of 'truth' in an abstract way, but that he is very God who is the Truth. As such the doctrine acts as an organising principle with explanatory power. But as we shall see below, lying at the heart of the *Myth* debate is the challenge that such an understanding is both misplaced and outmoded, requiring a radical overhaul. Before we turn to this challenge, however, we would do well to look at the way truth at one level can provide the basis for development at a higher level.

In a highly stimulating paper, John Macquarrie [9] draws attention to three levels of truth constitutive in theological investigation. These are: historical truth, theological truth, and metaphysical truth. Macquarrie proposes that there is a progression in significance as one proceeds from one level to another. This means that theological truth builds upon historical truth, so metaphysical truth is an outworking of the theological. Although Macquarrie himself does not suggest it, the relations between the three levels tend to be conceived like three stories in a building, thus:

Fig.1

| Metaphysical Truth |
| Theological Truth |
| Historical Truth |

Increasing order
of significance

The problem with this model is that it creates the impression that as one moves from a lower level to a higher level, the lower is left behind and is devoid of further relevance. Or to change the metaphor slightly, it can be likened to the different stages of a rocket: once the upper stages have been launched into orbit, the lower stages can be jettisoned as superfluous.

One suspects that something like this is occurring in the writings of those who would advocate a more existential approach to theology. A much more satisfactory way of conceiving the relations between the historical, theological and metaphysical would be as a series of concentric rings or spheres, with the historical elements providing the inner core which is taken up into, and transcended by, the theological and metaphysical, thus:

Fig.2

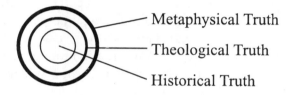

Metaphysical Truth

Theological Truth

Historical Truth

This representation safeguards the essentially historical nature of Christianity which has at its centre an historical person and particular events, providing not only 'raw' material for theological and metaphysical reflection, but checks and controls as well. It should be pointed out, however, that the actual relations are more subtle and complex than the diagram suggests, since metaphysical presuppositions and beliefs will to some extent 'colour' one's view of the 'historical', as well as the 'historical' shaping the 'metaphysical'. Nevertheless, in serving to underscore the main features of interdependence between the three levels of truth, the above model provides a useful aid.

In speaking of historical truth, we are referring to what happened. The procedure adopted in order to ascertain this will involve some measure of sifting through the available evidence and attempting some sort of reconstruction. Theological truth arises out of a careful reflection upon that historical core, drawing out the significance in terms of God and man.

Metaphysical truth is the result of further exploration into the philosophical and conceptual implications of what is said to have occurred as having theological significance. To a large extent it is this process which underlies the formulation of the great creeds, themselves having been woven within a metaphysical matrix. But in terms of language, the creeds contain a fine mixture of statements which are historical ('crucified under Pontius Pilate'), theological ('died for our sins') and metaphysical ('being of one substance – *homoousios* – with the Father'). But are any of the credal formulations to be considered 'mythical'? Traditionally, much theological language, including incarnational language, has been taken as factual, informative (telling us about something) and explanatory (unpacking the significance). But some, like John Hick, are of the opinion that very early on in the church's history, the mistake was made of taking certain statements as explanatory in nature (akin to scientific hypotheses) when they should have been comprehended mythically. The upshot of this position is that while the idea of the incarnation might be mythically true, it is not literally true (i.e. factually true). Whether such a contention can be shown to have any solid foundation will in part be determined by one's understanding of what constitutes 'myth', and it is to a consideration of this question that we now turn.

Myth

One of the major criticisms levelled at the book *The Myth of God Incarnate* is the way its different contributors tended to use the term 'myth' in a plurality of ways, often without specifying the sense in which the term was actually being used. Invariably this led to some confusion and obscurity of thought, which a book of such a highly provocative nature could have well done without. The reader who is perhaps entering this area of debate for the first time would be well advised to read Maurice Wiles' helpful paper, 'Myth in Theology,'[10] in which he discusses several different usages of the concept 'myth'. This would alert the unsuspecting student to the ways in which this term can be used in so slippery and evasive a manner.

Our starting point however will be George Caird's work in

Language, Imagery and the Bible, [11] in which he undertakes a most illuminating analysis of the various categories of myth in relation to different disciplines. In so doing, he clears away a lot of the fog which tends to bedevil most discussions of the subject. He begins by pointing out that 'myth' is used in two general senses. In common parlance, a myth is something which is essentially untrue and is thus a synonym for falsehood. Indeed, this appears to be the way the New Testament writers handle the word (cf. I Tim. 1:4; 4:7; Tit. 1:14). It would not be wide of the mark to suggest that it was this association that was in the minds of many when the notorious book hit the headlines, and so it was seen as an outright denial of the Christian faith. (This suspicion is corroborated by the appearance of the counter-book, *The* Truth *of God Incarnate.*) In theological circles however, the term has become linked with a movement which uses it as an overarching concept embracing all such 'God-Talk'. The name which is best known in this context is that of Rudolf Bultmann, who advocated a programme of 'demythologisation' in order to make the 'gospel' intelligible to modern man. This is what Bultmann has to say on the matter: 'Mythology is the use of imagery to express the other-worldly in terms of this world and the divine in terms of human life, the other side in terms of this side'.[12] In effect what Bultmann is claiming is that myth is a theological use of metaphor, a non-literal way of speaking. Caird on the other hand makes out a convincing case that as far as the Bible is concerned, where myth is used it is a *specialised* form of metaphor.

According to Caird, this special literary class of myth is capable of fulfilling a number of different functions. It may be performative – able to change things, possibly leading people to a deeper sense of commitment. It may be evocative – appealing to the imagination through that which is impressive, mysterious, sublime. Myth may have a cohesive effect, binding a group together by creating a sense of identity through an inherited tradition. But myth may also be referential, pointing to something beyond itself – an ontological aspect of reality. Caird therefore likens myth to a lens whereby the user in effect says to his audience, 'Here is a lens which has helped me understand the world in which we live and the way God relates to it; look through it yourself and see what I have seen.' Or to change the imagery, myth may be compared to a cartoon. At one level, a cartoon may be more representative of the character of a person or the hidden significance of a situation than a photograph. Of course, if it is a literal representation which is sought, then a photograph should do the trick, but if it is some underlying aspect of reality that is sought, then a sketch or cartoon might be more appropriate.

Caird cites what he considers to be an unambiguous example of myth in the Bible – Isaiah 14:12-15 – where the prophet makes use of a story about the planet known to us as Venus, but which the Hebrews would have called 'Heylel' ('Bright Shiner' or 'son of the dawn'). According to the Babylonian myth, Heylel aspired to make himself King by scaling the mountain ramparts of the heavenly city, only to be vanquished by the all-conquering sun. Within the biblical context, however, the myth is taken and reapplied to a different referent and so given a different sense, namely, the king of Babylon. He, like Heylel in the story, had aspirations for world dominion and he too would meet with a similar fate, but in his case it is the one true God Yahweh who will bring about his downfall. In this way, Isaiah, like any good preacher, is drawing upon stories common at the time and giving them a spiritual edge and application, and so bringing the point home in an evocative manner.

Given that there is some warrant for seeing the Bible as using myth in the way outlined above, is there any justification for claiming that the doctrine of the incarnation functions in the same way? This brings us to our final analysis in our trilogy: the use of the concept 'incarnation'.

Incarnation

The English word 'incarnate' can function either as an adjective or as a verb. Verbally, it literally means to 'render incarnate' or to 'embody in flesh'. Soderblom defines it as follows: 'The term incarnation is applied to the act of a divine or supernatural being in assuming the form of a man or animal and continuing to live in that form upon earth.' [13] However, both this definition and the verb 'incarnation' (Latin *incarnatio*) can be misleading, for they almost imply an entering *into* a man (incarnation – Greek *ensarkosis),* thus amounting to little more than a form of divine possession. Surely Professor Moule[14] is right when he suggests, somewhat guardedly, that it would be more in line with the traditional understanding of the incarnation to speak of 'carnation' or *sarkosis* – God *becoming* man while not ceasing to be divine.

However, in Christian circles the term 'incarnate' is rarely used as a verb. Instead it is the adjectival form which is predominant, acting as a sort of 'title': 'Jesus – God Incarnate'. Even so, the verbal idea is the one which underlies this usage and is the most pertinent to our discussion.

Upon closer inspection, both the denotation and connotation of the term 'incarnation' reveals something rather interesting. In speaking of divine action, in the main we have to resort to analogy, usually the sort of personal analogies mentioned earlier in the article. Accordingly, God can be spoken of as 'revealing', 'saving', 'forgiving', etc. – activities which are equally found in human affairs, but in this case heavily qualified in relation to the divine. But the concept of 'incarnation' is not analogical; it is not something which is to be found in the sphere of human activity which in some ways has a corresponding aspect in divine activity. This means that ironically, according to Bultmann's own definition of 'myth' given earlier, 'incarnation' falls outside this classification because it is *not* something which is 'common to this side' of experience. Nevertheless, it still might be argued that while 'incarnation' provides an instance where theological language is being used in a way that is strictly speaking not analogical, it still constitutes an elaborate and picturesque way of speaking, one which is akin to figurative speech, and so in this sense might be termed 'myth' to distinguish it from factual discourse. This appears to be the position of John Hick, and it is to an assessment of his attempt to provide an account of the relations between truth, myth and incarnation that we now turn.

Truth, myth and incarnation – John Hick

In his book *God and the Universe of Faiths,*[15] published before *The Myth of God Incarnate,* John Hick defines myth in the following way: '[Myth] is a story which is told but which is not literally true, or an idea or image which is applied to something or someone but which does not literally apply, but which invites a particular attitude in the hearer. The truth of myth is a kind of "practical truth" consisting in the appropriateness of the attitude it evokes – the appropriateness of the attitude to its object which may be an event, a person or set of ideas.'[16] Here Hick distinguishes 'myth' as a story which functions to evoke an 'appropriate attitude' in the hearer (which he believes the incarnation is designed to do) from factual discourse, hypothesis or model. Hick maintains that mythical language is not 'literally true', which presumably means that it cannot be taken as being descriptive or explanatory except in a very oblique sort of way. By way of example, Hick cites the story in Genesis 2 of the fall of man, which he says has this mythical quality of being able to convey a timeless truth common to human experience. In his treatment of the story of the incarnation, Hick places it logically on a par with Genesis 2, pointing out that when in the past the incarnation myth has been taken as being of a theoretical nature, a type of theological hypothesis, this has led to a dead end as well as a morass of logical contradictions. The only viable alternative, according to Hick, is that the story be seen as 'myth'. When that is done, then it functions perfectly well in evoking an appropriate attitude to Jesus as Saviour.

But one may ask, how did it come about, historically speaking, that Jesus of Nazareth, who was clearly human, was eventually conceived by his followers in terms of 'God and Man'? Hick provides an explanation. He suggests that in experience the early followers of Jesus did seem to encounter God in a remarkable way through him, and such was the nature of this encounter that their religious experience had to be interpreted in terms of the language of 'ultimates' – a step which occurred within two generations of Jesus' death. The end result of this interpretative process was the application of *the* ultimate language form, namely to speak of Jesus *as* God incarnate, which attained its full crystallisation at Chalcedon. Thus, according to this reconstruction of events, to say that Jesus is 'God incarnate' means no more than that God was encountered in Jesus.

Hick's position is backed up by two other considerations, one philosophical, the other historical. Philosophically, Hick is of the opinion that incarnational language, if taken 'literally' (i.e. as explanatory), is incoherent. It appears to be of the same order as speaking of a 'round square'. Historically, Hick, together with many of the other contributors to *Myth*, believes that the amount of reliable historical information that we actually have concerning Jesus is so scanty that it renders it impossible to construct such a lofty doctrine as we find attempted at Chalcedon. This means that if one is working to the model proposed in Figure 2, then the inner historical core is so insubstantial that the outer layers become very thin indeed. Of course this is of little consequence to Hick, for he considers it an error of the greatest magnitude to view the incarnation as 'metaphysical truth' anyway.

This, then, is Hick's basic thesis. But in the light of the foregoing discussion, how convincing is it? We would suggest that it is seriously to be found wanting for the following reasons:

1. Although there is some similarity between Hick's presentation of 'myth' and that put forward by Caird, in that both are a means of 'seeing-as', the function of myth on Hick's view is severely limited. While not denying the possible evocative effect of true myth, surely it amounts to something more than an effective tool producing some kind of 'practical truth' (whatever that might be)? It is not at all clear why 'myth' cannot have some explanatory role, providing some insight into the way things actually *are*. Neither has Hick satisfactorily demonstrated that the doctrine of the incarnation is of the same order as say Isaiah 14 or Genesis 2; rather it is simply *assumed* to be the case or, perhaps more to the point, it is placed within this category by default, on the premise that it cannot be of a factual nature, which again is an assumption and is not demonstrated.

2. As William Abraham has argued,[17] it is highly questionable whether there is the inner religious necessity to describe an 'encounter with God' in the language of ultimates, as Hick postulates occurred with the followers of Jesus. In the Old Testament there are plenty of examples where God was encountered, especially through the prophets, but there is not the slightest indication that there was an attempt to apply the 'language of ultimates' to such people. When one enquires why this is so, then one comes across one of the most salient features of Judaism, namely its ardent monotheism, which resisted any identification of man with the divine, except in terms of divine action. And yet this is precisely the milieu in which the 'high' Christology began to develop, with the type of language normally reserved for God amongst Jewish monotheists being applied to Jesus (e.g. 'author of life' – Acts 3:15; 'Judge of all men' – Acts 10:42; 'Creator' – Rom. 11:36; Col. 1:16; identification with Yahweh – Rom. 9:5; Phil. 2:10; *cf.* Is. 45:23). Pure religious experience (if there is such a thing) is surely an inadequate basis upon which to construct an account for such a development. It is more plausible to postulate a cumulative interaction of factors which were brought to bear upon the early church to look for categories to provide some sort of *explanation* for this remarkable person and the events surrounding his life. Jesus' teaching, his authority, self-understanding, lack of sense of sin, miracles, prophecies, resurrection and ascension, and the giving of the Holy Spirit, when taken together, would cry out for some explanation, an organising principle. Inevitably, the early Christians would have seized upon those categories which were ready to hand, especially those of the Jewish Scriptures, in order to apply them to Jesus under the inspiration of the Holy Spirit. Hick is therefore quite correct in saying that the followers of Jesus would need to search for a language of ultimates to be applied to him, but grossly wide of the mark in suggesting a sufficient cause.

3. Hick's comparison of the incarnation with the Fall also leaves much to be desired in that he ignores some very significant

disanalogies which bring into question a major plank in his thesis. First of all, while it could be maintained that the story of the Fall in some way reflects the common experience of man, that cannot be claimed with regard to the story of the incarnation. This is highly specific and does not flow from some general experience. In the second place, the story of the Fall is set in antiquity, whereas the story of the incarnation is firmly placed within history, and relatively recent history at that. This fact creates a significant distance between the events related in the New Testament and their accompanying importance and the world of 'myth'. Adolf Koberle's comment is most apposite at this point: 'The history of salvation that is directly linked to the name of Jesus is fundamentally different from the world of myth. By its very nature myth is without historical context, it describes events of nature that occur and re-occur in cycles.'[18]

4. Hick's main philosophical point is also open to question. Certainly the simple assertion 'Jesus is God' does appear to create the logical inconsistency that Hick describes.[19] But when this is said (and note that it is not a term used in the New Testament; the nearest we get to it is 'The Word of God', which is later identified with Jesus) it is often as a form of 'theological shorthand'. But surely, the great debates of the past resulting in the sophisticated formulations of the creeds in themselves testify to an awareness of the difficulties involved; hence the painstaking way in which formulations have been arrived at to ensure that such contradictions are avoided. Neither the New Testament writers nor the early Fathers ever thought that Jesus was God *tout simple*. Nevertheless, the conviction was expressed that although he was not *totum dei* (all that God is without remainder) he was *totus deus* (everything God himself is). Again this was forged out of the experience of Christ, moving towards some conceptualisation of Jesus' relation to God within the confines of monotheism. Certainly in so doing the church entered the realms of paradox, stretching human language to the limit, but nothing less than this would be

expected if anything like the traditional doctrine of the incarnation is correct.[20] As we saw earlier, why do the mythographers not allow for a greater amount of ambiguity in the realm of the divine as they no doubt do in the sphere of human relations?

5. Following on from this, one might also question Hick's censure that one should not treat the doctrine of the incarnation in a way similar to scientific models, i.e. as having explanatory value. If the reply is that it is a myth and myths are not to be treated in that way, then that simply begs the question. What is more, the alleged gulf between the function of 'myths' and scientific hypotheses is perhaps not as great as some suppose. The American philosopher W.V.O. Quine has remarked that 'The myths of Homer's gods and the myths of scientific objects differ only in degree and not kind.' After all, what are models, but abstract representations of a reality formulated in accordance with the evidential data? Traditionally, the doctrine of the incarnation has been seen in this way, and like the scientific models, some of which are antinomies (apparently contradictory), it has proved highly successful as a means of articulating and conceptually grasping something to which the biblical data decisively point, namely that in Jesus, God became man.

6. In our view Hick's historical scepticism is not warranted. The question of the historicity of the Gospels is outside the immediate scope of this discussion and the reader is referred to other works which deal with this.[21] Nevertheless, it must be pointed out that without sufficient historical warrants it is difficult to see how the Jesus story can even function as 'myth' in the way Hick suggests. Certainly it might provide a 'good read', maybe being evocative in some way. But what reasons can be adduced to convince a person that it should be accepted, even as conveying some general religious truth, which in fact it does not purport to do? The traditional claim is that the story is rooted in actual events, whereas on Hick's account what

these events are we do not really know, and so the story functions simply as story, perhaps tugging on the heartstrings, but having little, if any, epistemic power to elicit rational acceptance.

What is more, if the amount of historical knowledge about Jesus is as scanty as Hick believes it to be, then why not look to some more recent figure in history about whom we know much more and in whom 'God has been encountered'?

7. It is not true to say, as Hick does, that the language of incarnation was designed to evoke an appropriate attitude towards Jesus. The creeds were written for those who *already* had an attitude of reverence and belief. In some measure they were an attempt to *justify* that attitude rather than to evoke it. The matter of evocation is secondary and consequent upon the primary matter of explanation. If Jesus is factually the eternal Son of God, then it is appropriate that I respond to him in worship and gratitude. If he is not, then what is it I am supposed to respond to? On Hick's reckoning such a response is quite misplaced.

8. What one is left with on the basis of Hick's thesis is so vague as to be contentless. What does it *mean* to speak of 'encountering God in Jesus'? Indeed what value is there in speaking of God 'acting' in Jesus? To speak of God acting in Jesus is as helpful as saying that Jones is acting. Unless there is definite specifiable content (which the New Testament and traditional doctrines provide), such talk is little more than verbal padding. Indeed, one suspects that the ideas of Hick and the other mythographers only gain credence by cashing in on traditional Christian currency, which they have declared bankrupt. In other words, such views are parasitic upon traditional Christianity and can only survive at the expense of the host doctrines which they are trying to sap of vitality.

Concluding remarks

While it may be conceded that there is a literary category of 'myth' through which truth might be conveyed, it is not the category most applicable to the doctrine of the incarnation. When this is attempted, as in the case of Hick, the resulting construct is unable to bear the theological weight placed upon it. Neither is it able to provide as satisfactory an explanation either of the biblical data or the historical and phenomenological factors leading to the formulation of the traditional doctrine of the incarnation. By far the most satisfactory understanding of the function of the doctrine is that it is informative, possessing great explanatory power and operative within the framework of factual discourse.

NOTES

1. John Hick (ed.), *The Myth of God Incarnate,* SCM (1977.

    2. Michael Green (ed.), *The Truth of God Incarnate*, Hodder (1977.

    3. Michael Goulder (ed.), *Incarnation and Myth – The Debate Continued*, SCM (1979.

    4. Cf A. E. Harvey (ed.), *God Incarnate, Story and Belief*, SPCK; D. F. Wells, *The Person of Christ*, Marshall, Morgan & Scott; George Carey, *God Incarnate*, Arena; John Stott, *The Authentic Jesus*, Marshalls; H. H. Rowdon (ed.), *Christ the Lord*, IVP.

    5. John Hick, *The Centre of Christianity*, London (1977.

    6. Cf Martin Kahler: 'without the Cross there is no Christology nor is there any feature in Christology which can escape justifying itself by the Cross', cited in J. Moltmann's *The Crucified God*, SCM (1975, p.85.

    7. J. R. Lucas, 'True', *Philosophy* Vol. Xliv (1969), p.184.

    8. Anthony Thiselton, *The Two Horizons*, Paternoster (1980, pp.411-415.

    9. John Macquarrie, 'Truth in Christology', *God Incarnate, Story and Belief,* pp.24-33.

    10. Maurice Wiles, 'Myth in Theology', *Myth of God Incarnate,* pp.148-165.

    11. G. Caird, *Language, Imagery and the Bible*, Duckworth (1980.

    12. R. Bultmann, *Kerygma and Myth* 1 (1953, p.16.

    13. N. Soderblom, 'Incarnation', in *Encyclopaedia of Religion and Ethics*, ed. James Hastings, T. & T. Clark (1914.

    14. C. F. D. Moule, 'Three points of Conflict in the Christological Debate', in *Incarnation and Myth – The Debate Continued,* pp.131-141.

15. John Hick, *God and the Universe of Faiths*, Macmillan (1973.

16. Ibid., pp. 16 &17.

17. William Abraham, *Divine Revelation and the Limits of Historical Criticisms*, Oxford (1982), pp. 72ff.

18. Quoted in Carl Henry (ed.), *Jesus of Nazareth, Saviour and Lord*, Tyndale Press (1966, p.65.

19. For an excellent discussion of this see Richard Sturch's paper, 'Can one say "Jesus is God"?', in *Christ the Lord*, p.326

20. For a thoroughly readable presentation of this line of thought see Alister McGrath's *Understanding Jesus*, Kingsway (1987.

21. Cf. I. H. Marshall, *I Believe in the Historical Jesus*, Hodder; D. Wenham, R. France and C. Blomberg (eds), *Gospel Perspectives* I-VI, JSOT Press.

SCRIPTURE INDEX

SUBJECT INDEX